THE CORPORATE COUPLE

THE

LIVING THE
CORPORATE GAME

BY PEGGY J. BERRY

Franklin Watts 1985 *New York / Toronto*

Library of Congress Cataloging in Publication Data

Berry, Peggy J.
The corporate couple.

Bibliography: p.
Includes index.
1. Executives—Conduct of life.   2. Executives'
wives.   I. Title.
HD38.2.B47   1985   658.4'094   85-13576
ISBN 0-531-09592-4

CONTENTS

THE CORPORATE COUPLE

*For Dal, Jaime,
Leigh, and Me*

FOREWORD

It was December 1982. Six months earlier my husband had resigned from a large corporation to become president of a small start-up company. We were attending a pre-Christmas business/social cocktail party and talking with the company's attorney and his wife. As we were getting acquainted, personal credentials were exchanged: the man specialized in patent law; his wife taught English at a local college; my husband was a businessman. I wondered what I would say when my turn came. I had no impressive credentials; in fact, I had no credentials at all except corporate wife, outgrown mother, expert relocater, and burned-out volunteer. On an impulse I related that I was a corporate wife and had moved seven times, this time for good. For impression I stated that I was learning to use the word processor on our home computer and was thinking about trying to write an article on the corporate life-style. To my surprise the conversation became quite animated, centering on my wild proclamation. "Why not write a book?" they asked. I was in deep trouble. To escape I laughed and admitted that I was just filling time with the word processor—"I'm not a writer." After more urging and some uncomfortable moments the conversation finally shifted. But the idea remained.

After the new year began I was sitting alone one day, staring out the window and searching for some new direction for my life. I took an inventory of my present situation: my husband was engrossed in his job, my daughters were grown and gone, my volunteering was unfulfilling, and my tennis game never seemed to improve. Wondering where to go from there, I mentally retraveled my life's path.

That month, January 1983, marked my twentieth anniversary as a corporate wife. Dal and I married when we were sophomores at a small Alabama college. We both dropped out of school, but three years and one child later he returned to finish work for his degree. After graduation and another child Dal took a job as a sales trainee with a large corporation and was soon on his way to success. We began moving on to move up: from Muscle Shoals to Huntsville, Alabama; to Gainesville, Jacksonville, and Tampa, Florida; to Bloomfield, Michigan; to Newtown, Connecticut; and finally, to Dallas, Texas. We had lived in Jacksonville just long enough for me to return to college and receive my degree; in fact, we moved one week after my graduation. Corporate wives say that the minute you finish decorating your new home you'll be moved again. In my case relocation came the minute I decided to enter graduate school. I was accepted for graduate studies twice, but each time we moved before the term began.

In 1975 I borrowed a friend's copy of Robert Seidenberg's book *Corporate Wives: Corporate Casualties.* Reading that book was like reading a chronicle of my life since 1963, and I began to read everything I could find about the corporate life-style. While living in Connecticut I volunteered with a nonprofit organization, working on a project researching the personal and community effects of corporate relocations. I interviewed several corporate spouses, compiled research material, and helped organize community workshops on relocation. After moving to Dallas I continued my research and gave programs for and about corporate wives. And in January 1983 I was looking for a new direction.

Why not try writing an article about what I know best—the corporate life, I asked myself. I bought a "how to" book on writing, sent out several query letters, and received rejection slips for all except one. Six months after my query letter I received a reply from *Dun's Business Month* asking me to write a first-person article on some issue of corporate life. I wrote "Has Business Travel Gone Too Far?" under the pseudonym of Peggy Jay, and *Dun's* published it in November 1983. The response to that article initiated this book.

The Corporate Couple: Living the Corporate Game is not the typical corporate-wife-as-victim book. It is addressed to all three sides of the triangle: the employee, the spouse, and the corporation. This book is a depiction of the corporate life-style and the people who live it, with a few suggestions on how to improve it. *The Corporate Couple* is based on my own experiences and nonprofessional research and isn't meant to be a studied, psychological tome. I am not a psychologist, an author, or even a proficient writer. I am a corporate wife, and I do have something to say about that way of life. That's what *The Corporate Couple* is all about—the reality of living the game.

This book would still be just a cocktail party idea without the help of others. My thanks go first to Robert Levy, senior editor of *Dun's Business Month*, who opened the door for a naive novice. His kindness, courage, and wise counsel guided my decision to undertake this project. William Newton, senior editor of Franklin Watts, Inc., gave me the opportunity, and his keen eye and sharp blue pencil kept me hard at work. My appreciation goes to all the people I interviewed for their time, contributions, and interest; my appreciation also goes to my friends for their patience. I am grateful to Jerry and Marion Mills for their friendship and encouragement and to Marion, especially, for her assistance. I send my love to my family for bearing with me through the writing. Finally and most important, my loving thanks to Dal, my husband and biased critic, to whom everything I write is marvelous and without whom this book would have been impossible. His statement "You've supported me for twenty-five years. Don't you think it's about time I supported you for a change?" typifies his love, understanding, and attitude throughout this endeavor.

P. J. B.
Dallas, Texas

PART ONE

THE

PLAYERS

Corporations are people; without people corporations couldn't exist. A business organization is thought up, set up, and kept up by those involved in its activities; therefore, corporate people are a company's life, its existence. But who are these people, how are they involved in the corporation, and how does corporate employment affect their personal lives?

"Corporatites" are white-collar corporate employees, their spouses, and children. As a rule, most older employees came from blue-collar, working-class homes, where the entire family worked hard to provide the child with the college education needed to obtain a better job, better pay, and social mobility. Consequently, many of today's younger employees are children of these now middle- to upper-class corporate parents. Although their backgrounds differ, both older and younger corporate employees are college educated, and both are normally ambitious high achievers.

A corporate couple is a marriage in which at least one person is employed by a corporation in a position that, through promotions, can lead eventually to executive status. Contemporary corporate couples also might be dual-career couples in which both husband and wife are employed, but for our purposes the term "corporate spouse" relates to the wife of a corporate employee regardless of whether she is employed or not. The majority of corporate marriages remain traditional in the sense that the husband is usually the primary provider or corporate employee, and the wife, working or nonworking, is the corporate spouse.

Over the past thirty to forty years the role of the male employee has changed little if at all. His responsibilities, expectations, and ambitions have remained quite stable in the face of a changing society. Describe a typical corporate man, and that description generally is relative to almost all. The same is not true for the wives. The social changes of the past twenty-five years have affected and continue to affect the lives of all women, and corporate wives are no exception. Therefore, these women can no longer be lumped into one convenient stereotype. Today there are three distinct categories: traditional, transitional, and transmuter.

The *traditional* wife is usually thought of as the older woman, over fifty, although many wives from other age groups fit this mental set. She is content being wife, mother, housekeeper, and volunteer while her husband climbs the corporate ladder. The *transitional* wife is normally thirty-five to fifty years old, and she is the woman caught in the middle. She was socialized to the traditional role and spent her early marriage years as a traditional wife. Indeed, her husband, the company, and her senior sisters expected her cooperation and support for his career. But with the emergence of the women's movement society is changing; she now wants or feels pressured to accomplish on her own, to forge her own identity. Because of her middle position she is often confused and depressed, unfulfilled in the traditional role but unprepared to meet the new challenge. The *transmuter* is often the young wife, in her twenties or early thirties. She is the changer, the new breed, educated to and sometimes socialized to a personal career. She rebels against the antiquated traditional corporate wife role and refuses to live the corporate game by outdated rules. Her force is slowly changing the corporate environment and life-style, but her numbers are still few. One must be cautious of categorizing company wives solely by age; there are always exceptions. The attitudes of wives often fluctuate with variables such as socialization, children, and life cycle: one might find a fifty-year-old transmuter and a twenty-five-year-old traditional. Therefore, age can be only a general determiner of psychological type.

To understand the lives of corporate couples one must first understand the phases or stages of a successful business career and the personal and career dynamics of each stage. Part I concentrates on the gradual and subtle changes which can occur in attitudes, personalities, and lives during the progression up the corporate ladder. This evaluation is not exclusive to the corporate environment; personal change is the essence of life and can be related to various career choices. Although some of the changes may seem quite negative, they are in fact part of the maturation process in the making of most successful corporate careers. Couples learn to accommodate the metamorphosis, perhaps not as a positive, but as a consequence of the chosen life. The purpose of Part I is to articulate rather than judge this corporate evolutionary process.

Most corporate careers are divided into three stages: lower, middle, and upper management. Each is distinct in positions and character. Promotion from one level to another is never guaranteed, but an employee usually must pass through lower and middle management to reach the top levels of the corporation. In presenting each career level I include an overview of a fictional, composite corporate couple to provide a better understanding of the personal and career dynamics of each level— the rookies, the stars, and the coaches—and to give a clearer picture of career progression. Each stage prepares the employee and spouse technically and psychologically for the next stage. This psychological preparation is subjective and often subliminal; therefore, it's difficult to recognize and verbalize. But it is the basis of living the corporate game.

1

THE ROOKIES

LEARNING
THE GAME

The scene: college campuses across the nation. The players: young men and women soon to be graduated— eager, enthusiastic, ready to conquer the world—and corporate recruiters. The action: interviewing for employment with a large corporation, that first job, that first rung of the ladder to success. Corporations systematically participate in these college employment seminars, searching for outstanding recruits. Anxious business majors nervously enter these sessions hoping to win the security, training, benefits, prestige, and growth potential offered by big companies. Hundreds of these scenarios are played each year, but there is never a shortage of recruitable talent, because each year perpetually replenishes the supply. Annual estimates show that IBM conducts 50,000 campus interviews and hires about 6,000; General Electric interviews 23,000, hiring 2,000; and Procter and Gamble talks with 23,000 and employs 1,000.[1] Corporations skim the cream of each year's crop of college graduates; many are interviewed, some are selected for employment tests, a few are called for a second interview, but only the best are chosen.

For the recruits this hiring-in process is gratifying and exciting. After years of education and preparation the preemployment games are their first tastes and tests of real world competition, and winning feels good. They have survived the critical challenge of the corporate choice; from here on the path is marked, the sky's the limit, and the journey to a gloriously successful career and life begins. The corporate recruiters painted pictures of bright, prosperous futures that contained no dark hues, highlighting only the positives. In their euphoric state naive new recruits are so complimented by being chosen and so excited about the future that they rarely inquire about possible negative aspects that might arise in the coming years. They begin their careers oblivious of or unconcerned about the fact that corporate employment has two sides, and they have seen only the side of affluence and opportunity. Neither education nor the employment process reveals the personal and family sacrifices required for success in the corporate game. They are the optimistic rookies.

"The tasks of this period are as enormous as they are exhilarating: To shape a dream, that vision of one's own possibilities in the world that will generate energy, aliveness, and hope."[2] This quotation from Gail Sheehy's *Passages* eloquently describes the aspirations and expectations of young rookies embarking on their voyage into life. It is an emotionally sensitive time, filled with the sadness and fear of relinquishing the dependent parental ties of childhood but also filled with the happiness and anticipation of forming an emotional bond with a mate and beginning a new life of independence and interdependence together. This is a stressful time because young people must simultaneously launch three lifeworks or careers: adulthood, marriage, and work. Usually during this time a fourth career, parenthood, also begins. Each member of a newly formed couple brings separate socialized expectations of life roles and goals to the marriage. The melding of these often divergent expectations into a solid unit and partnership requires time and mutual attention. Invariably, each person knows his or her preferred role and chosen goal and assumes the other's role will be complementary in the accomplishment of that goal. Men come to marriage socialized to the priority roles of providers, husbands, and fathers and expect their wives to be supporters, wives, and mothers. Women are socialized as wives, mothers, and partners and expect their husbands to be lovers, fathers, and providers. For most women career comes third, after marriage and family; for most men career comes first, before marriage and family. This difference in role expectations and priorities is a major source of discord for corporate couples of all levels.

Today's generation of corporate rookies is more knowledgeable about the life-style and its problems because many were corporate children. In 1984, the Census Bureau reported that three-quarters of American men and more than half of American women under age twenty-five were still single. The report stated: "Many of these young adults may have postponed their entry into marriage in order to further their formal education, establish careers or pursue other goals that might conflict with assuming family responsibilities." Others choose less binding cohabitation ("living together") over a legal marriage. I received a letter from one such young woman expressing her distress over the workaholism of her companion. In the letter she stated, "And as we're not married, I could walk away at any time even though I love him dearly and would rather not." Living-together couples face the same problems as married couples, but if the stress becomes too great, the relationship can be dissolved without legal entanglement. Of those who choose marriage most are dual-career couples, with husband and wife building careers at the same time. They usually agree to postpone having children until both are settled in their respective careers and are financially secure. They vow allegiance to spouse and eventual family and confidently dedicate themselves to maintaining the vitally important balance between work and family. They set limits beyond which they refuse to go for the sake of career. But their youthful exuberance and the glamorous corporate rewards tend to negate realistic appraisal. Corporate employees always swear first priority to spouse and family, but their subsequent actions rarely fulfill their vows. And the rookie stage is where it all begins.

Rookie Stage Overview

Jeff and Carole have it made; they're on the road to success. Their journey began with graduation from college, he with a degree in business management and she with one in industrial psychology. Jeff accepted an employment offer from a large electronics company in the position of sales trainee. Being practical, Carole postponed looking for a job until after their wedding. On their short Florida honeymoon they dreamed and planned their future: careers, children, houses, and cars. On their return Jeff started his job and one month later left for two weeks of training in Washington. Carole began her job search and eventually accepted a promising position in the human resources office of a local plant. The head of the department was near retirement age, and Carole stood a good chance of promotion to the job. Jeff returned from training, Carole began her job, and with their combined salaries they began house hunting.

But things were different somehow. Jeff came home from training on an almost-spiritual high, enthusiastic about his work and pleased with the company. His work hours became longer, and he often stopped for a drink with the guys after work. This new devotion to his job made Carole a bit jealous, but she chastised herself for selfishness and offered to help him with his sales reports. Most of their conversations now centered on his job, or so it seemed to Carole, but she always listened intelligently, eager to learn about and share in this part of his life. Jeff showed little interest in her job and usually changed the subject when she tried to discuss it with him. This bothered Carole, but she said nothing. They found a lovely "starter" home and moved to the suburbs, but because of work schedules they made few neighborhood friends. Most of their socializing was with Jeff's office friends, but that was all right; the people were nice even though talk always centered around work and the company. Jeff did well at work, winning the Trainee of the Year award that first year. Carole too was happy with her work and loved the new house, but she worried about the distance that seemed to be developing in their relationship. Jeff was so engrossed in work that they spent less time together and shared fewer common interests.

After only two years Jeff received a promotion and raise. He now had the largest territory in the city and a new wardrobe to match the new importance. His zone manager invited them for a dinner celebration. They needed to make a good impression on Mr. Phillips to gain his support for Jeff's career, so Carole took the day off, bought a new dress, and had her hair done. The boss and his wife were extremely pleasant, sophisticated, and kind; Mrs. Phillips even asked Carole to substitute in her bridge club. Carole was impressed by these people but a little nervous in the situation. Jeff, on the other hand, was quite comfortable, talking business with authority and sureness. Carole was proud of him and secretly hoped he wouldn't work so much now. They had bickered about his work hours several times, but Carole knew how much this promotion meant to him. She too was involved in her work and understood his need to prove his ability.

Because of the new territory and more important clients Jeff started attending business dinners and traveling occasionally. He particularly enjoyed these new duties because he'd never before had the money or opportunity for expensive dinners and travel. Still, he felt a little guilty because he couldn't include Carole. That year he surpassed his quota, and Carole accompanied him on the President's Club trip to Hawaii. Three months later the doctor confirmed Carole's suspicions: she was pregnant.

Although the pregnancy was unexpected, they were pleased and began altering their plans. Carole would continue work until the baby arrived and return to her job after a six-month leave of absence; the chance of that promotion to department head wouldn't wait long. All went as scheduled until the seventh month of the pregnancy when the company offered Jeff a position as zone sales manager in Birmingham, Alabama. It was a crucial step in his career, and Carole had to stop work anyway, so of course they took it. During a fast four-day trip they bought a new house, a better one this time because of the salary increase included in the promotion. The old house sold quickly, Carole quit her job, the packers came, the movers loaded, and they were off to Birmingham.

This was their first big relocation and it went well, even though Jeff was at the office when the movers unloaded the furniture. The next few weeks were exhausting for Carole; the settling process took time and sapped her energy. She was forever tired, and Jeff was unnaturally tense. He was unfamiliar with the new situation and unsure of himself in the new job. As work consumed more and more of his time, he often left early and returned home after 10 P.M. Carole felt neglected and lonely, but Jeff explained that he "had to get his arms around his new job."

Finally, the baby arrived, changing Carole's life drastically but making little difference in Jeff's preoccupation with work. When the baby was six months old, Carole went to work with a consultant firm, and although she liked the job, she was uneasy about leaving the baby. Jeff traveled more now—he was out of town when Bobby cut his first tooth and had his first birthday. The branch manager, Mr. Borden, really liked Jeff, encouraged his efforts, and became almost a surrogate father. It wasn't long before Mr. Borden moved to the larger Memphis branch, and a year later Jeff too was promoted to a larger zone in Memphis. Once again Carole quit her job and followed.

Memphis was the same act, different scene. Jeff's work transition was easier because he already knew and liked the boss; in fact, the promotion had come through Mr. Borden. But Carole had difficulty finding a job that paid as much as the last one, and she became discouraged. It really didn't seem worth the effort and worry.

During this time she reassessed her life's goals and decided that Jeff and Bobby needed her more than she needed a career, so she devoted herself to being the best possible wife and mother. Her family became the center of her existence; she was superwife, supermom, and superhostess. Bobby was well adjusted, Jeff was happy, and except for wishing Jeff could be home more Carole was content. Life was good and Memphis was fine—until Jeff came home with champagne and an offer for a district staff position in Atlanta. Now she was really glad she hadn't gone to work, because the relocation process started all over again.

Atlanta was a great place to live, and the entire family loved it. The new job involved coordinating and assisting all of the company's branch offices in that district, which demanded constant travel, but the experience was valuable for Jeff's career and he thrived on his work. Although the travel was tiresome, he enjoyed the special attention he received at each branch. His knowledge, ability, and ego soared. Carole hated the travel and her resulting loneliness, so she became involved in the community by joining the Newcomers Club, garden club, and PTA. She volunteered at the local hospital one day a week and soon became president of the Grey Ladies group. Her days were filled with activity, but she was still terribly lonely in the late afternoons and nights. On the rare occasions when Jeff was home he was either exhausted or preoccupied. Carole now took full responsibility for Bobby and the home. She could never depend on Jeff's being there when she needed him, and it was just easier not to rely on him. He was in Chicago for more training when Bobby had his emergency appendectomy.

Carole understood the demands of the job and Jeff's need to accomplish; she understood that their pleasant life depended on the comfortable salary; she wanted him to be successful for himself and the family. But she worried that he was losing touch with and interest in her and Bobby. Subconsciously, she became bitter and began to resent his work. The company was demanding too much, Jeff was giving too much, and the family was sacrificing too much. Several times she tried to talk with him about this problem, but she was never able to express her concerns and feelings well enough for Jeff to really understand. He accused her of nagging, and each discussion ended in anger. He was happy and she should be happy too. After all, he was working to provide a good life for all of them; she had everything she wanted and much more than most. Carole was always left defenseless. There was no rebuttal to such rhetoric, so she stopped bringing up the subject, accepted the way life was, and silently seethed. This was not what she had bargained for in life, but Jeff and Bobby were satisfied, and perhaps it was her fault for being unhappy. The other wives seem happy and fulfilled, so maybe it's just me, she thought; maybe things will be different when he becomes a branch manager.

Learning the Game

Major corporations exert great effort and expense to induct a continuous flow of new rookies into company ranks. They canvass the universities for candidates with the desired qualities of intelligence, leadership, appearance, and ambition; above all, these candidates must be eager to succeed. For sales positions especially, corporations judge each candidate on personal and professional qualities that eventually might lead to management, and both the company and the candidate are aware of this projected goal. Much like social clubs, businesses choose as their employees those most likely to assimilate to the established corporate culture. Shortly after hiring-in, employees enter company training programs. (American corporations annually spend between $15 billion and $20 billion on training alone.) Although the training period involves subtle initiation into the company culture, it is always referred to with the inoffensive but inclusive term *training*. Training produces a technically productive employee; initiation is the rite of passage into the cult and is continuous throughout the career.

Company initiation generally applies to sales, marketing, finance, and human resource personnel. Blue-collar and clerical people aren't hired, trained, or initiated for future management. Such people *work for* the corporation, whereas the others, because of their backgrounds, positions, and initiations, are considered and consider themselves *part of* the corporation. (Personal statements of employees often reflect these attitudes. Assembly workers will normally say "I work for Megacorp"; computer sales people state, "I'm with Megacorp.") Both the company and other employees expect these bright initiates, if they're successful, to run the company someday. They are the company's future, and they must learn to think in the corporate mode and for the corporation's benefit. Their philosophy becomes: what is good for the company will in the long run be good for me. This mentality is characteristic of future managers.

Initiation involves indoctrination of shared attitudes, values, roles, language, and emotions. It is learning and accepting the corporate ethic of working, living, and behaving. I talked with a young man, newly graduated, newly married, and newly employed by a large corporation. He had recently returned from his first training session full of excitement, glowing reports, and praise for the company. He was so impressed that he planned to build his entire career with this company. His wife and future children are very important to him, and he firmly believes in balancing work and family. When I questioned him about this balance, he adamantly stated there would be no problems because his company was truly family-oriented; his boss had told him he should never let his work take precedence over his family. Moving on to his training, I asked how many hours he anticipated working in an average day. He quickly replied that he was in sales, and sales is not a nine-to-five job. Innocently, he recalled the specific slide from the training course showing a man at his desk, a clock on the wall showing 6:30 P.M., and the caption: "Sales is not a nine-to-five job." I then asked how he rationalized the family-oriented company philosophy with the overt call for long hours that would take away family time. For a moment he was stunned; then he replied that it would be no problem, he would handle it. This young man has been with the company less than three months, and already he works ten hours a day, plus an hour or so at home on some nights.

The training period marks the beginning of the attitude alteration that gradually changes carefree students into success-oriented "corporatites" who see the success examples of others and yearn for like rewards. Training illuminates the path to that success. Each step and position of career progression is clearly marked: trainee to sales representative to account manager to zone manager to so on and so on to president and chief executive officer. Rookies subconsciously learn that to attain this success personal and family trade-offs and sacrifices must be made. By the end of training, each rookie knows sales is not a nine-to-five job and realizes that the company knows the best career path for him. He knows promotion and relocation are compliments, because the company feels he earned the opportunities, and he would be foolish to turn them down. All the sacrifices one must make for success are disguised as career opportunities; therefore, the personal and family problems that accompany the corporate climb do not seem so severe—not to the rookie, anyway.

Training teaches knowledge and skills; initiation inculcates subjective corporate messages. Thought and behavior modifications aren't taught from textbooks or in formal, organized sessions. They come through a form of osmosis, unnoticed and unrecognized by the employee but nonetheless effective. Architects design company training centers for teaching skills, but they also design these centers to teach specific, subliminal lessons about company traits and culture. Nearly every detail conveys the corporation's image and character. In such an environment the corporate mentality becomes part of the employee's psyche, and the employee becomes part of the corporation, a welcome new member. It is indeed a subtle process, but assimilation into the culture is critical to individual success within the corporation.

Aside from the company initiation, relocations produce a major impact on rookie couples. College-educated rookie employees usually choose equally well educated marriage partners. Today most young corporate couples have dual careers. Corporate relocation brings these two careers into direct confrontation for the first time, and the repeated relocations typical of the rookie stage can severely strain careers and personal relationships. Some couples are fortunate enough to begin their careers in a large city such as New York, Chicago, Los Angeles, or Dallas, where branch, district, and perhaps even corporate headquarters are located. In this situation both husband and wife could possibly move up in their respective organizations without relocation problems, but there are no guarantees. Slots for promotion are seldom created; they come when and where there are open positions, and relocation is usually a prerequisite.

Stable, parallel careers are rare in dual-career corporate couples because of relocations and/or promotions. As a general rule, one—normally the wife—sacrifices her job for the husband's promotion and becomes a "trailing spouse," looking for a position in the new place. To preserve both careers a couple might elect an alternative to moving. One such choice is the commuter marriage, in which one will travel to be with the other on weekends, but this arrangement is personally expensive and emotionally unsatisfying. Relocations alone are physically and mentally stressful, but the resentment and often jealousy innate in dual-career relocations can be destructive. The rookie stage of corporate employment can entail three to five relocations, occurring approximately every two to three years.

The Rookie Employee

After talking with corporate rookies, I always come away deeply impressed by their idealism, ability, and confidence; I'm envious of their high spirits and sureness. They seem to have all the answers to life's questions and plan to mold their destinies as they wish, vowing to control effectively any hardships the future might bring. This new generation of rookies is different from the previous generation; they know what they want, how to go about getting it, and the price they're willing to pay for it. One's career is not happenstance but a formally or informally planned sequence of achievements. One couple knew exactly where they wanted to be on the career ladder five, ten, and fifteen years from now. Interviews with older employees revealed career plans formulated during, not prior to, progression. Their career progress has been much like an explorer cutting a path through the jungle, with only vague knowledge of a desired destination. This isn't the case with today's youngsters. Their exposure to the corporation has been greater, they have more knowledge of the structure and workings of the organization, and they are confident they can live and play the corporate game by their own rules. While I admire their idealism, I find one flaw in their logic. They do not consider the subconscious, transforming effects of corporate initiation.

Although rookie employees visually and verbally display self-confidence, uncertainty is characteristic of everyone in the twenty-two- to thirty-year age bracket, the life stage when one normally enters adulthood and begins both marital and professional careers. Faced with a multitude of new challenges, untested rookies are unsure of their personal capabilities and potentials but are eager to meet the challenges, test their abilities, and prove themselves competent. The first job is their proving ground, and company training/initiation marks the route by which success can be attained.

In their book *Must Success Cost So Much?* Paul Evans and Fernando Bartolomé propose that "people focus their psychological attention above all on their work

careers until such time as they find a sense of fulfillment there. The family is important, but major preoc-
cupations are elsewhere."³ Inspired by their own uncertainty and the training/initiation, rookies attack their first
jobs with enthusiasm, working hard to prove themselves, to achieve recognition and reward, and to gain
personal satisfaction. Thus, they begin climbing the
perpetual stairway of success that high achievers scale
throughout their careers. This stairway is also known as
the infamous corporate rat race, the race starting in the
rookie stage and ending in retirement. Professor Doug-
las Hall of Northwestern University described this stairway as the "success spiral syndrome," in which early career success generates more success opportunities and
more personal desire to be successful. This success spiral or stairway is part of the corporate culture passed from
generation to generation of employees. In an equation
the progression would be as follows: Effort = Performance = Reward = Higher Goals = More Effort
at Work and Less Involvement at Home.

In my opinion personal participation in this success
stairway has three basic motivations: socialization, company initiation, and ego. American men know from early
age that they will be providers, breadwinners for themselves and their future families. "What are you going to
be when you grow up?" is a question constantly asked
of boys and young men; only recently has this question
been asked with any sincerity of females. Men also know
that winning comes through competition. In the business world winning equates with a good salary; therefore, success in work provides a better living. The concepts of competition, achievement, and success are part
of our American heritage, and for corporate employees
material success in life comes via the success stairway.

Second, the corporate mentality gained through initiation hones natural competitiveness and enhances the desire for achievement and advancement. On the stairway employees compete with their peers, test their abilities with higher goals and more important duties, and gain promotions. Company initiation teaches pity for those employees who falter on their climb. It becomes a matter of pride to strive for and attain the next career level.

Finally, the career success stairway provides overt, concrete ego gratification that is partly innate and partly learned through company initiation. Corporate people show material signs of success and receive public recognition for success. Success in personal life is abstract. It isn't material or monetary; it cannot be seen, touched, or spent; it cannot be displayed; and it does not receive public praise. For many high achievers the desire for overt ego gratification is as great as their desire for achievement. The success stairway gives the opportunity to become an excellent provider, to compete and achieve, and to be recognized as an outstanding member of the company. This theory holds true for all successful corporate employees with whom I'm acquainted.

High-achieving rookies start the success climb early. Career gradually takes precedence over the family, in action if not in mind, and this devotion to work becomes a major stress on and a major distress in rookies' marriages. From their research, authors Evans and Bartolomé concluded that during this career and age level an ambitious rookie's priorities fall into this order: work, children, and spouse. Establishing the career, finding a mentor, proving ability, and gaining success are the central issues of the rookie employee's life. Private, marital lives are peripheral and are viewed as mere support systems for careers.[4]

Men especially tend to be arrogantly secure about their marriages and easily rationalize their conscious or subconscious choice of work over family. Sometimes there are valid reasons for this choice: the demands of the job and boss must be met to retain employment, and often the rookie has no viable alternative but compliance. But when the success syndrome is in effect the rationalizing mentality is time-structured: work long and hard, perform well, get the promotion, and things will be different then. The thought process goes something like this: If I work hard now, after the goal is reached, I'll be in a more powerful position and will be able to control my schedule. Then I'll concentrate more time with the family. But once the promotion is attained, the long hours continue under the "I have to get my arms around the job" justification, and the cycle begins anew.

Although the rookie's intentions are good, the time is seldom, if ever, appropriate to fulfill them. Rookie employees might be truly concerned about their marriages and families, but they naively assume the relationships will remain stable and develop according to plan regardless of neglect. Once the career is established, they envision taking the family off "hold" and returning it to first place. They simply intend to pick up right where they left off years before, but they'll have money and success in addition to family. This kind of rationalization often results in disappointment and sometimes disaster for the entire family.

Company initiation is intense during the rookie career stage. Older employees and selected role models lay down the patterns to follow. Peers and unspoken company attitudes impose work hours, senior managers teach duty performance, mentors teach office politics and maneuverability, and all management-level employees project the proper corporate mental and physical image to which rookies aspire. Friends and social functions take on career importance, and personal sophistication becomes a necessity. With ability, ambition, initiation, sophistication, and a well-inculcated success syndrome, the rookie will soon become a star.

The Rookie Spouse

A new, disconcerting breed of spouse is evolving and stirring up the placid waters of the corporate sea. This new woman is intelligent, educated, and ambitious; she refuses to row the home/boat obediently and smoothly while her George Washington mate stands in the bow charting his corporate course. These are the transmuters of corporate wifehood. They enter marriage with aspirations to goals and careers of their own, and they create shock waves throughout the business world by demanding recognition and consideration in their husbands' career decisions. Some of the new breed stand firm for their personal goals and work to find solutions that will accommodate both careers; these are the true avant-garde transmuter corporate spouses. At present, however, they are the exception rather than the rule. Traces of traditional socialization are still apparent in the values of most young women, and they subconsciously give their husbands' careers precedence over their own.

The first clash between the two careers comes with the first child or first relocation—either can be a critical event for the career woman. At this time the most common pattern of thought and action of transmuter rookie wives is to leave their careers temporarily with the intention of resuming work after settlement in the new city or after the child reaches a certain age. They put their personal goals on hold to concentrate on home and family, much as rookie employees put home and family on hold to concentrate on careers. Once settled, ambitious spouses start their careers anew, but as the years progress and the moves continue and/or more children arrive, a spouse's grip on her career normally weakens. The repeated job searches, in addition to the repeated settlings, become too difficult. She is never in one position long enough to make much career progress anyway, so she shelves it until later. Her direction in life converges with her husband's, and she gradually strays so far from her original path that the distance back to the career is overwhelming. As a result, most women eventually give up their personal ambitions and search for contentment by supporting and aiding their husbands. Traditional socialization wins out over avant-garde beliefs, and the majority of young wives come to resemble the transitional spouse more than the transmuter.

Evans and Bartolomé identified four types of modern corporate wives: the supportive wife, the working wife, the career wife, and the "family as career" wife. The supportive wife is basically the much worn traditional corporate wife. She is unemployed, dependent, and home-oriented. Her husband and children come first in her life, and she supports their needs and ambitions. Although she has many friends, she is often lonely. This woman blames herself for any family unhappiness, whether in herself, her husband, or the children. She is a corporate wife model and martyr. The working wife is employed, usually part time, but remains supportive to the husband and kids. She usually works to alleviate her loneliness, and her husband approves of her working so she won't bother him. This wife feels guilty about taking time from husband and kids to work. The career wife is the avant-garde woman committed to personal goals and professional identity. Home and family life are tense and stressful from trying to maintain two separate careers; this is the classic dual-career home. Because this life-style is so difficult, many abandon their careers and take on one of the other roles. The "family as career" wife is a misplaced career woman whose family is her profession and sole occupation. Her goal is the perfect, happy, and successful family, and she's usually disappointed because her husband refuses to play his "ideal" family role. Such wives are often uncertain of themselves, unhappy, and discontented. This wife normally blames her husband and the company for her unhappiness.[5] I see little difference between the supportive wife and the "family as career" wife except personality traits; one is self-sacrificing and the other is domineering. Their goals and orientations are the same: the traditionally happy, successful home and family. Therefore, I prefer to combine the "family as career" wife with the supportive wife and use the trite term *traditional* for both.

I believe that many of today's rookie wives begin their marriages as transmuter career wives and end up as either traditional or transitional unemployed or working wives, all of which roles are supportive of their husbands' careers. The difficulties of the corporate life-style and female socialization motivate this role change. In a *Wall Street Journal* article on child-rearing responsibilities of dual-career couples, one father was quoted: "Despite lots of honest feelings about the importance of feminism, we wound up with a very traditional pattern." His wife now works part time. I talked with a transmuter rookie wife about her probable action if her husband was transferred or when the first child arrived. She discounted any relocation because she felt her husband would move up his career ladder in the present city. As for children, they don't plan to have any for ten years, and at that time she will stop work until the child is school age. As rookies slowly change into gray-flannel personas, young wives too evolve into more traditional corporate spouses.

Wives are more cognizant of the transformation than their mates. Men tend to be objective, accepting at face value, whereas women are more subjective, searching for underlying meanings and trends. Women sense the gradual change in priorities and relationships; men rarely realize a change is occurring, and if they do, they rationalize it as a phase that eventually will revert to normal. Spouses hope tomorrow will be different; rookie employees rely on it.

Uncertainty is as pronounced in rookie wives as in employees. They come into the stage filled with emotional dreams of his career, her career, and their romantic marriage. Whatever is wrong, they'll make right through love. It's the start of their personal fairy tale. The euphoria lasts until the villain, the company, interferes. The company/villain casts a spell over her handsome prince and the plot turns sour. The poor princess is upset and heartbroken by the turn of events. She waits for the prince to break the spell, return to his senses, and restore their dream. Forgive the cruel analogy, but many American daughters are reared to romantic dreams rather than to reality, and reality can sometimes be cruel, especially for the corporate spouse. When the dream goes awry, uncertainty floods her being; this is not the life for which she prepared, and she's unsure of how to deal with it.

As the husband becomes more deeply involved with work and climbing the success stairway, the wife searches for ways to establish a personal link with his professional life and retain mutual interests. First she tries to help him in his work. This effort normally fails because the work becomes too technical and she has no training. She becomes frustrated and feels cut off and shut out of her husband's life. For self-preservation she directs her anger at the company for demanding so much of him. Admitting that he often chooses work over togetherness hurts too much. She tries to talk with him about the situation, but he is unable to understand her concern; he's happy and satisfied. Failing as a job assistant, the wife renews her search for a meaningful role in her husband's work life and usually finds her link: company entertaining. She attends many company parties given by other wives, and they seem to have the answer to her quandary. Entertaining also provides the opportunity to learn more about the people with whom he works. Swapping the assistant's job for the hostess position, the rookie wife establishes the vital link to her husband's work, receiving praise for her efforts, and her initiation into corporate wifehood progresses.

Rookie wives seldom refuse to accommodate their lives to their husbands' career wishes. Women are still socialized to almost sole responsibility for the marital relationship, and most fear the results of a confrontation between marriage and career in which the relationship might be damaged. Women also fear later regurgitation in the form of "If you hadn't kept me from taking that promotion, look where I would be by now." When a career decision such as relocation must be made, wives freely express their positive and negative opinions, but most leave the final decision to their husbands. If the wife doesn't want to move, she hopes her husband will consider her opinions, read her mind, and decide not to move. Usually, the man decides in favor of the career move; the wife is disappointed, hurt, and bitter, but the marriage evades a direct confrontation. No matter how strong the marital relationship, most women are afraid to test its strength against their husbands' careers. This socialized fear and insecurity lock many women into the traditional, supportive role.

Once settled into the traditional role, a clear division of duties occurs in the marriage. The man is responsible for providing the money, and the wife's duty is to support him in his efforts by taking care of most or all other facets of their private life. She frees him of worry and responsibility so that he can concentrate on his career. By trial and error she concludes there's simply less hassle and upset in the home when she is supportive of husband and children. In addition, other traditional company wives provide role models for the rookie wife; they personify the success of supportiveness. Being well initiated into the corporate culture themselves, these women strive to project the proper corporate image, and their facade rarely fades. They proudly proclaim their happiness and satisfaction verbally and through their successful husbands, well-adjusted children, and gracious entertaining. Never a negative crosses their lips. They are the conduits through which the corporate culture passes to the novices.

The lives of the rookie employee and spouse are stressful, each striving to bring a personal dream to reality. The male employee, socialized to provide, works hard launching his dream career. The wife, socialized to romance, finds her original ideals of marriage and career unrealistic and her dream destroyed by the unfamiliar roles, expectations, and difficulties of the corporate life. As the husband becomes part of the corporation, he receives great satisfaction and rewards for his work; as the wife assumes the traditional role, she receives little personal satisfaction and few rewards for her efforts. The career support provided by rookie wives is seldom recognized by themselves, their husbands, or the company. They never receive promotions nor raises and are rarely included on business or convention trips. During this stage initiation into the culture begins, the climb of the success stairway starts, and roles and patterns are established. But rookies retain the hope that it will be better when they are corporate stars.

2

THE STARS

PLAYING
THE GAME

Thirty-five, the threshold of middle age, arrives too early.
Just yesterday the mirror reflected lively hair, glowing
skin, sparkling eyes, and trim body—but disaster struck
overnight. This morning's image showed a gray maver-
ick sticking straight up, laugh lines, crow's-feet, and a
slight paunch in the torso. Only a few short years ago
the corporate couple looked and listened with disgust and
disdain to anyone over thirty-five and swore to end it all
before joining the middle-age brigade. Yet here they are
at thirty-five. Youngsters now look with disapproving arrogance at them and call them Mr. or Mrs. The middle
years came so quickly. Where do they go from here?

Thirty-five, or thereabout, seems to be a pivotal age
for most individuals. As one author said, it's "the end of
growing up and the beginning of growing old." Thirty-
five is generally accepted as the midpoint of an average
life span, and around that age the mirror becomes an
annoying standard of truth, attesting to the verity that

years do indeed take a toll. Heedless of expensive creams, enhancing hair colors, and rejuvenating exercise programs, mortality becomes a fact rather than a rhetorical issue. The end of life is as near as the beginning, but there is no going back, no retreat, and no escape. The humanness of existence dawns with shattering impact, affecting lives both physically and psychologically. The corporate couple reacts to the entrance into middle age just as noncorporate couples do. The passage is difficult for everyone, but the corporate environment, mentality, and life-style can be added burdens in this already upsetting phase.

To understand the midcareer, midlife corporate couple better, one must first examine some of the classic charactistics and dynamics of the age level. Men and women go through three stages between the ages of thirty-five and fifty: recognition, reaction, and reevaluation. The first stage, recognition, is generally the same for both sexes, but the stages of reaction and reevaluation usually vary according to gender.

Recognition has two elements, physical and psychological. Physical recognition comes early, presented by the mirror's image. The adage of being as old as you feel has little meaning when one discovers the first signs of advancing age. True, attitudes and behaviors may remain youthful, but the testimony of the physical is undeniable. Many people respond to these signs of aging with a rush of activity. With the intent of postponing the inevitable, they jog each morning, join the nearest health spa, go on the newest fad diet, consult a cosmetic surgeon, or buy a hairpiece. It's a shock to discover that one cannot sustain youth by sheer force of will. However upsetting, the truth of physical vulnerability is the initiator of middle age. But there are no

temporary or permanent antidotes for psychological recognition that time is not endless. With the coming of
middle age, most people consciously or subconsciously
take an inventory of their lives thus far. They recall
youthful dreams and ambitions and measure accomplishments accordingly. For most, accomplishments fall
short of early expectations; they are not where they
planned to be at this age. Yesterday the availability of
time was taken for granted, but now time is a measured
quantity. Half of life is over, and there is still much to
do.

Research finds that men and women usually react
differently to their physical and psychological recognition of middle age. Time becomes a primary issue to
both, but their mental concepts of time often are polar-
ized. It's a matter of perception, much like seeing a glass
as half empty or half full. Having taken stock of their
accomplishments to date and found themselves wanting, most men begin to think of time as too short; time
that is needed to attain their dreams is running out.
Feelings of failure or fear may follow; some attempt escape through the "middle-age crazies," trying to reclaim
their youth through extramarital affairs and/or eating and
drinking excessively. The majority of men, however, re-
new their commitment to career success with a dedicated urgency in an effort to make up for lost time and
prove themselves superior to their peers in the competition for places in the ever-narrowing pyramidal corporate structure. Uncertain of the future, they shift into
high gear because time is growing dear. Disappointment, fear, and temporary or prolonged depression are
symptomatic of the male reaction stage of middle age.

Women also often encounter depression with the
onslaught of the middle years. Much has been made of

the demoralizing effects of physical and numerical age on women, and for some these effects are valid. The former beauty queen no longer turns heads when she enters the room; now there is someone younger and prettier getting the attention. Women too experience uncertainty about the future. As a young rookie, she probably postponed her career to have children and devote herself to the home. Normally, the last child goes off to school as a woman enters middle age; the full-time job of mother and wife evolves into a part-time occupation. Time now becomes a major issue in her life too. In early middle age some women, much like some men, have extramarital affairs and some even become runaway wives. But unlike most men who see time as too short and running out, most women tend to have too much time on their hands and no meaningful way to use it. Men become upset because they haven't accomplished their goals; women become upset because they have accomplished their immediate goals and haven't defined new ones. In both cases reevaluation is mandatory.

In the reevaluation stage of middle age, the sexual diversity of the concept of time can present major problems in a marital relationship. Middle-age male reactions usually result in one of two conclusions: (1) their spurt of urgency and energy at work can propel them onward and upward and reinforce their dedication to careers, or else (2) they realize they have attained as much success as possible and scale down their career expectations. Regardless of the career results a man's midlife reevaluation normally makes him more sensitive to personal life. He acknowledges personal feelings and emotions, perhaps for the first time in his life. Wife and children become very important, and home becomes a solace and haven. But just as a man begins turning toward home and family, the home empties, as wife and children turn to the outside world.

Women's midlife reevaluations can culminate in surprising results, which are sometimes upsetting and frightening for their husbands. Most women look on this abundance of time as a long-awaited opportunity. With the children in school they are no longer encumbered by the socialized restraints of the dutiful wife and mother; time has made that job relatively obsolete. At last they have time to do as they wish, and most women eagerly and enthusiastically greet this new freedom. The majority of women see this point in life as a new beginning rather than an ending. They are ready to assert themselves, to look for a new purpose, and to establish their own identities separate from husband and children. For most, this stage is characterized by returning to school, going back to work or career, or becoming involved in gratifying community activities. Others, the ones who find fulfillment in the supportive wife role, continue in earlier patterns. The remaining few also continue their previous roles, bitterly trapped by indecision and fear.

The years between thirty-five and fifty are traumatic for both men and women, individually and communally. As men are drawing back disappointed, their wives are forging ahead eagerly. Such reversal of roles, attitudes, and behaviors normally effects changes in relationships and patterns of marriage. Middle age can be both frightening and invigorating.

Star Stage Overview

Jeff spent three years on the Atlanta district staff before receiving the Falls Church, Virginia, branch. Because of the continuous travel, those three years were physically difficult but professionally profitable. He gained valuable experience and insight into the finite workings of the organization, and the new assignment resulted from his outstanding performance and popularity with his superiors and peers. For Carole the years of Atlanta were emotionally difficult. The long work hours and travel were a constant source of irritation, and although she was busy with her volunteering and chauffeuring, her life seemed only a meaningless scurry of activity. She was just marking time until this promotion to branch manager came through; both Jeff and she felt things would be better now. Bobby cried as the moving van pulled away from their old house, but Carole breathed a sigh of relief even though she knew the hardships of another settling awaited her in Falls Church. She didn't mind the hardships, because Falls Church was where they were finally going to make their home and put down roots. Jeff had attained his career goal, and now they would build a new life together.

And indeed the dream did begin. Jeff was now the boss, and after the initial adjustment period his work days averaged about ten and a half hours, and his travel tapered to mostly one-day jaunts. Carole played and thoroughly enjoyed the role of branch manager's wife, giving company parties and ladies' teas, attending business dinners and out-of-town conventions with Jeff, and volunteering her time for community projects. Life settled into a manageable routine. Jeff was assistant coach for Bobby's baseball team and attended most of the games. They joined the country club, took up golf, and played every Sunday afternoon with their friends. Carole became almost as well known in the community as Jeff was at the corporation, and their relationship had never been better. After three straight years of having the top branch of the district, Jeff was awarded a special commendation by the company and a week's all-expenses-paid vacation; he was the golden boy. It wasn't long until headquarters called and invited him up for a conference about a possible position. Carole was upset, but Jeff assured her he wasn't interested in a corporate job, although he felt he had to listen to their proposal. He returned a different man. At headquarters Jeff talked with the man who wanted him for the staff job and turned it down, but then the vice-president of sales called him into his office, served coffee from a silver service, and talked about Jeff's future. The VP offered to have Carole flown up and promised to give a cocktail party so they could meet some of the other staff people. Jeff came home excited about the prospect, but Carole refused to go for the party. They talked long into the night, with Carole saying she didn't think it was a good move and Jeff saying that after two years on the corporate staff he would be a district manager. Finally, Carole said the decision was up to him to do as he thought best. He accepted the job. The dream had lasted four years.

Jeff went to Chicago to start the new job while Carole stayed in Falls Church to sell the house and let Bobby finish the eighth grade. Jeff knew he'd made a mistake after less than two weeks. The position was at best mediocre in prestige and boring in execution. There were two hundred other guys, just as bright and golden as he, all vying for twenty district manager jobs. The competition was fierce and the corporate bureaucracy frustrating. As a branch manager of seventy-five employees he had had power. Yes, that power was limited, but most of his decisions went uncontested. Now he had no one to manage and couldn't make even the simplest decision. He fought the disappointment and uncertainty at work, but when he finally returned to his empty apartment at night, depression decended. Consequently, he started working later and stopping for a couple of drinks on the way home. By the time Carole and Bobby arrived he had decided that the only way out of this misery was to double his efforts and get that promotion as soon as possible. He never mentioned his dilemma to Carole.

Carole was bitter about the move and was prepared not to like Chicago. She didn't like it; she hated it. Bobby, who entered the ninth grade that fall was at the age when mothers are an embarrassment. Jeff worked on the international corporate sales staff, and the travel began again, only this time a trip could last two weeks or more. That first winter tested Carole's sanity with snow and ice, Jeff's traveling, and Bobby's attitude. There were several calls from the school counselor about Bobby cutting classes and leaving school. Sessions with the counselor became routine, but Jeff never went. He was either in an important meeting or out of town, but he did try to talk to Bobby when he was home. Carole considered finding a job but quickly dismissed the idea because of her son's recent behavior; she was genuinely afraid of what he might do. He did it anyway. When he was sixteen, Bobby was arrested for driving while intoxicated.

While in Chicago, Jeff and Carole played the corporate game. They attended parties and gave parties. Jeff played golf with his boss, and Carole attended ladies' teas and went to the symphony on the company bus. They met the president of the company and his wife and dutifully wore their name tags. Carole smiled graciously when people complimented Jeff: "That young man will go far." Everyone thought them the ideal couple; no one knew of the turmoil at home and their problems with Bobby. They played their parts to perfection. And it finally paid off.

Jeff became the district manager in San Francisco just before Bobby entered his senior year of high school. By this time his "teenage" antics had somewhat abated, but he flatly refused to move to California, threatening to run away if they forced him to go. Carole was hurt and Jeff was angry, but after many emotionally heated discussions arrangements were made with Bobby's best friend's family for Bobby to stay in Chicago for his last year of school. Dejected, Jeff and Carole moved to San Francisco.

Jeff's district covered a large geographical area and contained many branch offices, which necessitated two or three days of travel each week. When he was in town, his commute to and from the office was tedious. With the house finished, Jeff gone most of the time, and Bobby in Chicago, Carole decided to return to school for her postgraduate work in psychology. Her corporate wife duties were few because the people on Jeff's staff were scattered over the entire San Francisco area, and most of the entertaining was done at a centrally located restaurant instead of in their home. Now was her time. Jeff was happy with the arrangement: she was happily occupied but was home when he returned from work, and she was still available for company occasions. It was better to have her busy and happy so she wouldn't gripe and nag about his work. A year later Bobby finished high school and came home for a month and a half before entering college in Illinois. Knowing no one except his parents, he was miserable and made them miserable too.

Two years after entering school Carole received her degree and immediately took a job in the city. And with that job things changed.

Jeff felt that he should be getting overtures from the company about a promotion to regional manager, but there had been none. He became concerned that he might be passed over, and he wanted to talk to Carole about his uncertainty. But she was seldom home when he needed her anymore and rarely sympathetic when she was there. Her job was so demanding that he had to take his own shirts to the laundry. She had missed the last staff party and seemed truly unconcerned about his travel. She even hired a maid to clean the house, and he felt uncomfortable if the maid was there when he was home. Jeff couldn't understand what had happened. Their lives were going in different directions just when they should be closer than ever. And Bobby was no better; he came home only for a week each summer and at Christmastime. For the first time Jeff began to wonder where his life was taking him. He seemed to be going nowhere, fast.

Playing the Game

Middle management is the make-or-break phase of a corporate career, and ambitious employees are fully aware that their performance at this level determines their professional future. Company initiation accelerates to a more sophisticated, subjective pace and encompasses elements of loyalty to the company, assimilation and dedication to the success stairway, and social and professional maneuverability. This job level is the period of learning and testing for employees. They gain experience in varied facets of the business and learn management techniques while superiors watch and test them to evaluate qualifications for upper management. To pass this midlevel testing, stars must relinquish a major part of the control over their personal careers by accepting almost any promotion offered and relocating to wherever that promotion dictates. Spouses are a major, but unrecognized, influence in relocation decisions, and their agreement is often fundamental to positive test results. Compliance with company decisions that affect a star's personal and professional lives relays the message that the star is obedient and realizes that the company knows what is best for his career. It also tells superiors that the spouse is supportive of career goals or that at least the star controls the home situation. During this stage superiors monitor stars closely to make sure their actions and decisions reflect company rather than personal benefit. Hungry rookies are apt to give personal benefit first priority, but middle managers must shift their thinking to what is good for the company. The shift to company mentality is critical and is a harbinger of advancement.

Competition is intense among middle managers. As stars climb higher in the corporate pyramid, next-step positions become fewer in number. Therefore, many managers vie for the same position, and the infighting can be fierce. Performance is the key to this test: long hours, travel, aggressiveness and results. Continued peak performance shows superiors that the success syndrome is firmly in place and is still active.

Professional and social maneuverability is purely political: can the star play the corporate political game? Although middle managers have little power, they must demonstrate that they can get things done and make things happen through themselves and others. Mentors are important in passing this test because they are political allies, teaching, showing, and backing their protégés in the art of office politics. Stars must learn to subtly manipulate bosses, peers, subordinates, and clients to assist in accomplishing tasks and attaining goals. Social maneuverability is a hallmark of middle management and is judged on two levels. First, middle managers seek to initiate or enhance ties with superiors, mentors, and peers through socializing over lunch, drinks after work, sports activities, and during travel. Being a fun guy and one of the gang is advantageous, part of "old boy" networking. Getting to know fellow employees, especially bosses and mentors, on a personal basis is politically profitable to one's career.

The second level of corporate social politics involves the star's spouse and requires her cooperation and contribution. Attending and giving business/social affairs increase in the middle corporate level, as social contact with immediate superiors and upper management becomes more common. Both stars and spouses become more visible and are judged on physical appearance as well as social and entertaining skills. Middle managers and their spouses must prove adaptability to and assimilation into the corporate social culture.

For stars middle-management positions are frustrating and thankless. Upper-management executives hold the reins of power; they make the decisions, point the direction, and assign the tasks, but middle managers are the functionaries of the organization, the workhorses that pull the corporate wagon. Stars have responsibility but little control and even less power. They may work a month on a special project, present it to upper management, and have the project completely canceled. Middle management decisions must be okayed by superiors before implementation—the chain of command must be followed—and sometimes approval can take months. If stars are politically astute, they can influence decisions, but they never truly make decisions.

Middle management/midlife is the most potentially dangerous of all phases, professionally and personally. Stars are a dime a dozen, and there are always eager young rookies ready to play the game. Many employees reach this level and go no further; dead-end jobs, demotions, and terminations proliferate. Many fall from the steep grade of the corporate pyramid, their careers stymied. In bad economic times when reductions in work force are necessary, secretaries and clerical workers go first, but middle managers are second. At such times, when the ranks are trimmed, the pyramidal incline becomes more pronounced, and promotions are harder to achieve. On the personal front, middle age approximates most middle management, and just when work life is toughest, personal and home life becomes chaotic. A dichotomy sometimes develops: work negatively affects personal and home life; personal and home life negatively affect work life. One seems to feed off the other and vice versa. Without a thorough understanding of the dynamics of this age and career stage, the results can be disastrous in both areas.

The Star Employee

Diligence in the rookie stage pays off; the career is launched, company initiation is inculcated, and the climb of the success stairway has begun. With promotion to middle management the game gets rougher and tougher, and the corporate culling out process begins. A rookie must prove fundamental ability in order to advance this far; further career advancement depends on the star's overall performance in middle management. Basically, there are three categories of stars: the superstars, the stabilizers, and the dropouts. For all of these stars, middle age and middle management determine the future. Superstars are the brightest stars in the corporate game, and they work hard to distinguish themselves as such. They invest long work hours at the office and at home; they travel extensively; they move anywhere for promotion; and they are adept in both office and social politics. In middle management these employees strive to separate themselves from the pack, to outshine all of the other stars and establish themselves as leaders among their peers. Superstars are classic gamesmen, reveling in competition, achievement, and winning the game. Their greatest fear is failure, being labeled a loser in the corporate game.

Superstars are the high achievers who climb the success stairway in enthusiastic leaps. Entering middle age, these employees have attained their early goals with ease and realize that those goals were set too low. They realize too that their capabilities could take them to the top of the corporate pyramid. Now the game takes on a new seriousness. These corporate men recommit themselves to their career, play the game with renewed energy and vigor, and shoot for the top. The corporation is their world, and they feel lost and displaced outside that environment. Social lives revolve around business/social affairs; leisure activity becomes occasional; community involvement is rare. Private life is stripped to the basics. Superstars are often one-dimensional people, career- and ego-centered. Work is the focal point of their lives and many become workaholics to ensure continued fulfillment and success.

At this stage a supportive spouse is a career asset. As the man recommits to his career with a fury, more home responsibility is off-loaded to the wife just as she is going through her own upsetting midlife stage. Superstars depend on their mates to keep the home running smoothly and to be listeners, relocaters, hostesses, business/social event attendees, and role models for younger wives. A spouse's cooperation is important in middle management; she has great influence, positive or negative, on her husband's career.

In their late thirties and early forties stars show little concern for the problems festering in the home. They often rationalize the problems as passing nuisances, manufactured by wives and children to divert attention from career and to themselves. Younger superstars tend to react angrily or ignore the adverse situation at home, shifting the responsibility for resolution completely onto the spouse; there's always some event or project at work that takes precedence over the pestering problems of home. But as the problems increase and the reevaluation stage of middle age begins, older stars realize the problems are not made up; they are indeed real and will not go away. This period of confrontation is very stressful. The personal and family sacrifices made for the career cannot be denied, and feelings of intense guilt and failure are overwhelming. But being sensitive and understanding doesn't necessarily alter their course and behavior. They are locked into their superstar ambitions, and although there is more awareness of families, careers normally retain the prominent place in their lives.

The reevaluation stage of middle age is often difficult for golden boys. Their dreams are geared up, but they are uncertain of the outcome and fear failure. During stressful times, even superstars become more dependent on their wives for encouragement and support. If the spouse continues to be traditionally supportive and satisfied with herself and her life, the marital relationship carries on in familiar patterns with little conflict. But if the wife is dissatisfied with her supportive role and eager to establish her own identity, marital conflicts often result.

The stabilizer stars are the backbone of the corporation, providing strength and continuity for the structure. These employees are usually ambitious, but for some reason they failed the advancer tests, and the promotions stop at the middle-management level. Stabilizers go neither up nor down, but they do sometimes make parallel moves. Corporate employees never know why their careers stall; they simply realize they will go no further up the success stairway. Some, much like the superstars, increase their work efforts in hopes of dislodging themselves and continuing their climb, but most remain trapped in middle-management dead-end jobs. Stabilizers are usually loyal, well-initiated company people who feel a sense of belonging in the corporate structure even though their career progress stops.

In middle age these employees inventory their careers and recognize they have reached their limits. Self-esteem plummets and depression ensues; families become their emotional support systems. Demotion is the stabilizer's greatest fear, and he clings tenaciously to his position through hard, productive work and politics but is psychologically unfulfilled by the work. As a result, most men turn more and more to their private lives to find the needed fulfillment, and spouses, children, and leisure take on a new meaning. A middle-management captive normally regrets the sacrifices that the whole family made for his career and decides that success isn't worth the personal cost. With this decision, private life takes precedence over work life. The job provides money, but emotional satisfaction comes at home. Stabilizers gear down and settle into acceptance and, sometimes, enjoyment of the situation.

The midlife psychological readjustment of the stabilizer, like that of the superstar, is related to his spouse's midlife reaction and reevaluation. If, as he is turning toward home, his mate is looking outward to find a new purpose, the stabilizer's sense of failure often magnifies unless there is good understanding and communication between the two. On the other hand, if the wife is traditionally supportive, the man's turn toward home can be emotionally rewarding for him and is often the wife's dream come true.

Dropout stars are those employees who reach middle management but do not stabilize or advance. Most are demoted or terminated by the company. Included among the dropout ranks are superstars and stabilizers who resign their positions either in frustration, to accept more lucrative jobs elsewhere, or to start their own businesses. Dropouts who are demoted or fired or who resign in frustration generally feel a sense of total failure, of being completely devalued and stripped of all accomplishment. Egos suffer severe damage, and depression is commonplace; uncertainty and fear of the future can retard psychological adjustment and action. The dropouts too turn to home for solace. But in this case traditional wives are normally as frightened and devastated as the dropouts and can offer little support. Life changes for both.

Regardless of the category—superstar, stabilizer, or dropout—the middle-age/middle-management life and career stage is traumatic. It is a stage of psychological upset and readjustment for everyone, but for the corporate star this period determines the future.

The Star Spouse

Middle age with its changing attitudes and purposes affects corporate wives as it does all other women, but the circumstances of corporate life increase the severity of the psychological impacts and often retard satisfactory resolution of those impacts. Unemployed traditional and transitional wives tend to have more problems at this age level than do working transmuter wives. In the rookie stage most women give up working to relocate or care for children, but in midlife, when they feel the urge to explore new options, other family and life-style problems often surface that can delay or completely cancel readjustment. If one is married to a superstar, transience remains an overriding factor; relocations are as common in middle-management levels as in the rookie stage.

Also, star husbands expect more physical and emotional support from their spouses. There are business functions to attend, parties to give, home chores to supervise, and child responsibilities to fulfill. When the star is distressed, a common condition for the middle-aged star, he turns to his wife for consolation and encouragement. In most marriages the wife is the ego booster and sounding board, and the husband is sometimes hurt or angry if she is unavailable for consultation. Marital conflicts are common in midlife corporate marriages.

Finally, in my opinion the strong bond of responsibility to children is one of the major restraints binding a wife to the traditional or transitional status. Middle age is the dumping ground of family problems, and everyone's problems seem to emerge at once. Most corporate children in their teens have buried resentments of frequent relocations and absentee fathers that often explode into rebelliousness. If the situation is serious, as is the case with many families, women feel duty-bound to remain the principal stabilizing force in the family. The husband is rarely available because of business "forces beyond his control." Middle age is a nightmare for many unemployed corporate wives. Research finds that of all groups housewives are the most prone to emotional upset and depression; numbers of unemployed corporate wives suffer prolonged depression, many seek therapy, and some require hospitalization for their distress.

Authors Evans and Bartolomé outlined five patterns of corporate marriages that evolve during midlife and middle careers.[1] The first and most prevalent pattern among executive marriages is confirmation. The employee feels secure and fulfilled in his job, much like the superstars. His mate is the traditional supportive wife who wants his happiness above all else. She continues to absorb family responsibilities and problems, and he continues his career concentration. There is little real communication in this marriage because both hide their feelings, doubts, guilts, and resentments. Their marriage pattern is accepted and confirmed for the future; nothing changes.

The second pattern is renegotiation and is normally brought about when a wife finally says "no more" to the present situation. After she forces a confrontation, marital problems are discussed. The two major issues are normally the quality of their private life and the wife's identity. Renegotiation often involves bitter arguments and marital upset that can last a year or more, and the outcome is often unpredictable. If renegotiation succeeds, the relationship changes for the better as communication opens and behavior alters; if unsuccessful, the couple might settle on another pattern or choose divorce. Regardless of outcome, communication starts and change occurs.

The third pattern is uneasy status quo in which the wife tries to renegotiate understanding and change, but the husband is so focused on the success stairway that he refuses to budge. He knows and sees the problems but justifies his actions and seeks no solutions, refusing to change his career-centeredness. The wife finally gives up trying for change and either bitterly accepts the situation or builds a separate life for herself, usually by going back to work. Some choose separation and divorce. But the bitterness and resentment remain.

The fourth and fifth patterns relate to specific situations. Reversal relates to the stabilized star's stalled career. He turns away from his work and deposits all his interest in home and family. The final pattern, the late climber, evolves when the success drive begins in the star stage rather than the rookie stage. Until now the employee has been mostly family-centered but suddenly starts climbing the success stairway with a passion. This situation completely changes the former pattern of marriage.

The traditional wife's marriage usually evolves into the confirmation pattern, and the transitional wife's marriage becomes the uneasy status quo. Transmuters and some transitional wives normally reform their marriages into the renegotiated pattern. Of course, not all relationships are easily categorized; variations often occur. I'm familiar with one marriage in which the husband became a stabilized star ready to settle into the reversal marriage pattern, but the wife returned to her career and quickly became a superstar. Their marriage pattern seems to be a reversed status quo. It is my belief that at the present time the majority of middle-age corporate marriages settle into the confirmation or status quo patterns, both of which leave wives in unhappy situations. In 1970 Lois Wyse stated in her book *Mrs. Success* that the unhappiness of the wife seemed to be in direct proportion to the success of the husband.[2] Although this is often valid, I would add that the husband's success is not the sole factor in her unhappiness. The dynamics of middle age, the restriction of viable choices, and female socialization also play important roles in her distress.

This is not to say that middle-aged women are necessarily doomed to unhappiness and depression. The corporate life offers many exciting positives at this career level. Salaries increase and material things are more attainable: better homes, superior education, expensive cars, country club memberships, and the like. The woman returning to school usually can do so without worrying about the tuition. Corporate wives often deny the importance of these accoutrements, but affluence does enhance the life-style. Also, being more involved in business/social affairs widens social contacts and increases personal sophistication. Business dinners are rarely held at the local pizza parlor; with the company paying the expenses, you go to the best restaurant in town. With such exposure one usually learns the social game and therefore feels comfortable in most situations. And perhaps most enjoyable, some middle-management positions offer travel opportunities in which mates can be included. Most women enjoy travel, and even though most trips are business-related, travel can provide exposure to new areas and sometimes even foreign countries. Many wives take that dreamed-of trip to Europe by accompanying their husbands on business trips. The company pays his expenses and the couple pays hers, thus cutting the cost in half. During the day he works while she sightsees, but at night they're usually free to do as they please. In the past most corporations frowned on this practice, but today it is more accepted. If the business trip is for an extended time, a few liberal companies even pay the spouse's expenses. So being the wife of a star isn't all doom and gloom; there are indeed good points too.

Changes and problems bombard middle-aged stars and spouses more than at any other career and life stage. It is a difficult time for both, but most corporate couples survive the blast, settle into the selected marriage pattern, and eventually accept and accommodate the lifestyle.

3

THE COACHES

CALLING
THE PLAYS

Upper management: corporate decision makers, company leaders, the tip of the pyramid. In most corporations upper management consists of the chief executive officer and/or president and all vice-presidents; in companies split into business units or divisions, division presidents are usually considered among the elite. Top-level corporate management is the ultimate career goal for the majority of ambitious rookies and stars, but those who actually attain the goal are few. In large companies, the odds can run as high as fifteen thousand lower and middle managers to one corporate officer. With odds such as these, numbers of talented superstars of necessity stabilize in middle management or become disenchanted with their progress and search for employment elsewhere. Many reach for the corporate brass ring, but few receive the coveted prize, especially at the company in which their careers began.

If asked to describe a typical top executive, the picture that comes to mind is usually a well-dressed, gray-haired male about six feet tall, approximately fifty to sixty-five years old. Generally, the image is much like the models in liquor advertisements—a sophisticated elderly man in a gray flannel suit. The public concept of upper managers has changed little over the past twenty years, but the managers themselves have changed. In 1984 a *Forbes* survey found that of the 800 highest-paid chief executive officers in the United States, 109 were in that position by the time they were forty years old. The assumption of the older man as the leader of the corporation is rapidly becoming passé; those reaching the upper level attain their goals earlier and more quickly.

Since the twenty-five-year age span is now seen in upper management, the typical, traditional profile of the corporate executive and wife is also outdated. Although most executive couples work through their midlife transitions during the middle-management level, some of the younger coach couples are still in the throes of those transitions, and this influences their reactions and life-styles in the upper levels of management. Life at the top is changing, just as the technology, management techniques, and personal qualifications needed for corporate leadership are changing.

Coach Stage Overview

The longer Jeff stayed in the district manager position, the more dissatisfied he became. He was frustrated with corporate bureaucracy, angry with his boss, and uncertain about the future. Was it possible that he would go no further in his career? Was he to remain stuck in the middle until retirement? Carole sensed that something was wrong, and when he told her of his fears, she was sympathetic but certainly not empathetic. She suggested he start looking at other companies if he was so unhappy. Jeff remembered having received several calls from headhunters, which he had never returned. Now he became more interested.

After many false starts and much deliberation Jeff eventually resigned his district manager's job and took a position as division president for another large company. The new office was in Boston, and relocation was mandatory; but it was quite a boost to his career and included a substantial salary increase. At first Carole resisted because of her career, but the new company eased her apprehension with their spouse job assistance offer, and finally she agreed. With the company's help and her degree and experience in counseling, she felt she would be able to find suitable, maybe better, employment in Boston. Bobby was nonchalant about the entire matter. It really made no difference where they lived; he was building his own life in Illinois but would, of course, visit on holidays and vacation. Although a little disappointed by Bobby's reaction, Jeff was delighted about the new job. Carole was anxious but satisfied with the prospect.

The company division of which Jeff became president was in bad shape. It had operated at a loss since its creation three years before, the product line usually obsolete by the time it reached the marketplace. Because of this discouraging record rumors of closing the facility floated throughout the plant, and employee morale was low. Jeff not only had a new position, he had a gigantic reorganizing and revitalizing job. Although the division was part of the larger corporation, it was set up as a small company, with its own vice-presidents of finance, manufacturing, sales, service, and human resources who reported to Jeff. Jeff had overall responsibility for the operation and in turn reported to the executive vice-president of the corporation. It was an exciting challenge that provided opportunity, prestige, and power. He had finally made it; he had reached upper management. But staying there depended on the division's performance.

Carole wasn't so excited. Shortly after they moved into their new home Jeff invited his staff for a cookout. The next week business visitors came for cocktails; one brought his wife, and Carole was delegated as official tour guide. It was an enjoyable two days, but Carole had to postpone a job interview to entertain the guests. Even with the corporation's assistance she was having a difficult time with her job search. Her credentials were good, but at forty-four it was hard to compete with the fresh young graduates of the prestigious Boston area colleges. Sometimes she didn't really mind not having a job, since being the wife of the division president had many benefits. In addition to the company picnic, Christmas parties, and business affairs to hostess there were foreign distributors to entertain and corporate affairs to attend in New York. But Jeff worked twelve hours a day and traveled extensively. That spring he made a tour of all the European distributors and was away almost three weeks, but he promised to take her on the next tour.

Carole was in a quandary: the good points of being the corporate wife were very, very good, but the bad points were horrible. Weighing the positives and negatives, Carole recommitted to finding employment. She didn't want to slip slowly back into the lonely, traditional-wife syndrome. After eight months she found her perfect job with an industrial psychological consulting firm.

The firm assigned the accounts, but she was free to set her own schedule and work periods. Occasional travel was necessary, but that too was kind of exciting—let Jeff experience sitting home alone for a change. All things considered, the job was ideal. She could still participate in most of the enjoyable parts of corporate life but also find fulfillment in her work. Finally she was content.

However, contentment didn't come as easily for her husband. Being division president gave him prestige and power, but he also had problems. Jeff's previous experience in running a branch and district gave him a good foundation in sales, sales budgeting and finance, sales personnel, and service, but now he was accountable for facets of the business with which he had no experience: manufacturing, research and development, overall budgeting and finance, and strategic planning. There was a lot to learn but a short time—two years at most—in which to show results by transforming the money-losing division into a profitable organization. It was a challenging but very precarious situation. Feeling that his career was on the line, he made running the company his major concern. Carole was once again a peripheral person in his life, loved but ignored unless needed for support and assistance. She sometimes felt like a prized possession, shown on special company occasions. She jokingly complained to others that Jeff had a new mistress: the company.

Jeff succeeded in reorganizing and revitalizing the division and remained president for seven years, the longest they had stayed in one location during their married lives. Their relationship during the first one and a half years in Boston was tumultuous. Jeff often got angry when Carole's work took precedence over helping him with company social and community affairs, but gradually they worked out an agreement. She would gladly participate in the events that didn't seriously interfere with her work, and he would understand that her work was important to her and therefore she couldn't accede to his wishes every time. He learned to be neither embarrassed by nor apologize for her absence, and in time he came to be quite proud of her accomplishments. On the other hand, Carole learned that she enjoyed some of the duties as the president's wife and made a special effort to attend the functions Jeff considered most important. Their priorities sometimes conflicted—both jobs were demanding and occasional compromises were necessary—but on the whole, the changes in their relationship and expectations worked quite well.

At age fifty-two Jeff was appointed president and CEO of the corporation. They moved to White Plains, New York, and Jeff commuted to corporate headquarters in New York City. Carole became a free-lance consultant for the Boston company, working when and where she chose. They had reached the pinnacle. Jeff still worked as hard and long as ever, but he had learned the lessons of corporate management well and felt more secure in his ability. His travel was extensive because the position demanded public appearances and speaking engagements, and Carole's presence was often requested and sometimes required on these jaunts. Consequently, she too traveled, but she tenaciously clung to her career, becoming professionally respected in her own right. All the while technology and the market continued to change. Jeff realized that the corporation was losing some of the market share to competitors, but the realization came too late. When he was sixty, the board of directors promoted him to vice-chairman of the board and brought in a new, forty-eight-year-old president and CEO from an outside company. Vice-chairman of the board sounded important, but in actuality it was a "do nothing" job. Jeff knew this was the end of his corporate career.

In moments of reflection Carole and Jeff tried to evaluate the long climb to success and its rewards. Looking back, they pinpointed several actions and events that could have been handled differently and better, but given the same circumstances and knowledge they had had at the time, they agreed that they would probably have made the same decisions. Yes, the climb was hard and hazardous: the moves, the problems with their relationship and with their son, and the sacrifices made for the corporate career. They also had regrets: no place to call home, no longtime close friends, lack of closeness with their own families, the loneliness of the rootless. Conversely, there were many points of pride: personal growth, seeing and experiencing new places and people, financial security, and the sense of accomplishment and goal fulfillment. They went over all the positives and negatives of the life-style, but there was one question on which they could never agree: is corporate success worth living the game?

Management Styles and Duties

Basically, there are two contemporary ways in which corporations are managed, and the management style determines the choice of upper-management people. The autocracy is the oldest and most familiar management method, in use since the industrial revolution. The top person is quite simply an autocrat: running the company, setting all goals, making all decisions, dictating all policies, and rewarding whomever and whenever he chooses. Such a person is usually egocentric, chooses "yes" people for upper management, and uses fear or termination as the principal incentive for employee productivity.

A different type of autocratic executive is more benevolent and manipulative. Instead of using fear and threats to motivate employees, the benevolent executive provides such things as recreational facilities, annual picnics, turkeys at Thanksgiving, and parties at Christmas to show concern for the welfare of workers. In return the workers are supposed to show gratitude through loyalty and hard work. Autocratic management methods are still evident in the corporate world, but participatory management is gaining prominence.

Participatory organizations inspire rather than threaten, consult rather than dictate. The top official sets goals and guides the accomplishment of those goals but invites subordinates' input and opinions as to the methods used to attain the goals. After consultation, he makes the major and final decisions and accepts responsibility for the outcome. Participatory management motivates by stressing employees' personal goals, and it rewards commensurate with personal contributions to overall accomplishments. The needs of the managed influence, or should influence, the methods used to manage. With this management philosophy, tasks and authority are delegated, and the power base is broadened. Participatory management is considered more productive and democratic, but it demands a strong, self-assured leader.

The January–February 1954 issue of the *Harvard Business Review* contained an article "Man-Hunt for Top Executives." Author Robert N. McMurry wrote that a good leader in participatory management "must ideally combine in himself the initiative and willingness of the entrepreneur to take risks with the judgment and administrative skills of a good manager." Although McMurry wrote the article almost thirty years before participatory management and entrepreneurship came into vogue, the same holds true today. A leader in the participatory corporation possesses the personality traits of the entrepreneur and the business skills of the autocrat.

Entrepreneurs might be described as having innate drive, aggressiveness, and creative imagination. These leaders are self-reliant and able to take calculated risks with minimal anxiety. They have intuitive judgment of people as well as problems and can see and feel others' points of view, sense the total situation, and make decisions quickly. Entrepreneurs normally are not "detail" people; they rely on others to study the minutiae. [1]

Second, a candidate for participatory corporate management must possess good administrative judgment and skills, but skills can be learned through instruction and experience. These skills include seeing the broad perspective of problems, setting and achieving long-term goals, delegating authority, developing open-mindedness, thinking independently, and coordinating numerous projects. [2] Corporate training and experience inculcate these skills during the lower- and middle-management career phases, but success in middle management does not necessarily qualify one for upper management. On the other hand, an entrepreneur without basic administrative skills can be disaster for a company. Top positions in today's evolving participatory organizations demand upper management with both entrepreneurial traits and management skills. According to McMurry's estimate, only one or two people in ten thousand possess this combination of traits and skills.

With the growing need for participatory management and leadership, many American corporations of necessity are looking outside their own organizations for candidates to fill upper-management positions. Corporate employment, with its protective umbrella of insurance, retirement, and educational programs, attracts many talented recruits, but such people usually have strong needs for security and lack the risk-taking traits needed in the decision-making positions of upper management. Most people with entrepreneurial traits opt for self-employment in the professions, free-lance activities, or small businesses of their own.

Probably the primary reason for looking outside the company for top managers is that large corporations tend to inhibit and stifle employees who do possess the personality traits and skills needed for corporate leadership. These employees become frustrated with the bureaucracy and the demands for conformity. They leave the company voluntarily or are forced out by conflicts with superiors. These dropout stars start their own businesses or join other companies where their talents are more appreciated. Some go to other large corporations in management positions, but many seek out small start-up companies offering lucrative stock equity as well as challenges. Corporations are beginning to recognize that the traditional organizational environment can lead to a deficit of leadership and are attempting to remedy the situation by setting up more flexible, entrepreneurial projects, divisions, and even start-up operations that foster innovative thinking.

Misconceptions about corporate upper management abound in our society. People enviously think of company officials and their spouses in terms of money, power, ease, and sophisticated life-styles without considering the magnitude of the duties, responsibilities, stress, and personal sacrifices that accompany the positions. Given to-day's business world and the rapid pace of technological change, contemporary executive couples no longer breathe a sigh of relief, settle back to enjoy their accomplishments, and plan for affluent retirement.

Just as being a superstar doesn't insure becoming a coach, being a coach doesn't necessarily guarantee tenure in the position. Coaches are constantly judged on overall company performance, and if results do not meet expectations, top executives are quickly asked to resign. Executives move from one department to another, new positions are created then abolished, and top-level resignations or terminations are commonplace. Executive search firms (headhunters) have grown into big businesses with the insatiable demand for new executive blood. Upper-level corporate positions may be the epitome of success to rookies and stars, but success can be fleeting.

Positions regarded as upper management vary, but regional managers are usually considered among the elite. Normally, regional managers report to vice-presidents, vice-presidents report to either an executive vice-president or the president, and the president reports to the board of directors. Describing the charter of duties expected of top executives is difficult because the duties vary from position to position, company to company. In participatory managements, presidents and/or chief executive officers (CEOs) are responsible for overall company policies, planning, organizing, and controlling; they are the final authority in decisions. In addition, the top official is accountable for company profits and losses and the company's interface with the larger community or world. Vice-presidents' duties fall into the same categories, but their responsibilities are departmental rather than companywide. Being a member of the senior staff, vice-presidents also consult with the president and/or CEO and assist in making company decisions, just as departmental managers consult and assist the VP.

In addition to work duties, coaches and their wives become corporate representatives in both the company and the general public; this is especially true for presidents and chairmen of boards. Within the company they are the most elevated and envied role models for other employees and are acknowledged as hosts and hostesses at any company affair whether in their homes, at the office, or elsewhere. Both executives and spouses are expected to represent their company favorably in the community, attending dinners, volunteering for projects, and presenting charitable donations. Their image is the corporation's image. Some top executives of large corporations even become national public figures. Private life is invaded and therefore becomes very dear.

The Coach

Today's corporate leader is a different breed from most of yesterday's corporate executives because the business environment is different; the evolution of the dynamic, fast-changing age of technology requires new, innovative management. The figurehead executives of the past, as much concerned with their leadership in the local Rotary Club as with their company duties, are fast becoming extinct in the new and hostile corporate climate. With the decline of figurehead managers, former corporate mavericks are ascending, their entrepreneurial traits and talents now in demand. Yesterday's outcasts are today's leaders.

Most modern top executives fit the description of a "prisoner of success".[3] They devote their lives and careers to climbing the success stairway, and their work is the essence of their existence. Having found the professional niche and identity that perfectly suits their talents and personalities, they are good at their jobs and find personal satisfaction and ego gratification in work that private life cannot equal. The careers of these egocentric, ambitious high achievers are models, envied and emulated by other climbers of the success stairway. Success seems to accompany their efforts regardless of hills and turns in the career paths. For the "prisoner of success" work/career is more than an occupation, it is a passion with overtones of a divine calling. Private life is also important to success prisoners, and many often feel guilty about the "necessary" neglect of themselves, wives, and children. Although their careers are well launched, coaches are much like rookies in regard to their private life: it's important but not primary.

Many coaches act as if the office cannot run without them, but few admit to feeling that way. This attitude has both practical and psychological bases. In the rapidly altering and intensely competitive marketplace, "running the railroad" requires constant vigilance. Coaches must stay abreast of and if possible ahead of the current business trends and competition. Information is the key to evaluating business conditions, and the office is the information center, much like the command center of a military operation. It is practical and important that coaches have access to necessary information and be available to make decisions.

There are two psychological motivations for accommodating and sustaining personal importance at the office: fear and satisfaction. An executive's position is never so secure that replacement isn't a threat; there are always contenders for upper management. Performance is the bottom line in high-tech corporations, and those found lacking are quickly deposed, regardless of seniority or past record. Second, as mentioned earlier, most coaches simply enjoy their work; they need the work as much as or more than the work needs them. Work demands sometimes cloak individual needs for the personal gratification received from the work, and numbers of upper-management people work for satisfaction rather than money. They take pleasure in their prestige and power and the respect and deference shown them by others; they relish controlling their own and others' destinies and find fulfillment in the ownership of plans brought to fruition. Coaching is the ultimate ego trip for "prisoners of success."

But upper management is not all fame and glory. Pressure and stress are pervasive in the professional and personal lives of modern coaches. In addition to work pressures, families demand more time, communities demand more social responsibility, and the judicial system demands compliance with increasing numbers of laws. And all are measured against time, performance, and bottom-line profit. Coaches must accept responsibility for corporate results, whether good or disastrous. Regardless of how the corporate buck is passed, it always stops in upper management. There's no place else to pass it.

Time is one of the greatest pressures on top executives. Time is a limited quantity, but the demands for an executive's time are not limited. He is bombarded from every angle for "just a few minutes of your time": wife, children, subordinates, clients, investors, and community. Trade-offs have to be made, and someone is always disappointed—too often that someone is the executive's wife or child. Importance carries obligations and burdens that require time for visiting clients and company facilities, attending industry seminars, and representing the company through speaking engagements and public appearances. The private life of most upper managers is pared down to essentials because of the never-ending demands for time that can impair mental and physical health. As one president of a large company said, "If you work twelve hours a day, you finally get to be boss so you can put in sixteen to eighteen hours a day."

The upper-management environment can affect an executive's life and personality in more subjective areas. On attaining success, executives often enjoy sharing their expertise with younger people and find much satisfaction in taking on a mentor's role. But on a less positive note, some executives become so impressed by their own ability that they lose faith in the abilities of others to accomplish tasks alone. As one executive told me, "People do what you *in*spect, not what you *ex*pect." Others' weaknesses and failures are intolerable. Trust in others is also vulnerable, but executive suspicions about others' motives are often valid. The prestige and power of executives are very attractive to unscrupulous people wishing to gain personal benefit from association with the source of power, and this situation is as prevalent in private life as in professional life. To guard against being unwittingly used, executives often mentally question the motives of others: Are they attracted to me or to my power? What do they want from me? Allowing others to manipulate their power can damage coaches personally and professionally. Paranoia? Perhaps. Reality? Certainly.

The final steps of the success stairway are a difficult climb, but once at the top the view can be rewarding. Chief among the objective rewards are the financial benefits which allow an affluent if not opulent present life-style and freedom from money worries about future retirement. Subjective rewards vary with individual personality, attitudes, ambitions, and values. Not all chief executives are prisoners of their success, and not all of those who are prisoners exhibit the same psychological characteristics. Many ambitious corporate employees are sincerely devoted to their families, achieving and maintaining that delicate balance between home and work as they climb toward the top. For them, upper management is a psychologically rewarding culmination of their dreams, plans, and efforts. For the others, the top of the pyramid may give professional fulfillment but personal emptiness. Becoming more sensitive to loved ones and turning toward home with advancing age, compulsive climbers often realize that the sensitivity was too long coming and the hoped-for personal relationships are unattainable. Neglect has taken its toll. Their only rewards are material.

The Coach Wife

Coach spouses can no longer be placed in a one-size-fits-all package. The changing business environment is lowering corporate expectations of wives, and the changing societal environment is expanding their personal choices. Regardless of these changes, corporate couples define their own relationships through individual and mutual expectations, commitments, and roles. Although most women disagree, I maintain that corporate wives have always been free to determine their life course for themselves, but in adhering to tradition socialization they often allow society, mates, and corporations to make life decisions for them. When a person allows others to make her personal decisions, she abdicates self-responsibility and must play the role assigned her. A free woman who refuses to think of herself as free and refuses to accept the responsibility of her freedom is enslaved by her own choice.

As stated earlier, technology altered the American business environment in the marketplace and in the office. Previously, products were fairly stable, and companies were content with slow, steady growth. With competent management in place and manufacturing running on schedule, coaches could afford the time to expand their company's influence beyond the executive office. In that era executives and their wives were expected to entertain often and attend outside affairs as representatives of the company. But technology is altering the stable business environment and changing the company roles played by coach couples. Running a profitable business in today's high-tech climate demands constant, concentrated attention, and executives have less time and inclination for outside activities. As a result, the number of corporate duties and expectations imposed on upper management wives is decreasing. Today there seems to be less mandatory public exposure and official entertaining. This doesn't mean the duties have ceased, only that the occurrences seem to have decreased.

In addition to fewer corporate expectations, women as individuals are changing. During the past twenty years the feminist movement hasn't radically affected female socialization, but it has affected female mentality. In the past women felt locked into traditionally supportive roles because of their socialization; today women realize they can change their roles regardless of socialization. With this mental change society has been forced, through Title IX of the Civil Rights Act, to accept women in roles and positions formerly closed to them. As a result, women now have a range of opportunities and options and feel freer to choose without fear of ostracism. It is a woman's personal choice even if she chooses to remain the unemployed, traditional corporate wife, aiding and abetting her husband's career.

According to Allan Cox, author of *The Cox Report on the American Corporation*, top executives tend to be staunchly traditional in their marriage and family life. Of the coaches surveyed 90 percent replied that their spouses are "always" or "usually" supportive, and 87 percent said that the spouse's support was "very" or "somewhat" important to their career advancement. Only 3 percent said their spouses were "never" supportive, but 10 percent said spouse support was of only "marginal" importance to their careers.[4] Although this report does not state the ages of the executives (older couples might tend to be more traditional) nor the employment status of spouses, the 90 percent support is very revealing. One concludes that even today the number of supportive mates is phenomenal. But of course this doesn't necessarily mean that all these spouses give their support in the traditional, unemployed manner. Many middle-aged women are opting for paid employment, and employed wives also can be supportive wives.

Let's examine the role and life of the traditional, supportive upper-management spouse as described by several authors and researchers. Mrs. Coach has an official role as representative of the company and her husband: hostess, link to the community, mobilizer of other wives, and public relations person. The couple's private life is restricted because of the public and business involvement, and it becomes difficult to distinguish between business and personal life because friendships take on business importance. Anything this wife says or does might be held against her and will reflect on her husband's reputation. Therefore, she seldom feels free to express her own opinions or feelings or simply to be herself. Because she represents her husband, she plays down her talents, abilities, and interests, and plays up her husband's attributes; she is content to bask in his reflected glory. For all this the wife receives financial security, status, the joy of her husband's accomplishments, and perhaps a stable, happy marriage. This description sounds dreadful, but it was generally true in the past. One hopes this epitome of old-fashioned womanhood is disappearing.

By the time corporate couples reach the top they normally have worked through their marital relationship, have settled into a confirmation, status quo, or renegotiated marriage pattern, and have accepted their lives together. The corporate wife exerts power and influence on that resulting pattern. Some choose and are happy in their choice of confirmation, but many others are opting for renegotiation. The latter seek a more equitable marriage partnership that accommodates mutual supportiveness and independence within an interdependent relationship. As a result of the feminist mentality, the range of available choices, and fewer demands from the corporation, there is no longer a typical corporate spouse. The influence of a husband's career on the life of a spouse is undeniable, but growing numbers of young, middle-aged, and older wives are freeing themselves from obligatory corporate duties and refusing to be the victims of their husband's careers. Instead, they are choosing their own roles and the extent to which they wish to be involved in their husbands' careers. The majority of wives remain supportive, but most expect their husbands' support in return. Consequently, the traditionally supportive spouse is fast becoming an endangered breed. Corporate wives are demanding and gaining consideration and respect if and when they choose to play the corporate game.

PART TWO

GAME

PROBLEMS

In the progression up the career ladder from rookie to star to coach, or at any stop along the way, corporate employment and its accompanying life-style present persistent problems for couples. Rookies believe these problems to be related to career phase and hope that with time, hard work, and promotion the circumstances will ease. Stars realize that the problems are innately related to corporate life, will not be solved by the next promotion, but will in all likelihood intensify. The uncertainties of midlife compound these work-related problems, often making middle-management couples bitter and resentful, although material rewards ease part of the pain. For the coach couples at the top of the pyramid the problems remain and pressures increase. Although they have more control, these couples usually accept, assimilate, and accommodate the demands and try to make the best of the situation until retirement. Rookies hope, stars resent, and coaches accept.

Few people realize at the outset of their careers that major problems exist, and even fewer understand the tremendous personal and family impacts common to living the corporate game. The United States is swiftly shifting from an industrial to a technological era, which is altering the way a signficant portion of the population lives. But neither socialization, education, nor the company instruct these people about the problems of corporate employment or the hardships of the life-style. The hardships are difficult to define without complaining, to verbalize without whining, so corporate couples are silent. Publicly, they display the proper, happy facade and hope someday it will be different, if not for them, then for their children. Is it any wonder there is so much pain?

The problems of corporate life have existed for thirty years. During this time a few researchers and writers surveyed, probed, and reported on life within the corporation, but society showed little interest in the personal difficulties of this seemingly fortunate segment of the population. Concern is focused on the less fortunate, and rightly so, but symptoms of discontent such as drug abuse, alcoholism, and mental distress are appearing in the previously stable middle and upper classes. The reasons for these symptoms are thus far unexplained. Corporate people make up a significant portion of these economic classes, and their personal difficulties and discontents sometimes surface in these same symptoms. Our society must acknowledge these problems and seek to alleviate them by altering socialization, education, and the corporate environment to address the needs of corporate people more effectively. Otherwise, the problems will remain, will continue to distress corporate families, and will eventually impact society, the educational system, and the business community.

4

PRACTICE
MAKES PERFECT

LONG HOURS

Within the American population is a tribe of people who without additional compensation donate many extra hours of work to their employers. They are a special breed of employee, motivated by compulsion to compete and ambition to achieve. They thrive in the salaried, white-collar jungles of corporations, and they believe in the philosophy of meritocracy.

Meritocracy is defined as an "educational system whereby the talented are chosen and moved ahead on the basis of their achievement: leadership by the talented." This is a misleading definition because meritocracy is not limited to the educational system; its concepts have spread from the schools and have become accepted by society as part of the culture. Babies are introduced to achievement in the cradle—a simple "goo" brings claps of glee from Mom and Dad. Children are rewarded for doing their best at home, but once in school they quickly learn that *doing* their best isn't enough. They must *be* the best to gain recognition, reward, and success. Remember the Thanksgiving play in the second grade? Only the brightest and most talented kids were Pilgrims and Indians; the rest were trees and turkeys. With reading, writing, and arithmetic the lessons of meritocracy are taught and learned early, and these lessons are never forgotten.

Competition is fundamental in our society, and few dare question it; our country and our political and economic systems are founded on competition and free enterprise. Everyone recognizes the cliches: "America, the land of opportunity," "a self-made man," "climb the ladder of success," and so on. Pardon another cliche, but the philosophy of meritocracy is "as American as apple pie." The message is clear: Work hard, prove you are the best, and you will be rewarded.

Achieving success is synonymous with winning in our society. It is no mystery that Michael Maccoby's 1976 book on corporate executives is entitled *The Gamesman: The New Corporate Leaders.*[1] Maccoby's executives are talented, smart, and competitive. They are the captains of corporate teams, not just presidents or managers. Achievement is the challenge, the corporation is the arena, business is the game, and success is the victory.

Long Hours and Meritocracy

Maccoby's gamesman is termed a success in the business world, but that success is often dearly won. Devotion to career and hard work are assets in professional life but can be real liabilities in a businessperson's personal and family life. Work is a motivational force in life, and existence often depends on it. Freud recognized this fact when he wrote, "The communal life of human beings has . . . a twofold foundation: a compulsion to work, which was created by external necessity, and the power to love." For many corporate employees, the key word in that quotation is *compulsion*.[2]

There seems to be a consensus among recent surveys that executives devote an average of sixty hours a week to business. These hours usually include commuting, actual desk time, business lunches and dinners, and reading and working at home. The survey conducted by Diane Rothbard Margolis for *The Managers: Corporate Life in America* concluded that managers most commonly worked between sixty and seventy hours per week.[3] Using the conservative sixty-hour figure as the average for managers and comparing it with the accepted forty-hour week of blue-collar workers, managers work 50 percent longer. But because they are salaried employees, they receive no extra pay for extra work. Why do they do it?

Psychological studies give many reasons for workaholism, all of which center on some emotional premise and all valid in specific cases. But despite individual variations, devoting many hours to work is common among corporate employees. Although my layman's view is generalized and perhaps simplistic, I conclude from experience, observation, and interviews that the excessive work of most employees is based on belief in meritocracy, that hard work brings personal recognition and rewards. The American culture inculcates this philosophy so deeply into our psyches that achieving career success becomes a major motivation in the lives of many people, especially men. And corporations are astute enough to encourage these ideals of meritocracy because it is to their advantage to do so.

To illustrate this point, let me cite my own experience. My husband's office was located in downtown

Detroit, and we lived in a suburb eighteen miles outside the city. The freeway traffic into the city was horrendous, so in order "to beat the traffic" my husband left home at 6:30 A.M., arriving at the office shortly after 7:00. He breakfasted at the cafeteria and was at his desk by 7:30. As his day progressed, he had lunch—again at the company cafeteria—and continued his work until 6:30 P.M. If he left earlier than 6:30, he reasoned, he would be in traffic for an hour. Normally, he arrived home a few minutes past 7:00. This was a long workday: ten and a half hours working, one hour eating, and one hour commuting. In all, he spent twelve and a half hours from the time of leaving home in the morning to returning at night. In winter he left in the dark and came home in the dark. Although these long hours reduced his time with the family, I could certainly understand the frustrations associated with bumper-to-bumper traffic.

Later, after moving to Dallas, I began to suspect that heavy traffic wasn't the sole reason for working excessive hours. Now my husband is president of a small corporation, and the office is only fifteen minutes from our home. Normally, he leaves for work at 8:15 in the morning and is at his desk by 8:30. Yet he still doesn't get home until 7:00 at night; occasionally he arrives a few minutes earlier, but sometimes it's much later. A psychological test, taken during his latest physical checkup, shows my husband to be mentally sound, well-adjusted, and happy.

I have concluded that, apart from demands of some urgent problems that must be resolved, my husband devotes so much time to business for two basic reasons:

1. He loves his job. It is exciting, fulfilling, and interesting. He derives pleasure from his achieve-

ments and satisfaction from doing his job to the best of his ability.

2. He covets success and seeks the continuous competition of striving to win. His success drive probably never will be completely gratified.

Although most employees state that long hours are an unspoken but expected part of their job and there is subtle pressure from both the company and peers, most of the incentive for working extra hours comes from a personal, internal source rather than external pressure. E. Jerry Walker, executive director of the Center for Family Studies, wrote an article entitled " 'Til Business Us Do Part?" in which he summarized the meaning of "career success" as related by a group of all-male managers. He stated: "To a high achiever career success is an entity in itself. While many executives pay lip service to being a good provider, good husband, and good father, these are not the driving motivations behind their efforts. For most executives career success appears as a goal in and of itself."[4]

I would add that being successful and achieving success are not synonymous, although both are elusive. For ambitious people, simply attaining career goals is not success; success is competing, proving one's ability and worth, and winning—not once but repeatedly.

The One-Dimensional Person

In 1981 The Wall Street Journal and the Gallup Organization surveyed 476 wives of senior corporate executives. Most of the women indicated that their executive husbands believed that significant sacrifices in their personal and family life must be made in order to succeed.

Most ambitious corporate employees, whether in the executive suite or on their way, share this belief. In the never-ending competition, work often becomes a passion. As one woman stated in the survey, "I feel that sharing my husband with his career is probably worse than sharing him with a mistress because there is no end to it and there is nothing I can do about it."

Devoting so much time and energy to work and giving it priority over all other parts of life often causes a personal imbalance. When the job becomes all-consuming, one is in danger of becoming a one-dimensional person. Such a person doesn't have to wear a brand, "1-D," on the forehead; a 1-D person is immediately recognizable.

Perhaps the easiest place to spot the 1-D people is at a company cocktail party. Be a good guest. Mingle. Chat with the people you meet. You will encounter several 1-Ds. Casual conversation with such people is a monumental task; they talk only about work or sports. Their sports are enjoyed mainly via television because there is too little time after work for playing. If the conversation moves into areas other than achievement and competition, 1-Ds become visibly uncomfortable and drift away. Outside their limited arena Mr. and Ms. 1-D are social voids.

In February 1982 *Self* published an article entitled "Ambitious Men—Can You Afford One?" The author, Jane Adams, asked an ambitious sales executive to calculate how much of the time spent away from his job was totally unrelated to business. His answer: fewer than twelve hours a week. No wonder there are so many 1-D people populating the corporate world. Time belonging to family, friends, and leisure is sacrificed to satisfy the compulsion to compete and win. The majority of driven high achievers do not realize the personal cost of winning that next promotion, being number one in a field of fifty.

But to employees, there are always valid reasons for devoting many hours to a job, and these reasons always focus on external forces. Perhaps the most often cited explanation is "I do it for you, my family." How does one rebut such self-sacrifice, especially when a person truly believes it? In most cases, the employees work excessively for personal ego satisfaction. The material status symbols they provide for their families are often displays of achievement. Granted, the families enjoy the lovely homes and country club memberships, but given a choice, most families would opt for more time over more money.

Another popular reason for working long hours is "I have to work late. It shows the boss I have the proper attitude for promotion to management." Such reasoning is encouraged by management and even by the press. For example, an article in the April 1975 issue of *Money* stated, "Bolting for the door at five o'clock betrays a blue-collar mentality and can keep you in a low-paying job." Along with insulting both blue- and white-collar mentality, this advice implies that promotions are not awarded solely on the quality of work, but just as important, promotions also depend on the quantity of hours devoted to that work.

Most ambitious people are reluctant to admit simply enjoying their work and wanting to succeed in their corporate climb. When confronted about the length of their workday, these people "stonewall," denying any personal control over the matter. Stonewalling shifts the blame for excessive hours away from that person's internal drive and onto external pressures—the family or the corporation. Owning even part of the responsibility might necessitate change in work habits as well as attitudes. There is nothing obscene about enjoying one's work, nor is the desire to compete and win shameful. The situation becomes destructive only when the high achiever's inner drive to win is so pervasive that noncompetitive life holds little or no interest, and as a result, time for family, friends, and leisure is compromised.

On the basis of my interviews and research, there seems to be a consensus among corporate employees that their compulsion to achieve has few, if any, negative repercussions on themselves or their families. While this opinion may be true in the employees' minds, after talking with wives and children, I find its validity is certainly questionable. The highly competitive environment of the office nurtures employees' desire to prove themselves through superlative performance. They feel they must be supermotivated, superstrong, supersuccessful; the list is endless. Mr. Superman and Ms. Wonder Woman recognize only the positives, because negative thinking has no place among super-attitudes. As a result, it is extremely difficult for the high achievers to evaluate accurately the effects of long hours on themselves and their families. Nonetheless, negative results for both employees and families do exist and eventually have to be reconciled. These people live in a pressure chamber at home and work in one at the office. Pressures for time, family, performance, money, decisions, quotas are with them constantly. Rarely do supermanagers discuss these pressures with others, and personal realization of the intensity of the problem usually comes too late.

Living under continuously stressful conditions often results in burnout or breakdown. Apple Computer, Inc., provides a excellent example of the effects of stress. Being a highly competitive company, Apple is populated with eager high achievers. The company is dedicated to winning the battle against IBM for first place in the personal computer industry. An article in the January 16, 1984, issue of *Business Week* described the company as a "counterculture" with an "underlying attitude that gives far more weight to doing an interesting, important job than to possessing the trappings of power." The competitive enthusiasm of many of Apple's 4,645 employees resulted in extraordinarily long hours devoted to the company's projects. Team members working on developing Apple's Macintosh computer wore T-shirts boasting: "Working 90 hours a week and loving every minute of it." But all was not well at Apple. Poor health began to plague members of the Macintosh team. Employees began "burning out" and leaving the company.[5] The hours were too long, and the pressure schedules were too stressful. After all the hyperbole, corporate supermanagers are mortal; the negative effects of long, pressured hours demand physical and/or mental compensation eventually.

Almost invariably, ambitious employees assume that no matter what, their marriage and family relationships will remain stable and fulfilling. Their confidence in this belief is astonishing. All relationships require maintenance, but because of their compulsive work habits, many corporate workers alot little time to the upkeep and enhancement of relationships with spouses, children, and friends. Although businesspeople are admirably diligent in making financial investments for future security, these same people are often nonchalantly negligent about making emotional investments. Relationships are much like savings accounts: if you make steady deposits in them, they will pay off with interest later. No investments, no payoffs; there is nothing there to grow. Those extra hours at the office have to come from somewhere. Time added to work is time subtracted from the family. As a result, family bonds are jeopardized.

Effects on the Spouse

Generally, corporate employees are reluctant to talk about the effects of extended work on themselves and their families, but spouses usually welcome the opportunity to verbalize the anguish, anger, or advantages that result from such job devotion. Emphasizing a spouse's eagerness to share experiences is not to be translated as derogatory; in fact, quite the opposite is true. Being a corporate wife myself, I realize that most spouses are relieved and elated to discover that others share the same problems. They can finally remove that "everything is lovely in Corporateville" facade.

Most corporate wives are just as ambitious for their husbands as the men are for themselves. Unemployed spouses adjust their lives to accommodate the career, knowing that success is important to their husbands' egos and monetarily beneficial to the entire family. Of course, they enjoy all the things the handsome salary enables them to buy. Women, on occasion, even enjoy being introduced as the "wife of John, the company's golden boy." But they wonder if these rewards are worth the sacrifices.

The problems resulting from an employee's lengthy day differ among spouses, depending on age and life phase. Loneliness is said to be the major complaint among American women, and this is certainly true for the older unemployed corporate wife. But it is not necessarily true for the unemployed wife of a young rookie. If the couple have children, loneliness rarely becomes a major problem for the wife during the rookie and early star stages of the career. A young wife and mother is normally too busy and too tired to miss her husband's company to any great extent. During the day, time to be alone is one of her life's great rewards. But the nights can be lonely. After the children are in bed, she still needs company and conversation with someone above juvenile level.

For the older wife whose children are past the age of requiring much of her time and attention, loneliness is an ever-present threat. Her day may be crammed full of activities—working, attending meetings, playing tennis, or cleaning house—but by four or five o'clock these time-fillers wind down. Other women return home to greet the children from school or start preparing for dinner, but in her home there are no children, no husband arriving from work, no dinner to prepare—business dinners often preempt dinners at home. There is nothing interesting on television until seven o'clock, and until then the pesky poodle is her sole companion and best friend.

"The job always comes first" is a common complaint of the high achiever's wife. One woman surveyed by *The Wall Street Journal* gave this advice: "Be sure you are ready to play second (or last) fiddle in the band your husband conducts. . . . Your needs will come last, so you should want his success at most any cost." Another executive wife from the same survey said her husband's job was "all-consuming" and he "expects everything else to take second place."[6] Corporate employees are notorious for altering or canceling personal plans if these plans come into conflict with work: birthdays postponed, anniversaries missed, outings canceled, theater tickets unused. Everything personal runs the risk of being axed at the last moment. A seasoned corporate daughter once asked her father, "Where are you going on my birthday this year, Dad?"

Spouses can easily feel displaced by the job because their wants and needs are so often put off until a more convenient time. Everyone, male or female, wants and deserves to have top priority in life of his or her spouse; that's what marriage is all about. But wives of ambitious employees know they come second, and this knowledge erodes their egos—only the strongest, most self-assured women escape this damage. Unemployed wives are especially susceptible to ego erosion. If long working hours become habitual for the employee/husband, many wives begin resenting his job and hating the company. It's easier to hate the company then admit to second place in a husband's life. Other wives fall into self-doubt, asking themselves: What have I done to make him stay away? Is there another woman? Is he so unhappy at home that he would rather be at work? Somehow these women blame themselves for his work habits. Perhaps this relates to that old fallacy "A man won't run around if you keep him happy at home." Nevertheless, working excessively causes ego damage, both real and imagined, for most wives.

Many spouses complain of worry and anxiety about the effects of extended workdays on the employees. The employee's health is the greatest source of worry. A wife, especially, knows all the latest statistics on heart attacks and knows her husband is not immune, even though he thinks he is. For many couples the husband's health is a taboo topic. Superman refuses to entertain any thought that he happens to be a prime candidate for the intensive care unit because he equates poor health with personal weakness and vulnerability. Discussion of his health only makes him angry, so his wife worries silently.

Physical safety is a second source of worry and anxiety for the spouses of superachievers. Normally, late workers don't telephone home to inform spouses of late arrival. "Real men" don't call home, and Superman is no exception. The other guys might think he has to ask permission from his wife. When my husband worked in Detroit, it was not uncommon for a late worker to be mugged in a well-lighted parking lot. Of course, I worried when he was late coming home. In addition, employees have been known to meet occasionally for a drink before going home. Here again, having received a telephone call or not, a spouse grows more tense as the hours pass. One woman related that she became well known at the local police station from calling to see if any accidents had been reported. Each time her husband arrived home safely, she was relieved to see him and yet angered by the worry he caused—not to mention the embarrassment of having called the police station again.

Corporate spouses live each day with the ominous danger of blowing a fuse from the chronic overload under which they function. Employees who work long and hard at their careers have little time or energy left over for home chores and responsibilities. However, high achievers are superbly adept at delegating these duties to spouses and kids. All the wives I know should have the title secretary/treasurer after their names. Without exception, each takes care of the household finances, pays the bills, deposits the check, balances the checkbook, and so on. Never have I met that famous stereotype who is always spending, buying expensive clothes, and overdrawing at the bank. She certainly isn't the run-of-the-mill corporate wife.

Mrs. Achiever either hires someone to do the majority of male-oriented household chores or she does the chores herself. In addition to their other duties, many wives cut grass, care for the yard, see to repairs, and wash the car. One friend of mine has full responsibility for their swimming pool. She explained that her husband was at work when the builder finished construction of the pool, so she listened to all of the maintenance instructions. One weekend she went over the care routine with her husband and left the pool in his hands. Within a week the pool was a disaster. Now she maintains the pool herself, saying that her husband would just "screw it up again." I'm not convinced that the "screw up" wasn't intentional.

I have a homespun adage that has become my guideline concerning household chores: If you consent to do one of your husband's chores one time, it is yours forever. For twenty years I have flatly refused to do certain chores for two reasons: (1) I don't want the chores to become my responsibility, and (2) I want my husband to know he had specific household responsibilities, so home won't become simply a place to eat, sleep, and change clothes.

There is an overload of a different kind that plagues many spouses: parental overload. The gathering of the family at the end of the day has long been a custom in American homes. For the corporate couple this is no longer a traditional practice. By the time the late-working employee arrives, the children have been fed, the younger ones are ready for bed, the older ones are busy or preparing to go out. The employee says "good night" to the little ones, "see you later" to the teenagers, and "what's for dinner" to the spouse. Family sharing around the dinner table has become archaic in the corporate home.

When an employee extends the workday with added hours, a gap appears in the family unit that must be filled. Once again the spouse takes over, becoming stand-in father as well as mother, or vice versa. Women often play dual roles in the family scene. I would guess that the mother in a corporate family makes perhaps 90 percent of the decisions regarding the children, not because she wants to but simply because the father isn't around when the decisions have to be made.

Have you ever been to a Little League ball game or any juvenile sports event in a corporate neighborhood? Go. You will see a few mother-and-father couples, but mostly you will see mother-and-mother pairs. Try the PTA or any elementary school program. The results will be the same: few fathers and many, many mothers.

Being both mother and father much of the time is an extremely heavy load. I often feel that the corporate wife/mother should be included in the statistics on single-parent households headed by a woman. Are there any differences between her and an aid-to-dependent-children mother other than the amount of money provided? If ambitious employees continue to abdicate their parental responsibilities, who will provide the vitally important male role models for the children? No matter how diligent her efforts, a woman can never provide this.

The time taken from the personal side of life and donated to the company robs the spouse of not only her mate's companionship but also in many instances social interaction with other men and women. An employee/husband finds social interaction with both sexes at the office; generally, the wife has contact during the day with other women whose husbands are at work. Most nightime mingling is couple-oriented; an extra woman is rarely welcomed. The wife of the habitually late worker must choose to decline graciously, or if she goes alone, be the uncomfortable extra woman who hopes her husband will show up soon. Most women I know have learned to decline graciously, limiting their social contact primarily to daytime gatherings with other women.

More important, extended work hours usurp vital time couples need for companionship and communication. Employees who work ten to twelve hours arrive home exhausted and detached. They are mentally and physically drained, ready only to fall into bed. Spouses learn quickly that attempting to converse at such a time is useless; therefore, unless the issue is urgent, it's better to postpone discussion until a more propitious time or forget it altogether. Bluntly speaking, long hours strain marital relationships.

Sensitive wives of overambitious employees know that confrontations about excessive work are unproductive. Spouses have only partial knowledge and experience concerning long workdays. They can be sure of the effects of excessive work on home life but can only speculate about the business necessity of that work. Only the employees know both the home and business sides of this problem. Honesty and understanding, from both man and wife, are essential to positive discussion of the problem.

The effects of long hours might be condensed into one sentence: The socialized need to compete and win, when carried to the extreme, can be destructive individually to employee and spouse and collectively to the marriage itself.

Benefits of Long Hours
for the Company

When rookies join a corporation, they come well-prepared to enter the competitive white-collar jungle. The corporation doesn't have to train employees in the philosophy of meritocracy; the American social system has already instilled those values. The company simply encourages and utilizes the philosophy, thus profiting from employees' work without wages.

For corporate employees, promotion is the "carrot in front of the mule's nose." Always just out of reach, the mule/employees work long and hard striving to obtain the carrot/promotion. If they work long enough and hard enough, the carrot is usually won. A promotion, an exciting new job, a new challenge, and a brand-new carrot—the next promotion. It's a perpetual cycle: As soon as one promotion is obtained, another appears just out of reach.

According to an Associated Press report of a three-year study conducted by Harvard professor James Medoff, non-union employees are often promoted on what he terms "the four P's: personality, performance, potential, and politics. Of these four, performance and office politics are most important in white-collar jobs. I find the use of the word *performance* rather ambiguous, because an employee's performance depends on the superior's definition of the word. For some managers, performance is how well a job is done; for others, performance includes not only how well a job is done but also how long and hard an employee works at the job. A friend related that when he was at corporate headquarters one senior vice-president had a habit of strolling the halls each day about six o'clock in the evening, checking to see who was still at the office. The week between Christmas and New Year this same man checked each morning to see who came in and who took days off. Under these circumstances performance was judged by time devoted to the job, in addition to how well the job was done.

Companies never specifically define the hours of a workday. Normally, the beginning of work is clearly designated as eight, eight thirty, or nine o'clock, but companies make no attempt to define the end of the day. That is left open-ended. This omission is understandable. Why should the company want to limit its employees' working hours when it's to their advantage not to do so?

On occasion extended hours of work become mandatory for obvious reasons; there are deadlines to meet, projects to complete, quarterly quotas to accomplish. At such times the job requires extra time, and most employees willingly give the hours. As a general rule, however, company pressure for longer hours with no pay is more vague and less recognizable because the pressure is subjective and very subtle. Manipulating an employee's belief in meritocracy, his company initiation, and his dedication to success, companies use the "carrot" psychology to motivate increased productivity. The employee knows that the carrot, usually promotion, is gained through talent, diligence, and hard work. Superiors allude to promotion but rarely specify exactly what promotion and never guarantee attainment. When this tactic is used, the employee must set his own standard of achievement and work as hard and long as he thinks necessary for that achievement. There are no company guidelines or parameters, and most high achievers believe that more is better: more work means better reward. But corporate superiors seldom mention that a large number of employees from all over the country may be vying for the same promotion, although only one person can win the position.

Corporations often use this ploy to entice employees to corporate headquarters. These employees perceive that spending time on the corporate staff is an important career stepping-stone and recognize that valuable experience can be gained at headquarters. Junior employees happily join corporate staffs, thinking they will be there perhaps two years and will then be promoted to a district manager or an equivalent position. Once settled into the job, they find fifty or a hundred other people of the same rank, and all expect a promotion to district manager. Suddenly, the arithmetic becomes obvious. One hundred people competing for five district manager jobs, two of which might be available in two years. The result: two out of the hundred will get the promotions, some will remain on the corporate staff indefinitely, and the rest will be sent back to the field at their previous level.

Corporate headquarters are hotbeds of job competition. Some reach their ambitious goals; others awake from their ambitious dreams to find themselves in dead-end jobs. But think of all the long, productive hours the company gains from the competition. There is no doubt about it: fierce competition among employees increases employee productivity without expense to the company. In essence, it's a financial gain for the corporation.

Here's a simple computation to illustrate this point.

Consider an employee, making forty thousand dollars a year, who works ten hours a day, or two hours over the official eight-hour workday. Excluding two-weeks paid vacation, he works five days a week for fifty weeks a year:

50 × 5 = 250 *workdays per year*

The official American workday usually consists of eight hours:

250 × 8 = 2,000 *accepted work hours per year*

The employee's salary is $40,000 a year. Divide the salary by the normally accepted 2,000 work hours to find the hourly wage if he was paid by the hour:

$$\frac{\$40,000}{2,000} = \$20 \text{ per hour wage}$$

If our employee works two hours more than the accepted workday each day of the 250 workdays in a year, he will work:

250 × 2 = 500 *extra work hours per year*

Multiply the $20 hourly wage by the 500 extra hours:

500 × $20 = $10,000 *yearly value of*
2 extra hours a day

This imaginary employee who works an average of only fifty hours a week (not the average sixty hours quoted in surveys) donates worktime valued at ten thousand dollars to his company each year.

Let's take our example one step further. The corporation is large, employing thousands of people. Being ridiculously conservative, let's estimate that only one hundred employees out of these thousands average working a fifty-hour week. Each of the hundred will donate ten thousand dollars worth of unpaid work per year to the company:

$$\$10,000 \times 100 = \$1,000,000 \; \textit{value of all extra hours}$$

As a result of the two extra hours worked each day by the hundred employees, the company saves one million dollars in operating expenses and/or wages.

Although never mentioned, corporations do indeed benefit from the long hours of their ambitious employees. Increased productivity and savings in operating expenses are certainly pluses, but these abstract profits will never show up as a line item in the corporate profit-and-loss statement. A few individual promotions are the only acknowledgment of the long hours of many.

Summary

One of the great pleasures in life is working in a job that is challenging, rewarding, and also enjoyable. Accomplishment in a job well done makes a person feel good. Although finding a fulfilling vocation is often difficult, for many high achievers the corporation provides the opportunity, challenge, and environment needed for a rewarding work life. But the corporation is an abstract, impersonal institution, whereas the employee is a living, feeling mortal. The only balance the institution has to maintain is between profit and loss. The employee must maintain a balance between a fulfilling career and a fulfilling private life, and these needs are difficult to keep in balance when one works in the corporate environment.

American socialization instills the ideals of meritocracy in everyone; some learn too well. An employee's desire for success is manipulated and reinforced by subtle company pressure, and for many ambitious people competition and achievement become an all-consuming passion. Such passionate ambition is as destructive to the employee's private life as it is productive for his career and the corporation. Professional life and the corporation gain, but personal life and family lose.

Marriage and family life in our country are in transition. A major factor in the so-called breakdown of the family is the massive shift from blue-collar to white-collar jobs and the inherent changes in work habits and lifestyle. If corporate employees' "power to love" is as strong as their "compulsion to work," the open-ended workday must be honestly and consciously monitored to lessen its negative effects on the employee, the spouse, and the family.

5

THE RIGHT
MOVES

RELOCATION

Relocation is as old as history; without it the population of the world would have remained crowded into the Garden of Eden. Our American heritage resulted from the Pilgrims' "moving on," and the tradition continues to thrive. America has experienced several mass relocations: the frontier movement in the middle 1800s, immigration in the late 1800s and early 1900s, the Depression migration of the 1930s. And we're on the move again.

Although historically unrecognized, occupational relocation influences American demographics. According to John Naisbitt, author of *Megatrends,* the 1980 census reported that for the first time in our history more Americans are living in the South and West (118 million) than in the East and North (108 million). His statistics reveal a shifting from an industrial society centered in the North and East to an information society locating in the South and West. California, Florida, and Texas are designated as the megastates of tomorrow.[1]

The latest census recorded our country's population at approximately 226.5 million people, with 45 million—one in every five Americans—relocating each year. Of these people, one-half, or 22,500,000, move as a result of corporate transfers. Petroleum, chemical, automobile, and business machine companies move their employees most often. Between 100,000 and 250,000 executives transfer yearly. Those in the twenty-five-to-forty age bracket are the most mobile: 68 percent move at least once every three years, 23 percent move every two years, and 18 percent move annually.

Logically, the number of relocations increases with national economic prosperity and decreases with recession. Such a decrease was noted during 1980–1983 recession. IBM, a company famous for transferring employees, moved 5 percent of its work force annually in the mid-70s but only 3 percent in 1983. As the economy goes, so go corporate transfers.

Company Rationale and Assistance

Ask any corporate person why a company transfers employees, and the most likely response will be "management development." The corporate world places great emphasis on developing candidates for management. One of the most important duties of any manager is training subordinates to become managers. The trainee is then promoted and transferred to fill a job slot left empty by another promotion and transfer. This train-promote-transfer cycle operates nationwide in most corporations and worldwide in many. Transfers are, in fact, necessary for an employee to learn the various areas of the business. Experience gained in the field is different from the experience at headquarters, and geographical location is usually different too. Relocations, accompanied by increases in responsibility, salary, and title, are considered vital for the development of well-rounded, experienced executives.

Another company reason for transfers is necessity: a vacant job slot needs to be filled; an entire facility is moved or closed; a merger or acquisition has occurred. Companies sometimes relocate their people en masse from one state to another. Union Carbide's move from New York City to Connecticut was a mass employee relocation. Having lived only in the city, with its public transportation, many Carbide employees had to be taught to drive at company expense. Others refused to move and found other employment. General Motors recently acquired Texas-based Electronic Data Systems (EDS) and is relocating well over one thousand EDS employees to Michigan.

Often companies use transfers as an "acid test" of an employee's willingness to make sacrifices for success. A corporate executive whom I interviewed related his early experience when he was offered and refused a promotion/relocation. "The next day the president of the company called me and said, 'Ron, I understand you've received an offer. You're in marketing. I expect you to move. It's part of your responsibility if you're going to be with this company and expect to get ahead.' " Accepting a relocation is taken for granted; refusing a move can be a black mark on the employee's record.

Transfers also are used for demotions or parallel positions instead of promotions. The message is clear: take the transfer or leave the company; move on or move out.

This practice is especially prevalent at corporate headquarters. Such a transfer is used by the company as a process for weeding out the unsuccessful and is a traumatic experience for the employee and family.

Corporate management believes in the necessity of transfers and spends millions of corporate dollars each year on relocations. Financial moving benefits or relocation packages offered by companies have greatly improved in the past two decades. When my husband and I made our first move in 1965, the company paid for the house-hunting trip, the moving company, and a grand total of three hundred dollars for incidental expenses (even in 1965 three hundred dollars didn't cover drapery cost for the new house). That was the entire relocation package. We were responsible for selling and buying our homes; no real estate fees were paid. If the old house didn't sell quickly, we had to make our own payments on both the old and new homes. Today companies are more generous. The greatest boon for the employee is financial assistance in selling and buying homes. If the old house doesn't sell within a two- or three-month period, a relocation firm paid by the company will purchase the home. Seldom will the firm pay the asking price for the house, but the employee is relieved of the anxiety of having to sell the house before buying the new one.

A 1983 *Forbes* article gave a breakdown of the typical company cost for moving a middle manager: house sale and purchase, $21,500; shipment of goods, $5,200; mortgage assistance and cost of living adjustment, $3,000; incidental expenses, $4,900; house-hunting trip, $1,800; spouse job assistance, $1,100. Estimates of company moving cost per employee range between the above $37,500 to $50,000. Because of more expensive hous-

ing, relocating a high-salaried top executive can be
$100,000 or more.[2]

Regardless of the improved benefits, employees
sometimes incur personal financial losses when relocating. To illustrate this point, let me cite the experience
of a corporate couple transferred from the Southwest to
the home office in New York City. They moved to
Connecticut, and the employee commutes to the city.
Although they purchased a home the same size as the
one they sold, each month they draw on their savings to
pay the bills. The promotion, salary increase, and moving benefits did not offset the higher cost of housing and
living. This couple considered only the career advantages, disregarding the financial loss. For them, management development is personally expensive.

Housing costs vary with sections of the country, and
company compensation often doesn't consider this difference. One might sell a beautiful home in Atlanta for
ninety-five thousand dollars, but one cannot buy an
equally beautiful home in San Francisco for the same
amount. After going through one such housing down-
grade I told my husband that one more promotion and
we would be back in Alabama with an outhouse. Although companies are much more enlightened about financial moving expenses, a transfer and promotion
doesn't always translate into an improved living situation.

Why Do We Do It?

Just as corporations have valid reasons for transferring
employees, employees also have sound reasons for accepting the transfers. A promotion offer is a compliment
to the employee and, vicariously, to the employee's

family. It announces to the world that this person's talent, intelligence, and hard work merit reward, and it says to peers that this employee is among the chosen, an example to follow. A promotion validates a person's worth in the business realm. The employee is congratulated, complimented, and sometimes compromised by all the praise received—the company needs *me!* How could I turn down such a grand opportunity? The company has so much confidence in the employee's ability it is willing to invest many thousands of relocation dollars for training and advancement. Ambition is the name of the game, and the arena is the employee's ego.

When a promotion is offered, the time to make a decision is purposely short. Many times a transfer/promotion is offered one day with a decision expected the next. From the company point of view this tactic is understandable, but it makes for a difficult situation at home. After receiving an offer the employee arrives home in a state of euphoric excitement, with ego soaring, ready for champagne and celebration. It is easy to be carried away by the compliments and promises; it is not so easy to put aside this delicious state of euphoria and look at the situation realistically. Decisions made at the height of the excitement are often pressured by time and emotion.

Other advantages accompany promotion/transfer offers besides employee ego satisfaction. If the prized job offer is accepted, the experience expands the employee's chances for future promotions within the company. The promotion also enhances a person's résumé. An excellent résumé is an important asset for the ambitious corporate climber and can be the passport to a bigger, better position with another company. A headhunter with just the right offer might call at any time, and a variety of experiences and qualifications makes the employee a more desirable job candidate to outside companies.

A relocation can be broadening for the family as well as for the employee's career. Moving offers exposure to new culture, education, and people. Whether or not the event actually becomes a positive experience depends on individual circumstances, personalities, and attitudes. Generalities are dangerous because one family member may profit from the move while another may be devastated. My daughter says she feels that each new place we have lived brought hardships and bad experiences that have affected her life. But each place also gave her at least one plus. She gained and kept a good friend in each locale; one place offered an advanced educational challenge; another was near New York City, which she enjoyed immensely. Basically, she was saying there were both gains and losses associated with each move, although at the time there seemed to be only losses. Hindsight tempers judgments.

Money is an important influence in the transfer/promotion decision. Increased job status is usually accompanied by increased salary, which can provide a better home, better life-style, and better education for the children. When in the throes of moving, most people would gladly exchange these monetary rewards for a settled life, but once the adjustment to the new place is made, the additional money and its attendant accoutrements are welcomed and enjoyed. Many corporate families also benefit financially from buying and selling homes. This situation is two-sided and depends on the housing market, locale, and national economy. The earlier example of losing money on the house when moving from Atlanta to San Francisco can have the opposite results when the direction is reversed. In moving from California to Georgia a corporate couple might make a substantial profit from selling high and buying low. During the housing boom of the late 70s many transient couples gained financially as a result of the housing market and their mobility.

But corporate couples sometimes accept transfers for negative rather than positive reasons. Fear is a powerful motivator and can be a persuasive influence in a couple's transfer decision. Just as a promotion/move enhances the employee's record and career, a rejection of that move can cause irreparable damage. Superiors rarely verbalize career threats, but the employee knows a turndown puts career progress in jeopardy. It is general knowledge in the corporate world that one relocation might be refused without severe job effects, but a second refusal puts a black mark on one's employment record. After the second rejection superiors generally assume the employee won't or can't move, and that employee is no longer considered for future promotion/transfers. A career can quickly stagnate into a dead-end job or demotion. A second fear involves job security. The choice is simple: accept a demoting transfer or find a new job with a different company. Either option is demoralizing and in such circumstances few or none of the positive aspects of transferring are relative.

Another negative reason for accepting a relocation is escape. An undesirable situation, within either the family or the career, might have developed in the current location. In either case moving offers escape from present circumstances and hope for resolution of the problem. But a problem is rarely solved by changing locations; it usually moves with you and is compounded. A recently transferred and recently divorced man related, "We thought the move might bring us together because we'd have to depend on each other. We were using the move to wipe the slate clean, but instead other problems developed."

It is to be hoped that corporate couples accept transfers more often for positive than negative reasons. Regardless of the reason, moving is basic to the careers of millions of people and is accepted as an unalterable consequence of their employment.

The Move

By its nature moving means change, and any change, whether a plus or minus, is upsetting. There is never a good move; comparatively, a move is either "not quite as bad as" or "worse than" other moves, and each is traumatic. Relocation isn't simply packing up at one place and unpacking at another. The entire process of relocating requires time, normally one of three years. From my own experience I have identified three overlapping yet distinct stages within each relocation; psychological separation, the physical move, and psychological settlement.

A friend of mine has a standard phrase, "This too shall pass," which he uses to lessen or dismiss the severity of a given situation. While driving to church one Sunday, this corporate family was discussing some minor problem that had arisen, and true to form, the employee/husband/father intoned his "this too shall pass." Silence. Suddenly, one of the children spoke: "Dad, does that mean we are going to move again?" The father had no such ulterior motive, but he had often used the same phrase relating to a move, and the child made the obvious connection.

The initial moving stage—psychological separation—is set in motion long before the boss calls the employee in to discuss the promotion/transfer offer. It begins with intuition: a feeling that something is in the wind, a discreet feeler from the boss, or an innocent bit of office scuttlebutt. Experienced corporate movers become supersensitive to subjective clues of an impending transfer. Even though nothing concrete has been mentioned at the office, the couple's thinking and planning shifts from long-term to short-term, and this shift alters the way they live their lives. Everyday decisions are affected by the probable move. "Why paint the house, plant new bushes, join a new activity, enroll in a class, make a new friend? We'll probably be moving soon anyway."

Finally, the day arrives; the boss formally proposes the transfer. Now the psychological separation stage becomes open and intense. By the time the employee leaves the boss's office work peers know the promotion/transfer offer has been made and assumes it will be accepted. Then begins the torturous decision process for the couple. The employee floats into the house on cloud nine, smiling broadly. One look at the bottle of champagne and the spouse knows without a word that a sales pitch is coming. The children are sent to their rooms, to a neighbor's house, or out to play—anywhere out of hearing distance—so the couple can discuss the details of the offer. No matter how secretive the parents are, the children instinctively know something momentous is afoot; their antennae are very sensitive. A transfer offer is comparable to an impending death in the family; you think you are prepared for it, but when it happens, it's still a shock. The employee is in a euphoric state; the spouse is already dreading the hardships ahead. Productive discussion of the issue is impossible until they manage to arrive at a common emotional plane; only then can a well-thought-out decision be made.

The transfer decision process varies with individual couples. All facets of family, individual, and career implications should be considered in the decision. After much discussion most corporate wives abdicate responsibility for and participation in the decision. For this reason the employee/husband usually makes the final decision on whether to accept or reject the relocation offer. Occasionally, an employee resists a promotion because of family difficulties, or sometimes he feels it isn't a good career move. In this event the standard reason given to superiors for the rejection is "family considerations." Regardless of the actual reason, the family excuse is more acceptable and causes less damage to the career.

However, corporate couples normally accept transfer offers, and psychological separation accelerates. By now news of the upcoming move is common knowledge. The "For Sale" sign in the front yard might as well be of flashing neon. A change comes over the entire family; personal interest and investment in the present location ceases. The employee departs for the new job in the new location, and a gap appears in the family unit; home life becomes abnormal. The children are lethargic and upset, uninterested in participating in usual activities and unhappy about having to leave friends. The spouse begins methodically to disengage from commitments: giving notice at work, resigning from the PTA board, dropping out of tennis league. Perhaps the most difficult element of psychological separation comes from outside the home. After the initial deluge of condolence calls from friends the telephone stops ringing except for business solicitation calls from real estate agents and moving companies. One's circle of friends contracts. Invitations slowly trickle to a halt, partly because everyone knows the employee is away but also because the family too will soon be gone.

This social phenomenon always upset me until a friend inadvertently explained. Joan had lived in the same general area all her life; her husband owned a small dry cleaning firm in town. Unknowingly, they bought a new home in a transient corporate neighborhood and quickly made friends in the new community. Couple by couple, their new friends were transferred by their companies. On the day I told Joan that we too were moving she exploded from frustration saying, "I'll never again make friends with corporate people. It hurts too much when they leave." Only then did I finally understand that the disengagement process is really two-sided. Nontransient people seek long-term friendships, not short-term relationships.

The second stage of the moving experience is the physical move or the actual mechanics of selling the house, buying a new one, packing up, traveling, and moving into the new home. This phase is filled with hard work, anxiety, loneliness, excitement, and at times enjoyment. It is the middle stage that overlaps psychological separation on one end and psychological settlement on the other.

Preparation for the physical move begins within days after acceptance of the job offer. Because the employee quickly leaves to begin the new job, the wife usually falls heir to the chores and details of moving. The wife and children routinely remain at the old place until the house is sold, the kids finish the school term, and the new house is ready. During this time the husband/father/employee works halfway across the country, lives in a hotel or an apartment, and returns to visit the family once or twice a month. Little assistance can be expected from him.

The first order of moving business is getting the house ready to put on the market. It must be in the best possible condition to sell for the best possible price. A thorough housecleaning, minor repairs, and sometimes painting are necessary. This is sell, throw-, or give-away time. Attic, garage, and basement empty as all unused items are discarded. But transient families are rarely "pack rats"; such accumulation is too much trouble to move around. Next all personal and sentimental items disappear from view—the bathroom looks like an ad in *House Beautiful*. The house is no longer a comfortable home; it is transformed into a piece of marketable merchandise.

After the house renovation a real estate agent approved by the relocation firm representing the corporation is selected. As a rule, three independent appraisals of the house are required in the event the relocation firm must, as a final resort, purchase the house. If this becomes necessary, the relocation firm usually will pay the average of the three appraisal prices. Finally, the decisions on agent and asking price are made, and the "For Sale" sign goes up. From this moment on it is open season on the family's privacy.

The selling process begins with open-house tour day for all realtors of the area to preview the house. It's advisable to leave home for the entire day because of the constant parade of people looking into closets, checking out the bathrooms, and prying into the pantry. This tour of the house is understandably necessary, but it is nonetheless an unpleasant experience. From the real estate listing of the house until the actual sale the home becomes a quasi-public building.

During the months that a house is on the market the seller seldom relaxes. The agent could call at any time for an appointment to show the house in fifteen minutes, or someone might simply ring the doorbell after seeing the sign in the yard. The seller rarely declines showing the house because this could be the very person who will buy. The house must be kept clean, picked up, and in showcase condition at all times. Such a state of living isn't conducive to relaxation.

Once the selling process has been initiated, the next step is visiting the destination to begin the buying process. This house-hunting trip is a mixed bag of emotions. There is the excitement of travel, eating out, visiting a new place, and looking for a new home, but all of these normally pleasurable activities are tempered by the pressure of selecting the new home within a specified time period. This buying period varies with the company, but the average period is four days. Finding the best house in the best location is stressful and time-consuming. Real estate agents routinely show houses just above or just below the mover's stated price range; for some reason few houses are available in the desired range. If a suitable home isn't found within the allotted time, some companies pay for a second house-hunting trip or allow the family to move, store their furniture, and rent an apartment until a desirable home is found. Of course, there are limits to this generosity. Most couples select a home in the assigned time, and the spouse returns to the old home to finish the selling details while the employee works on the purchasing details.

The physical stage of the move now shifts into high gear. The moving company is contacted, a moving date is set, and a representative visits to estimate the weight of the furniture and required van space. The spouse contacts the telephone, electric, gas, water, and newspaper companies about cut-off dates; the employee contacts the same companies in the new location about start-up dates. School, medical, and dental records are collected and change-of-address cards are mailed out. Activity is at fever pitch as the moving date approaches and the employee returns to the family. The sale of the house is finalized, and the packers arrive to carton possessions.

By moving day all the family's chores are finished. There is nothing to occupy time except watching a stranger carelessly wrap and stow grandmother's prized crystal. Friends drop in to say good-bye, and the children cry. The legs are removed from the lovely dining table, and the piano is almost dropped down the front steps, but eventually everything is loaded. Nothing remains but the empty house, the car, the corporate couple, the sobbing children, and the luggage for the trip. The door is finally shut on both the old house and the old life.

I always enjoy the interim between closing the old and opening the new. In this short space my life seems self-contained; the family is of necessity a solid unit sharing the same experience at the same time. There are no chores to do, no appointments to keep, no bills to pay, no responsibilities except to the moment. The past is gone and the future has yet to arrive. It is a period of aloneness and togetherness, a period of independence and interdependence—suspension of time and space. A sense of freedom prevails until the future necessarily intrudes.

On arrival at the new location, confusion and chaos reign; there is much to do and not enough hours in the day. The packing process is reversed; unpacking begins. The legs are replaced on the dining table, the piano is almost dropped coming up the front steps, and grandmother's priceless crystal is carelessly unwrapped. Find the linen crate, pull out sheets for the beds, cover the naked bedroom windows before dark. The movers finally finish unloading the van and leave. The corporate family stands, bewildered, in the strange house amid a forest of crates, boxes, and misplaced furniture. The future is now; a new life in this new place begins.

The employee goes to the new job, the children enroll in the new school, and the spouse establishes the domicile. At this point the employee and children normally modulate into the psychological settlement stage of the move, but the spouse remains trapped in the physical stage. Much remains to be done before venturing into the community. Contact new doctors and dentists, transfer medical, dental, and school records, locate the nearest hospital, find the most convenient shopping area, unpack the dishes and organize the kitchen, order draperies, hang pictures—the list of urgent tasks is endless. After months of turmoil household order finally emerges out of moving chaos, and the new house is transformed into home. The physical move is completed, and the spouse too enters the third and final stage of the relocation.

Psychological settlement might be defined as attaining a sense of well-being in the new place. A Harvard Medical School study cited these requirements for a personal sense of well-being: someone to give assistance if needed; intimate friends to like and trust; reassurance of one's own worth from others; and a sense of community to share social concerns and opinions. These same requirements are necessary for psychological settlement after relocating. There is no prescribed time frame in which the transient attains this sense of well-being. For some it's a matter of months; for others, it may be one to three years; some people might never "settle" in a specific locale. On an average most relocated people require twelve to eighteen months to adjust psychologically to a new environment.

Even as an adult, being "the new kid on the block" is an uncomfortable situation. In most locations a representative from Welcome Wagon calls on the newcomer, but in my experience this organization does little to promote a person's sense of well-being. The visitor is friendly and informative; she answers questions about local facilities; and many Welcome Wagon branches are authorized to invite new residents to join a local newcomers' club. However, the main thrust of Welcome Wagon is commercial, since local businesses pay Welcome Wagon to hand out their advertising and discount coupons. Personally, I resented being patronized by the sales pitch in the guise of friendship, but many new residents look forward to this call.

For numbers of women the most helpful organization in a new location is a newcomers' club, which usually has a luncheon meeting once a month. These clubs are specifically designed for new residents and offer social contact with others through such activities as bridge groups, sports leagues, and craft workshops. Membership is usually limited to a specific time period, one or two years, and many women use these activities to make new friends and ease the transition into the community. Such clubs focus on keeping the newcomer busy to alleviate loneliness, and many transient wives with "joiner" personalities contact this club immediately after their move. But newcomers' clubs offer little assistance for the less gregarious or the ones who are in the throes of moving depression. Most newcomers' clubs offer only social, not psychological, help.

As for neighbors, baking a cake for the family moving in next door is an almost-forgotten tradition and seldom occurs in today's busy world. In my relocations I experienced various welcomes from neighbors. I was warmly welcomed in one place, cake and all; in another, no one called; in a third location, my nearest neighbor visited, but I later wished she hadn't. As I was making coffee, Mrs. Poison Tongue informed me how I should conduct myself with the other neighbors: I should never visit unless invited because "this was not the kind of neighborhood where you would borrow a cup of sugar." I met no other neighbor for eight months. Shortly before Christmas I found a party invitation in the mailbox, so my husband and I gathered our courage and went. We didn't even know our hostess. The party was a great success, we met our neighbors, and they were delightful. I endured eight months of loneliness as a result of that unfortunate first encounter.

Indeed, friends and a social environment are necessary to adjustment after a move, but physical environment often influences the speed of establishing these friendships. People are more accessible in a densely populated subdivision than in a neighborhood zoned with two-acre lots. More effort is required to walk half a mile for a visit than to visit over the back fence. Consequently, physical isolation can retard adjustment.

The culture of the area is also an important factor in gaining acceptance by the community. One place may be warm and welcoming, eager for the infusion of new talent, whereas another area may be cool and aloof, threatened by any change. Seasoned transients often purposefully choose transient neighborhoods because the culture is homogeneous in that everyone is eager to make friends quickly. Neighbors are more welcoming because they have experienced the same lonely feelings, and this acceptance makes the newcomer's psychological settlement quicker and easier. Conversely, a stable neighborhood can be difficult. After moving to one rather provincial town my husband and I talked with a man we met in the park. He asked how long we had lived there, and we explained that we were newcomers. The man laughed and said, "Don't let it worry you. I've been living here for eleven years, and I'm still considered a newcomer."

Settling takes time: time to grieve for the loss of former friends and time to make new ones. Settling begins before separation is complete. Homesick for the familiar, new residents often compare the new area to the old, and these comparisons delay both adjustment to the new community and acceptance by the community. Texas provides an example of the important role of attitudes. During the entire decade of the 1960s only 214,000 out-of-staters moved into the state, but in the two years from April 1980 to July 1982 more than three times that number, 667,000 people, relocated to the Lone Star State. Car bumper stickers advertise the resulting attitudes: one proclaims proudly, NATIVE TEXAN; another bluntly states, IF YOU LOVE N.Y. SO MUCH, TAKE I-30 NORTH. On a recent trip west I was greeted by a bumper sticker reading, WELCOME TO CALIFORNIA. NOW GO HOME.

The middle stage of relocation, the physical move, might be compared to childbirth in that the pain is soon forgotten. But the first and third stages, psychological separation and settlement, often cause emotional pain that is not easily reconciled. These two phases of the moving experience are potentially damaging for any member of the mobile corporate family, especially if transfers occur frequently.

Personal Impact of Moving

Moving causes personal repercussions regardless of how well the move goes or how advantageous it is to the career. All relocating couples strive to concentrate on the positive aspects of moving. The negative get little pre-move attention because negatives tend to cloud the decision by allowing raw emotions to surface. But during the post-move adjustment the negatives refuse to be denied. Personal upset and stress are inherent in any change, and moving certainly qualifies as change.

For the employee the initial euphoria of promotion/relocation is short-lived; reality invades with a multitude of changes, chores, and confusing emotions. The elation becomes anxiety, and the celebration turns to mourning. Making the transition from old job to new and from old home to new results in prolonged stress. If the usual pattern is followed, the transferred employee starts the new job two or three months before the family arrives. Alone in an unfamiliar place, the man goes in early and stays as late as possible to fill the empty hours. The rented room is simply a sleeping place; work becomes the focal point of a solitary existence.

Once on the job, the transferee finds that the coveted promotion, which was glamorized by superiors, is in reality a brier patch of problems. Uncertainty and self-doubt replace arrogance and pride. After the initial shock the employee realizes that if all had been going well, the position would still be occupied and the promotion not offered. Unresolved problems are the primary reasons for empty job slots but are a discouraging welcome for the newly arrived promotee. Self-imposed pressure to perform miracles and prove worthy of company faith and money is enormous. The employee's reputation and capability may be well known, but credentials and creditability must be reestablished in any new job. Each office has its own set of politics, and the transferee is reluctant to act until this political system is deciphered, defined, and understood. The newcomer must find out who are friends and adversaries; he must determine where the power lies and how to gain access to that power. Other employees often resent incoming promotees, and this resentment can make the "get my arms around the job" period even more difficult.

While the employee is trying to adjust at work, family and relocation tasks demand attention. Time must be allotted to scout out the area, engage a real estate agent, locate desirable neighborhoods and schools, preview houses, and make the initial contact in securing mortgage money. These chores should be done before the spouse arrives for the actual house hunting. But the husband should never buy a house without his wife's consideration and agreement. A wife usually spends more time at home than the husband does, and it's important to her adjustment that she feels comfortable with the choice. In addition, transferees sometimes select areas and houses that are too expensive, from a subconscious urge to compensate the family for their uprooting. "Sure we can swing it. No problem." Such an emotional decision, if uncorrected by the spouse, strains the budget, adding a financial burden to the relocation.

Compensating the family takes many forms and is a normal routine in most relocations. Corporate couples feel guilty about moving their families; therefore, pets, new cars, trips, and swimming pools, to name only a few, are frequently offered as consolation prizes in an effort to ease the guilt and appease family discontent. In our traumatic move from Florida to Michigan my husband and I allowed the children to choose the carpet colors for the upstairs bedrooms of the new home. They chose red, hot pink, and purple, with the blue from the lower floor on the stairs and in the hall. The day we moved into the house, one of the movers had the audacity to ask me if I chose the colors for the upstairs or did we buy the house like that. However, when we were transferred again, this kaleidoscope house sold within two weeks. But most of the time such appeasement has little effect on personal emotion or home sale. Expensive items can't change feelings, and the consolation prizes for the children have the potential to backfire, adding resentment to discontent. Regardless of the effort, the couple's guilt feelings usually linger, sometimes for many years.

The businessperson moves into a relatively familiar community, the office. Talents and credentials are transferred, reestablished, and eventually accepted in the new office. But this ready-made acceptance doesn't provide immunity to the personal repercussions associated with relocation. Plagued with bouts of stress and guilt, the employee's psychological settlement is never complete until the job situation is comfortable and the family is content. Until then both personal and work life are disrupted.

The emotional impacts and the problems of relocating have no regard for proper timing. Before the employee's adjustment is complete, the spouse too begins to struggle with the "moving blues." The corporate couple's relationship is often threatened during a move because at the precise time mutual support is needed, little is available. Both are overwhelmed by their individual problems, with scant energy left to share. Furthermore, the concurrent but separate adjustments are often in direct opposition. It is difficult to relate to a spouse's loneliness when the employee has too little time for too many people at the office. Reaching a plateau of mutual support and understanding is vital to the couple's relationship, but excessive dependence on each other can be as destructive for the marriage as no support at all.

The term *trailing spouse* is the newest title conferred on the mate of a transferred corporate employee. In dual-career couples this spouse could be male or female, but in most corporate moves the trailing spouse is female. Although 57 percent of the married women in America now work outside the home, old customs and sex roles still prevail in most marriages and families. Most men are reared to be the major wage earner, and most women, whether employed or not, are socialized to be the stabilizers in the family. When relocation occurs, the woman feels responsible for the emotional settlement of children, husband, and herself—in that priority order.

Mother/wife emphasizes the positive and reconciles the negative. "Just think of all the new friends you'll make and all the things we can do. I know you miss your friends in Chicago, but you can telephone and write and we'll visit them next summer." "Of course there are problems with the job, that's why the company needs you here. You'll have it running smoothly in no time." Only after the children are settled in school, the husband is occupied at work, and the moving chores are completed does the relocated woman realize she has neglected her own well-being in the process of stabilizing everyone else in the family.

In the early career stages moving is often seen as a

great adventure and challenge for the young wife. It is exciting: new people, new places, new home, "on our own, at last." The children, if any, are under school age and adapt easily; mother and father are their security. Although the young wife misses her relatives and former friends, she adjusts quickly and wonders why there is such a fuss about moving. She prides herself on her accomplishment and boldly states, "If you have a good attitude, you will have a good move." But with repeated moves, growing children, and advancing age and career, her opinions of relocating change. The excitement of adventure and challenge fades into dread.

Loss of self or identity is perhaps the most common distress of unemployed corporate wives. Unlike the transferred employee, a housewife's credentials do not transfer. With each move she must once again start from the bottom to rebuild her community credentials. A woman might have left Chicago as president of the local PTA, but in the new community she is known only as the mother of the new kids in school. Husband and children automatically move into a community: office and school; the transferred spouse has to find her own community and acceptance.

A close friend, who has moved seventeen times, wrote a verse that clearly depicts a wife's loss of identity:

> Who is me?
> Where is she?
> Lost at sea?
> No, run over by a moving van.

In small seminars, I always ask the women to identify themselves to the group. Invariably, most will introduce themselves as follows: "My name is Mary Jenkins. I'm married and have two children, ages eight and twelve. My husband is a sales rep for Paper International, and we live on State Street." They define themselves only through husbands and children, not through personal interests and activities. Loss of self isn't confined to the mobile corporate wife—many women immerse their personalities in their families—but mobility is directly linked to the prevalence of loss of self in corporate wives.

As the number of moves increases, women tend to withdraw more and more into their families, expending less and less energy to rebuild. One woman, previously an avid church worker, stopped joining the local church after moving. She had moved her church letter so often and stayed such a short time in each place that it didn't seem worth the trouble anymore. This lady had had one too many moves. A second, more severe relocation repercussion on wives is depression, either minor or major. Although all family members go through some form of the "moving blues," most husbands and children reach settlement relatively quickly and unscathed. For the wife the blues are usually more profound and enduring, unnoticed until the rest of the family is secure and thoughts turn inward.

After the kitchen is in order, the drapes hung, and the redecoration completed, the wife awakes one morning with an empty day ahead. There is nothing to do and no one to do "nothing" with. Husband is at work and children are at school. Loneliness descends like an isolating blanket of snow. She goes into the living room, but the sofa she lovingly reupholstered cannot return her affection. Suddenly, all the beauty she created in the new home becomes meaningless. She is a solitary person in an unfamiliar place. The telephone never rings for her. She is lonely.

Loneliness is depressing and if unresolved can turn into major depression. A 1972 Yale University study on the effects of moving on women concluded that moving can cause depression, but normally the woman herself is unaware that moving is the cause. Women tend to blame themselves for being lonely and unhappy. They internalize the stress, burying the pain and anxiety of what they consider a personal inadequacy.

In my research I interviewed two professional counselors—one male, one female. The man had moved several times while employed with a large corporation in a noncounseling capacity. The woman was an employed trailing spouse with only one corporate relocation. In separate interviews I asked the same question to both: can frequent moving cause depression in women? The man answered that moving is only a catalyst that can bring to the surface an underlying pathology causing the depression. The female therapist emphatically stated that moves alone can cause depression. From her own experience she related: "Although I am a 'shrink' by profession, I became a victim to panic, frustration, and depression in an alien environment with no support system." Maryanne Vandervelde, psychotherapist, author and corporate wife, stated in *The Changing Life of the Corporate Wife* that 70 percent of all psychiatric patients are women. Corporate wives, usually showing symptoms of depression or alcohol abuse, make up a large category of these women.[3] From my interaction with other relocated wives I find that minor depression is normal, and major depression and breakdowns are not uncommon.

Kathy, a thirty-eight-year-old wife and mother of four, moved three times in five years. Although she has been in her present home more than a year, she is still unhappy, confused, and depressed. She worries about one child's problems at school. Her husband works long hours and travels, which he has never done before. She hasn't found her niche in the new community and misses her old friends. Finally, she sought professional counseling. Kathy ended her story by relating how ashamed she felt; she had always adjusted so well before and couldn't understand why she wasn't adjusting properly this time. Kathy too had had one too many moves.

For an employed trailing spouse, moving involves additional problems. Recent statistics reveal that dual-career couples now make up one-third of the yearly corporate relocations. Whether the spouse is male or female, job hunting is difficult and stressful. As stated earlier, some companies offer spouse job assistance in the relocation package. This broad term *assistance* ranges from hiring an outside placement firm to typing the spouse's résumé to passing on rumors of local job openings. Sometimes the company itself hires the spouse. There are no reliable statistics, but informed sources estimate that only 3 to 5 percent of American corporations offer any kind of spouse job assistance. The huge majority offers nothing.

Job hunting is a demeaning experience, especially if the person is a highly ranked professional. In the new location such positions are usually scarce; rarely is there an empty job slot waiting for the trailing spouse. The female psychotherapist/trailing spouse mentioned earlier related that she left the former location at the top of her profession. Her husband's company offered no spouse job assistance at all. After contacting twenty-five personnel agencies in the new city she found that professional organizations in her field do not use agencies for hiring, but she was offered many jobs working on a commission for the personnel agencies. After seven months she hired, at her own expense, a consulting firm with contacts in the field and finally found a position.

Her story is not unique; it occurs repeatedly in dual-career transfers. Many spouses end up with lower-ranked jobs and are forced once again to climb the career ladder. A promotion and salary increase for the transferee might result in demotion and salary reduction for the trailing spouse. These inherent difficulties of dual-career relocation have spawned the phenomenon of commuter marriages. The husband lives and works in one city while the wife lives and works in another city, their relationship depending on telephones and weekend commuting. Such arrangements are rarely personally satisfying or communally gratifying. For the relocated dual-career couple, personal and career impacts are dramatic and demand concerted pre-move consideration and post-move understanding and support.

Summary

Americans have always been a mobile people, but in the past three decades corporate families have become the nomads of our country. Relocating is perhaps the most serious problem encountered in the corporate life-style, and most couples move many times during their careers. Although moving employees is expensive, companies feel transferring is necessary for management development and are willing to pay the price.

For the corporate family, moving usually provides financial and career rewards but extracts personal and psychological penalties. Repeated frequent moves can be damaging for the individuals, the family, and the marriage. Employees are becoming reluctant to relocate because of these negative effects. Some companies have become sensitive to the relocation issues, but most still provide only financial resources.

Corporate people, like people in general, do not fit into convenient molds. Moving isn't required of all corporate employees, and negative impacts of relocation are not relevant to all who do move. Individual circumstances and reactions govern the individual results. But the impacts cited are possible, often probable, repercussions of the mobile corporate life-style.

6

THE ROAD GAME

BUSINESS TRAVEL

Travel is essential to business. Whether next door, in the next city, or across the country, personal interaction facilitates buying, selling, and/or bartering products and services. Historically, businesspeople traveled by foot, horse, ship, and later by rail to peddle their wares, but the Wright brothers' fifty-nine-second air flight in 1903 revolutionized transportation. Until the end of World War II airplanes were utilized primarily as military weapons and transportation for the wealthy. But in the late 1940s and early 50s air travel became increasingly affordable, available, and safe. The business world quickly recognized this fast, convenient transportation as a valuable business tool, and the race to the airport began. Today the modern version of the Wright brothers' invention enables even the smallest companies to claim the world as their marketplace. Ever-increasing numbers of corporate employees file into these winged, cylindrical machines, imprison themselves for a time, and later file off to transact their business. The airplane is to the businessperson what the fire truck is to the fire fighter, a tool that takes him or her where the action is.

But what are the consequences of jet-set life-style for traveling employees, their spouses, and families? If the job demands it, companies expect their employees to travel—some people travel up to 75 percent of the time. Such absenteeism from home and family affects not only employees, it also impacts on the lives of spouses and children. Travel is a requirement in corporate life, but corporations take little notice of any personal side effects incurred. That's the responsibility of employees. For companies, travel is simply a tool used to gain desired business results.

Travel and Business

Companies use travel for four major purposes: training, selling, meeting, and rewarding. Each is a necessary component of a successful business operation. In most companies marketing and · sales employees travel in greatest numbers and most frequently. Engineering and finance people travel less and usually for specific, time-structured projects, assignments, or meetings. Office and production personnel rarely travel for business purposes. Since sales and marketing employees are the most frequent travelers, their experiences are the main focus of this chapter.

The first business travel experience for most employees comes early, after graduation from school but prior to actual employment. In many cases a company-financed, preemployment interview is required, which is the rookie's exciting introduction into the world of business travel and expense accounts: free plane ticket, ground transportation, hotel, and meals. If the young candidate is hired in a sales position, this initial trip is a harbinger of what is to come.

After employment the first official business travel is usually for training. Initial training and periodic updates are vitally important for both companies and employees. For new employees this initial training period, normally two weeks, consists of education, orientation, and indoctrination. Rookies are educated in selling, engineering, and/or finance techniques; they are oriented in company opportunities and methods of operation; and they are indoctrinated with the company philosophy and culture.

For seasoned employees periodic training is required by the company to keep abreast of new developments in products, techniques, and policies. Most employees enjoy these periodic sessions because increased training denotes increased importance to the company. In addition, the trainees expand their company contacts and acquaintances in business and social settings. Enthusiasm and company loyalty, either instilled or renewed, are important by-products of training sessions, and most employees return to their homes and offices in high spirits.

Many large corporations centralize their training into one large institutional complex. Xerox, for example, has a magnificient training center in Virginia that resembles a university; it is an aesthetically designed campus containing classrooms, dormitories, restaurants, and recreational facilities. Other companies conduct their training sessions in or near their home offices. Regardless of location, widely dispersed employees of large corporations must travel to the training center.

The second and greatest use of business travel is the actual selling of the product or service. To date no machine, method, or technique has been invented or discovered that can replace conducting business face-to-face. Other than the written contract, nothing cements a deal better than a handshake. Trust is basic to business dealings, and this trust is built on the nuances of personal interaction. Worldwide, hundreds of thousands of corporate employees migrate every day to obtain this indispensable face-to-face contact, and company profits can depend on this necessary travel. Although business travelers make up the majority of air passengers, travel costs are considered an insignificant expense item in most company budgets. I talked with a vice-president of sales and marketing for a small electronics firm. Travel expense is approximately 10 percent of the sales budget, and he speculated that the percentage would be even less in larger corporations. For companies the costs are well worth the results; it is a minor investment for a major return.

Travel is a valuable asset in employee job performance. In an interview with a young purchasing manager I asked if he did much job-related traveling. He answered that he did some, but, he continued, "I'd like to do a lot more. I think I would do a better job." Face-to-face transactions enable employees to make better decisions, thereby earning or saving money for the company. Additionally, employees acquire knowledge of other operations and swap ideas that can increase productivity.

Third, various in-company business meetings, interbusiness conferences, and trade shows mandate employee travel. Meetings are the accepted method of communicating information to employees, and the number and frequency of such meetings in local offices, off-site, and at home offices continue to grow. In his book *Megatrends* John Naisbitt states, "Jet airplanes, as far as I can tell, have led only to more meetings."[1]

The same is true with interbusiness conferences and trade shows; there is a conference or show for almost any business interest, and they are always well attended. In the United States, trade shows have experienced a popularity explosion with the number doubling from 4,500 in 1974 to 9,000 in 1982. Trade shows are held periodically throughout the world, but the crème de la crème of these shows are the international fairs held each year, usually in Europe. Companies also participate in specialized producers conferences, users conferences, and educational programs. Companies benefit from being represented at shows and conferences in two important ways: (1) the company is publicized, the products are advertised, and sales are often improved by the exposure; (2) the experience, knowledge, and contacts acquired by the attending employees improve their productivity.

Finally, companies use travel as a reward for employee accomplishment. Sales-oriented companies normally function under a quota system, salespeople being assigned a specific amount of sales, dollar or unit, as their work goal or quota each year. Depending on the individual company, 5 to 25 percent of the highest sales achievers are eligible for each year's President's Club, Legion of Honor, or some such honorary program. As recognition for their work, winners (and usually spouses) fly to a chosen location for recreation, meetings, and banquets. In 1981 one large corporation flew more than five hundred people, all expenses paid, to Europe for a week of celebrating; the next year this same company took their people to Hong Kong. But most companies are more conservative, opting for resort hotels or cities within the United States. Employees who do well in their work sometimes win individual trips, alone or with their spouses. If spouses are allowed, the trip is usually a weekend vacation; if only employees are allowed, the trip is disguised as a business conference.

Travel is so prevalent in business that it is an accepted and expected part of corporate employment, and the prospects of future business travel often are used as subtle perks in the hiring process. I asked a young man soon to receive his master's degree in engineering management about his plans. His answer: "I want to hire in with a company as an engineering management consultant. I would like to do a lot of traveling before settling in one location and getting married." This young man has already received several offers promising the desired travel.

Because travel is considered essential, the privilege is often indiscriminately sanctioned by managers and abused by employees. Regardless of the misuse, for the corporation, the costs of business travel are worth the results.

Travel Business
and
Business Travel

Like the moving industry, the American travel industry's growth has paralleled the increased demands for services from the business community. Today the travel business is big business, and most of its business is business travel. Airlines and hotels in particular openly court the business traveler with special programs and rates, offering amenities that cater to the traveler's comfort and needs. No wonder Robert Seidenberg, psychiatrist and author on corporate life, termed traveling executives "elite hoboes."

Business travelers make up more than 50 percent of airline passengers; commercial airlines therefore focus most of their attention on these frequent flyers. For a nominal yearly fee, exclusive airport lounge privileges, personalized reservation and information services, speedy advance check-in, special seating, and custom in-flight meals are available. The lounge privileges include meeting rooms, coffee, and free local telephone calls. For a relatively small additional fee the passenger is enrolled in the seating upgrade program: if an unoccupied first-class seat is available, on request the passenger is moved into the first-class section with no charge. Although these programs are open to anyone who can afford the fees, business travelers are the majority of the members.

The volume of business flyers is so great and potentially profitable that in recent years a number of new airlines have been established to cater specifically to businesspeople. Although these airlines still have limited routes and schedules, their fares are reasonable and competitive. They usually offer more seat space and legroom. Their food, preceded by a hot towel, is considered better than the standard fare and is served on china, with a linen napkin and silverplated flatware. One company features an on-board concierge to aid passengers with hotel reservations; another supplies curb-to-plane minivans with baroque background music. Reincarnated Braniff Airlines hopes to lure the business trade with its adjustable forward compartment known as the "business cabin." A small California firm has on-board barbers, manicurist, and secretaries, but of course only top officers of huge corporations can afford such luxury. The largest portion of out-of-season European travel is done for business purposes, and the international airlines haven't neglected these lucrative clients. The programs vary by airline, but most have business-class seating with extra room and specialized services for the business traveler. Booklets are available that contain general tips for doing business in Europe, local customs, business facilities and opportunities, and diagrams of major airports. One airline even publishes a quarterly newsletter for its frequent international business passengers. Most airlines offer help for transportation problems, "meet and greet" services, and limousine transfers from the airport. KLM has a "Stay on the Way" program available to its first-class and full-fare business-class flyers who have connecting flights to other destinations; these passengers have a free overnight stay in Amsterdam. Business services are commonly available to international travelers and include office and meeting space, mail and message pickup, translators, secretarial service, telexes, and amenity kits containing a calculator and business material. One airline prints business cards in various foreign languages. What more could a business traveler ask?

But the most successful of all travel promotions is the frequent-flyer bonus program offered by most major commercial airlines. When initiated, such programs were time-limited, with a definite ending date, but the response was so great the termination dates were extended. With only one exception, these programs have no enrollment fees, and the impressive rewards include free tickets to such exotic places as Hawaii and Hong Kong, free cruises, and free or reduced-rate lodging.

Hotels also cash in on the business travel market. Several of the leading chains are partners in various airline frequent-flyer programs, adding bonus points for each night's stay. Other hotels have frequent guest programs of their own in which guests earn points toward a free weekend stay or an accommodation upgrade from a room to a suite. A new trend in hotel offerings is the VIP or "club floors," usually two top floors, accessed by express elevators. These VIP floors are designed to entice executives. Generally, each floor has its own concierge and a lounge area with an honor bar. The rooms contain such amenities as a stocked refrigerator, wine, toiletries, bathrobe. A senior vice-president of one hotel chain was quoted in *Time:* "In the morning, coffee, a roll and a paper are brought to the rooms, getting the executives off to a fast start." A concierge of a club floor said, "They love to be pampered."

Not long ago I noticed a billboard advertising a top hotel chain. This sign was simple, yet eye-catching and meaningful. In the upper left corner was a luscious sugar-coated strawberry and in the lower right corner was a filled brandy snifter. Across the center in huge letters was EXECUTIVE SWEETS. The message was clear. Not only does the hotel offer special executive rooms, it also offers the coveted executive life-style.

Today's phenomenal amount of business travel is very profitable for travel-related industries; thousands of travel agencies service only corporate accounts—no personal trips or tour groups, please. The traveling businessperson is a lucrative marketing target, courted and lured with specifically designed products to be bought with company money.

Personal Motivations
to Travel

Business travelers may be "elite hoboes," encouraged to travel by the company, but sometimes they are motivated to travel for other than business reasons. For many years I silently harbored doubts as to the validity of some so-called business trips. I often wondered if covert personal motivations might occasionally be hidden beneath the overt business reasons for travel. But in my position as a corporate wife this was a question I could not ask, a premise I could not state because of my lack of firsthand knowledge of the business situation. In talking with other spouses I found that they too expressed the same doubts and dilemma.

The question, Is business travel always done solely for business reasons? remained with me until I read *Tradeoffs: Executives, Family and Organizational Life*, written by Barrie S. Greiff, M.D., psychiatrist to the Harvard Business School, and Preston K. Munter, M.D., corporate psychiatric consultant and psychiatrist to the Harvard Law School. At last these two men, equipped with research and impressive credentials answered my question: some businesspeople do travel for more than business reasons.[2] From my research and interviews I find that excitement and freedom, self-esteem, status, and personal gain are the four most pervasive personal motivations for business travel.

When a lottery winner is interviewed, one of the first questions asked is "What are you going to do with your money?" Normally, the winner replies, "First, I'll pay my bills and buy a new car. Then I'm going to travel." Everyone wants to travel; we read the travel section of the Sunday paper and dream of someday seeing the world. Usually, the dream is as far as we go; most people simply don't have the money to turn the dream into reality. But not so for some dreamers. They are corporate travelers, and their companies inadvertently provide them with esoteric benefits rarely recognized. Corporate travel and expense accounts allow these employees access to a world that would be financially prohibitive otherwise. Their travel is on the company. Free.

A personal temptation to travel for excitement and freedom can be easily disguised by or translated into valid business trips. A relatively minor business call or detail that might be handled by phone or delegated to someone else suddenly becomes so important that a trip to New York or wherever is vital. And why not take in the latest Broadway hit and do the town while there? Many middle-income employees become so widely traveled— business, of course—they are personified travelogues, with firsthand knowledge of almost any destination. Neighborhood and company parties buzz with cocktail conversation comparing trips. Travel is the "in" topic. "Have you been . . . Did you see . . . Did you eat . . . Next time go to . . ." The corporate traveler can answer any question about the best hotels, restaurants, and sights. It all sounds sophisticated, glamorous, and very expensive to an unknowing noncorporate listener.

Valid and pseudo-business trips grant employees a sense of freedom, a convenient escape or short respite from the everyday boredom, restrictions, and/or pressures at home or office. Routines do sometimes become boring, and there is a bit of wanderlust in most of us.

Why not break the boredom and do a little business at the same time? Perhaps there is a pressing situation at home or at the office that an employee isn't quite ready to confront. What better way to gain more time than to take a trip, especially if the company pays? When talking about business travel, one corporate wife stated, "I know John needs to travel. He's not a nine-to-fiver. He's got the gypsy blood in him; he's got to be on the go."

Whenever I stay in a hotel frequented by business travelers, I always observe these trippers. Most business-people behave circumspectly; some do not—the accepted behavioral rules and restrictions seem forgotten, misplaced, or simply discarded. Travel evidently grants an anonymity that allows them to do and say things they would never dream of doing or saying in familiar surroundings. This anonymity, combined with corporate expense accounts, permits these on-the-road employees to eat, drink, and behave in a manner outside their normal moral and financial restraints. They seem to love these occasional tastes of jet-setting glamour and carefree activities.

Self-esteem is another important personal factor in pseudo-business travel. Most salespeople and executives display sufficient egos and self-confidence, attributes characteristic of the job. But everyone, self-confident or not, enjoys feeling important, and all of us "love to be pampered." Self-esteem is said to be a mirror image of how we perceive other people feel about us. For employees, travel can boost self-esteem. Required business travel impresses one's subordinates at the office, one's family at home, and one's friends in the community, because travel is an abstract symbol of importance. An employee's absence is often explained to children and friends as "an important business trip." This explanation translates into "important people conduct important business." Others' reactions mirror-image back to travelers, enhancing their self-esteem. Travelers are catered to on the plane, in the hotel, and in restaurants; they are valued customers. While away, employees often take important clients to dinner, or they are invited to dinner by clients. Either way, a feeling of self-importance complements the occasions. International travel can overinflate the ego because foreign businesspeople, especially the Japanese, often wine, dine, and entertain visitors royally. Certainly, such celebrity deference raises one's self-esteem.

Some corporate employees travel to emphasize their company position or status. The farther up the corporate ladder a person climbs, the more opportunity he has for travel. Although the need to display one's job status indicates a lack of confidence in one's ability, some corporate employees travel as much to exhibit rank and importance as from necessity. Nevertheless, business travel, valid or not, increases in direct proportion to job level. The use of travel as a job status symbol is particularly evident among midlife middle executives striving to prove their abilities; image is a primary concern for them. Upper managers and company officials usually travel only from necessity because (1) they become tired and a bit jaded; travel loses much of its excitement; (2) their self-esteem is by now well established and their company status well known and relatively secure; (3) "running the railroad" requires their presence at the office. (There is an exception: upper executives sometimes plan trips simply to add some variety to life. They become bored with the daily routine, and travel alleviates the boredom.) But even though upper managers often prefer to travel less, their travel can be extensive and very frequent.

Personal gain became a major personal reason for travel with the introduction of airline frequent-flyer programs. Corporate people, spouses included, are jetting everywhere; some even sell their free tickets through newspaper want ads, clearly a money-making scheme. Public and private debates rage over the ethics of personal use and monetary gain from these prizes. Nonetheless, frequent-flyer programs increase corporate travel abuse. The lure of business travel is difficult to resist because it is loosely monitored by superiors, easily rationalized by employees, and undeniably explained to corporate families. But the fact remains, as expressed by one spouse, that "a lot of these trips get made up."

The Travel Cycle

For employees and families each trip is a cycle made up of three stages. Greiff and Munter delineated the stages as anticipation, separation, and regeneration.[3] I prefer the term *reentry* to regeneration. Regardless of terms, I discovered that a travel cycle with distinct stages does occur, although most corporate families may be unaware of it. This cycle begins, ends, and restarts without conscious recognition. The following is merely definition and description of the cycle stages, not a psychological analysis of the causes of particular actions and feelings. In all stages the behavior of the traveler and the spouse differs. This is understandable because the traveler is the performer, doing the action, and the spouse is the supporter, dealing with the personal and family consequences of the actions.

Anticipation is the initial stage of the cycle. For both husband and wife this is the period of physical and mental preparation for the leaving. A stay-at-home spouse usually makes sure the traveler's needed clothes are clean and ready, she cancels the traveler's conflicting appointments and any couple social engagements, and she begins planning activities for herself and the children to fill the upcoming separation time. Some spouses pack the suitcases, others leave the packing to the travelers. Most employees do little physical preparation other than the necessary business planning of appointments, reservations, tickets, and presentations. For dual-career couples with shared home responsibilities this stage involves a flurry of rearranged schedules and shifted duties.

Mentally, trip preparation is not so routine. The individual feelings of both the husband and the wife about the business travel dictate the emotional atmosphere in the home as the traveler readies for the trip. Employees who really enjoy the travel and those who seldom travel are usually in high spirits, happy, and expectant. Spouses who remain home are often upset and resentful, dreading the separation. The resulting atmosphere can be quite tense. In an interview a spouse recalled an earlier exchange: "Jim said, 'You're ruining the time we have together before I leave because you're so upset about me leaving.' I said, 'Well, I can't help it.' " Then she continued, "I don't do that anymore."

Spouse resentment comes partly from the impending separation, but a traveler's excitement about the trip also plays a part. The excitement is often interpreted by a spouse as a personal insult, an abandonment or betrayal. For the wife of a frequent traveler, this anticipation stage is familiar and routine; her attitude and the home atmosphere normally relaxes into nonchalant acceptance over time: "So when are you leaving?" Although this attitude may sound callous, a wife eventually realizes there is nothing she can do to change the situation, so she pretends it really doesn't matter. But most corporate wives deeply resent their husbands' frequent travel.

The separation stage of the cycle begins with the actual departure. Loneliness is characteristic of this period, and almost every traveler and spouse experience it at some time during separation. Schedules and appointments structure most of the traveler's time, and loneliness usually intrudes only with solitary meals and empty hotel rooms. Many times business dinners are planned specifically to avoid lonely meals and empty rooms as long as possible. For the spouse, loneliness is most acute at the employee's normal coming-home time, but the nagging feeling lurks until the next day's round of activities begins. Both employees and spouses plan their days of separation so that little time for loneliness remains.

When employees travel, two voids appear in family units—one physical and one psychological—and stay-at-home spouses must fill these voids. After the departure spouses automatically assume all the familial functions of the travelers, becoming mother and father to children, taking responsibility for chores, and making all decisions. Most important, spouses fill or try to fill the emotional void felt by the children. Continuity is vital in all homes, and spouses of traveling employees strive to maintain this continuity single-handedly during the separation stage.

Separation is a difficult time for spouses because of the overload of responsibilities, but most corporate spouses discover that activity, staying busy, is the key to endurance, and many actually enjoy this stage. These spouses plan special outings with the children, do thorough housecleaning, or work on projects and hobbies. Any variety of activities is possible because regular schedules relax—Daddy won't be home for dinner so let's grab a burger at McDonald's and take in a movie. Business travel can provide stay-at-home spouses with a sense of freedom too.

A family might be compared to a circle. When a member leaves, the circle breaks and a gap appears; the circle's continuity is disrupted and its strength is lost. In order to regain its strength and continuity the circle must contract, close, and re-form. This is the separation stage. On return, the smaller circle must again break, readmit the returned traveler, and re-form to its original size. This is reentry.

Reentry can be boom or bust for employees and spouses. Employees fantasize joyous homecomings: Ares home from the war, Diana home from the hunt. They picture, and indeed long for, jubilation for safe return and appreciation for a job well done. Such homecomings sometimes await infrequent travelers; rarely does this scene welcome frequent travelers. Employees who seldom travel or novice frequent travelers usually return home bearing gifts, especially for the children. Gifts serve three purposes for the donors: (1) they help mitigate travelers' guilt feelings, (2) they remind those at home they were not forgotten, and (3) they are intended to ensure travelers of an eagerly awaited return. But as the trips increase, the gifts decrease. It's a standing joke around our home that I used to receive coming-home gifts of perfume and candy, now I get only dirty underclothes and souvenir matches. Gifts are expensive, and buying them takes time from an already busy schedule. And travelers soon realize that such gifts don't alleviate guilt feelings, nor do they ensure happy homecomings. Children tend to eagerly await the surprises rather than the returnees, and presents mean little to harassed or resentful spouses. Of course, most spouses and children are happy the wanderers are home, but many employees leave and return so often that the goings and comings are routine and therefore ignored.

Like the anticipation stage, the smoothness of the reentry depends on attitudes. Anger and resentment don't go away during separation; they usually intensify, resulting in a strained homecoming. One man related that he hated his wife's business trips because he is always suspicious of the male attention she gets while away from home. Such suspicions are sometimes well founded. Every corporate spouse hears jokes and stories of philandering on trips, and numbers of corporate marriages have ended as a result. In one instance pseudo-business trips were used by an employee to carry on a long-distance affair for two and a half years. Jealousy is not unfamiliar to stay-at-home spouses. Regardless of attitudes, spouses and families generally need at least a day or two to widen the circle and accept the returned members.

Employees also need time for reentry. The home environment is quite different from the travel environment, and a shift in behavior is necessary. It is dangerous to treat spouses like business clients and children like servants; home isn't an office or a hotel. The transition from business to home requires "gearing down," relaxing and regenerating. In some cases travelers return home in a defensive mood. This defensiveness can originate in guilt feelings about leaving, some event while away, or perhaps knowing that anger and resentment await at home. Couples with established travel routines seem to have the smoothest reentries unless, of course, some disaster upsets family equilibrium during separation. Nevertheless, every successful reentry takes time and demands cooperation from all—employees, spouses, and children. When reentry is accomplished, the family is a complete circle again and the travel cycle ends—until the next trip.

Personal Impact of Frequent Travel

Business travel influences more than business deals. Each trip affects the personal lives of corporate couples, and frequent trips alter relationships and erode family structures. Feelings of loneliness and guilt are common to both employees and spouses, perhaps the only shared effects of travel. And even the guilt comes from different sources. Employees berate themselves for being away, and spouses fault themselves for not being more understanding.

When asked to list the positive personal effects of travel, employees usually cite careers and excitement. But the negative effects of travel on employees are more numerous and aren't so easily identified or reconciled.

Travel is mentally and physically draining, a potential health hazard. Gail Sheehy stated in *Passages:* "The man logs so many hours on airplanes, he can barely remember how to eat without pulling down a tray."[4] Stress, tension, and frustration accompany each trip: late arrivals, lost luggage, long lines, unprepared hotel rooms, canceled appointments. Even the most meticulous schedule can go awry. Transcontinental and international flights produce jet lag that lasts for a couple of days. A person recovers just in time for the return flight. In essence, travel wears people out.

The loneliness of the road is always unpleasant, but for some people loneliness is threatening. Most find relief in positive actions such as visiting friends, sightseeing, or going to movies. Others indulge in less positive actions: overeating and drinking, hanging out in bars, gambling, going to X-rated movies, or spending the night with a prostitute. Reactions to loneliness vary with personalities, but loneliness is a definite negative.

A third negative aspect is the contrasting activities and living styles of home and travel. Meat loaf and iced tea is quite a come-down from veal Oscar and white wine; an elementary school play pales in comparison to a Broadway hit; and "take out the garbage" certainly isn't being "pampered." The distance between a million-dollar deal and the household budget is tremendous, and travelers must traverse this distance in the reentry stage of the travel cycle. Spouses often comment that employees have the best of both worlds: the love and security of home and the excitement and glamour of travel. Home-bound families have difficulty relating to the employee's other world because their travel experience is limited. Making the transition from travel to home, in body and mind, is the responsibility of the traveler.

Finally, when business trips are frequent or the absences are lengthy, corporate employees risk becoming visitors, and sometimes strangers, in their own homes. The longer and/or more often the family circle contracts, the more reluctant the circle becomes to reexpand and welcome the returning member. A family, consciously or subconsciously, can harbor deep resentment against the employee for using the home and their lives like a revolving door, and this resentment can be a vengeance against the "offender." Also, when a family member leaves, the remaining members rearrange their lives, individually and collectively. This rearrangement excludes the missing member and is an attempt to retain some semblance of continuity. I spoke with a woman whose husband, a ship pilot, was away about 75 percent of each year. She related that she dreaded his return because it always upset the family's regular routine. The exclusion of the traveler and the rearrangement had become the normal way of life.

The travel cycle often confuses small children. Children center on the constant parent for their security and find it difficult to define the family position and authority of the transient. In one family the small son always reminds his returning father that "Mom is the boss." Young children define their relationships from their experiences. A *Fortune* article cited this example: In anticipation of a visit from Grandmother, a corporate wife said to the small daughter, "We're going to have a visitor, and it's someone you haven't seen in a long time. Can you guess who it is?" The child replied eagerly, "Dad?" [5]

From my experience and interviews, spouses personally benefit in three ways from the employees' business travel. The most often cited plus is self-dependence. Necessity forces spouses to depend on their own resources and talents; otherwise, life is chaotic for the entire family during the separation stage of travel. In most corporate families disasters such as broken limbs and car problems seem always to occur when the employees are out of town. Such events require immediate action and cannot be solved over the telephone. Spouses learn to be self-sufficient, which is certainly a positive for any person. "Clinging vine" spouses don't last long in marriages involving frequent travel; either the marriages fail or the employees find nontraveling employment.

A second advantage for spouses lies in the relaxed schedules and unstructured time during separation. For unemployed spouses especially, this time is theirs to use as they like. Many become quite protective of this time and resent being asked to do something for other family members during "their" time. For companionship unemployed spouses often lunch with friends, and employed spouses sometimes stop after work for a drink with peers. But most spouse activities depend on whether or not there are children and, if so, their ages. Generally, a spouse uses the separation to cultivate a personal life that doesn't depend on the employee's presence.

The third major spouse benefit from employees' business travel is purely materialistic: free trips. Most traveling employees enroll in airline frequent-flyer programs, and each trip adds mileage points to the total needed for two free tickets. These tickets are normally for personal use, so employees and their spouses fly off on pleasure trips that would be unaffordable otherwise. In addition, spouses are invited on some, but very few, business trips at company expense. Such trips are usually company award programs to recognize top achievers and are sometimes strained, tense occasions for spouses. Nevertheless, a trip is a trip and a welcome respite from everyday routine.

The negative aspects of business travel are difficult for most spouses to discuss because such talk pricks at sore spots in a couple's personal relationship. Wives, especially, tend to blame themselves for feeling as they do. When relating their feelings, most preface their statements with "I should be more understanding, but . . ." or "I guess I'm selfish, but . . ." There are no buts about it—the negative repercussions of travel on spouses are real, and their feelings are justified.

For the majority of corporate spouses the difference in life-styles created by travel is a smoldering but active volcano that occasionally explodes, spewing anger, bitterness, and jealousy. Inequality is the foundation of this sensitive issue, and I always use a personal story to illustrate this point.

I remember how excited my husband was twenty-one years ago as he told his mother and me about his new job as sales trainee with a major corporation. He announced that his first assignment was to go to Detroit for two weeks of training, then on to Washington for a week of observation. I shared his excitement until his mother, listening quietly to the good news, turned to my husband and said, "Do you remember the old tenant farmer who lived down by the river? Well, during the Depression he would go hunting to provide food for his family; usually he killed a possum for his wife to clean and cook. At dinnertime the old man would eat the possum meat and his wife and children would share the gravy." Then her gaze shifted to me. "Seems to me that with this job Dal will be getting all the possum and you'll only get the gravy."

Being an inexperienced corporate wife at the time, I laughed at the anecdote, but I now know that such is the case with business travel. The spouse's life at home does not and cannot equate with the employee's life on the road at company expense. I dream that someday my husband and I will visit a place he has never been. I would like, at least one time, for us to share the discovery without his being the tour guide and my being the tourist. Spouses in presumably equal-partnership marriages sometimes feel cheated because they keep homes and families running smoothly, enabling employees to travel worry-free, but they seldom receive praise or reward for this contribution. I recently saw a cartoon relating to this subject. A disgruntled-looking wife stood, arms folded, watching her husband pack for a trip. The husband, laden with tennis racket, swimming gear, and golf clubs, said, "The way you carry on, you'd think I enjoy these business trips."

Overload of responsibility and role shifting are also among the negatives of travel. As already mentioned, spouses assume all the physical and familial responsibilities of the absent employees. This is necessary for continuity in the home but often results in physical and emotional exhaustion for spouses. When travel is frequent or lengthy, this unequal division of marital responsibility breeds resentment and unhappiness. If the family is traditionally patriarchal and the stay-at-home spouse is the wife, the family structure sometimes quietly transposes into a matriarchy. Travel-induced overload is the same as that caused by long work hours, discussed in chapter 4, with one distinguishing difference: female spouses must shift their familial roles when their husbands travel.

Most corporate marriages continue to be traditional, with the male as "head of the house" and the wife dependent whether she is employed or not. When the man travels, the woman switches from dependent wife, becomes the depended-on head of the house, and shifts back to dependent wife on the husband's return. For a self-sufficient wife authority and power are easy to assume but are sometimes difficult to relinquish, and when the traveler returns, a power struggle often occurs. The businessman is secure in his role; he leaves as head of the house and returns as head of the house. Only a wife has the difficult and confusing task of changing roles as as quick-change artist changes clothes.

The final major negative for travelers' spouses is loneliness and social boredom, which may be fought but never completely conquered. I consider myself a good housekeeper, but I rarely make the bed when my husband is away. I always thought this a mild rebellion on my part until interviewing several other corporate wives. It seems numerous "good housekeepers" neglect to make their bed when their husbands are away. All the rest of the housework is done, but the bed remains unmade. There must be a psychological inference somewhere in this laxity. In addition, women tend to plan their social activities for the day but rarely go out at night; men tend to be less inhibited about nighttime socializing. An extended trip can mean two or more weeks of children and TV set night after night. Weekend travel is especially hated, since weekends are considered family time. Spouses feel especially isolated on weekends; their own family is incomplete, and they can't intrude into another family's special time. As one spouse said, "Five days a week are theirs [the company's]. The weekends are mine."

For a couple as a union, I find that frequent travel poses two threats: the first is financial and the second is emotional. Although companies provide expense accounts to cover travel costs, without exception travelers spend more than companies reimburse. Whether it be gifts for the kids, a few drinks with the guys, or a ticket to a play, these expenses come directly from the family budget and probably wouldn't be incurred if the employee were at home. Such travel activities are understandable, but when the credit card bill arrives in the mail, the family finances reel from the shock.

Frequent travel is potentially threatening to a couple's relationship and is sometimes a real danger to the marriage. My interviews revealed several incidents of either/or marriage situations. The ultimatum was either find a nontraveling job or the marriage is over. One brave woman endured fifteen years with her husband traveling five days a week before issuing this ultimatum. She honestly stated that the marriage was in trouble as a direct result of the travel, and "you can't fix a troubled marriage in a weekend." I'm happy to report that the husband changed jobs, and ten years later they're still married.

This is not to say that all corporate marriages that involve travel are troubled; many couples and families adjust and cope very well. But few people enter marriage with foreknowledge of frequent travel, and although most spouses adjust, few enjoy the adjustment. My purpose isn't to predict failure for corporate marriages that involve travel but merely to mark the hazards.

Summary

Jet airplanes have caused a boom in business as well as transportation. Modern air travel is an indispensable, valuable business tool, and millions of air miles are logged each day in the name of business. Corporations use travel in four important ways: training, selling, meeting, and rewarding. Both employers and employees have valid travel reasons and both benefit from travel, but traveling is so necessary that employee travel is often loosely monitored and indiscriminately sanctioned by company managers.

Many employees travel for more than business reasons; personal motivations include excitement, status, self-esteem, and gain. Travel-related industries lure executives with glamour, sophistication, and "freebies." Both personal motivations and travel lures lead to abuse of expense-account travel privileges.

Each trip involves employees, spouses, and children in a travel cycle of anticipation, separation, and reentry, but most corporate families are so familiar with frequent travel that they settle into routines with the family circles contracting and expanding smoothly. However, even with a smooth routine business travel has positives and negatives, and the negatives can result in severe damage to the corporate couple's relationship and marriage.

7

THE HOME GAME

STRESS
AND SPILLOVER

Corporate couples lead two lives: private and professional. Corporate living demands accommodation of both
and combination of the two into one. The shift from
blue-collar to white-collar employment means more
couples face the difficult task of adjusting to the corporate life-style in which there is less of a barrier between
work and home. This adjustment is more than switch-
ing from one type of work activity to another; it involves
a shift in the individual's work attitudes and habits and
an increased psychological investment in one's work.
Blue-collar employees refer to their work as jobs; white-
collar employees speak of their careers. The dictionary
defines a job as a piece of work done for pay, a task, a
duty; a career is defined as one's progress through life, a
profession, an occupation. A job implies a chore that
must be done, a means to an end, work that provides
money to live. A career implies a lifetime commitment,
an end in itself, the life progress that provides money.

Both give sustenance through money, but a career is part of a person's identity.

White-collar corporate employees often have more personal involvement in their work, personal interaction at their work, and personal integration with their work. Their careers are avocations as well as vocations, and their career goals are life goals. Careerists seek fulfillment and achievement through their occupations; money is often secondary. Their long, unpaid work hours reflect this dedication to achievement and the secondary importance of money. Second, corporate employment involves interacting with other people more than with machines. Fellow workers and clients influence an employee's job performance; his accomplishments depend heavily on interpersonal relationships and cooperation. Finally, career people integrate work into their personalities; work achievements or failures affect their egos. Their work overflows into their homes, and occasionally business/social functions overtly mix personal and work lives. Careers aren't simply time given to work to provide money; careers demand personal investment from employees and consequently from their spouses. A job is left at the work place; a career is a personal identity and comes home.

Corporate Pressure and Personal Stress

The two words *pressure* and *stress* are often used as synonyms, but for corporate couples stress is a direct result of pressure. Pressure is inherent in corporate employment and life-style, and the well-publicized stress of employees and spouses evolves from this pressure. Hans Selye, an authority on the subject, distinguished two types of stress. Good stress, or "eustress," is "the spice of life," coming from pleasant, gratifying incidences, stimulating the body and mind. It is energizing and vitalizing. Bad stress, or "distress," comes from unpleasant experiences and can cause physical and mental discomfort and disease.[1] In popular reference and usage Dr. Selye's "distress" is simply stress and connotes the negative or bad.

Pressure and stress aren't new phenomena of the technological age. Selye emphasized that the complete freedom from stress is death. Even Stone Age people lived with the stresses of securing food, shelter, and safety. Living was stressful then, and the same is true today. But modern life is much more complicated, and contemporary ambitious corporate couples experience abstract, psychological stress emanating from careers and accompanying life-styles. Descriptive phrases such as "pressure cooker environment," "rat race," and "life in the fast lane" are common corporate imagery, and in truth the imagery is reality. Researchers estimate that work pressures cause between two-thirds and three-fourths of the major stress in employee's lives. In my opinion these estimates also hold true for corporate spouses. The pressures of corporate life are both external and internal. People and job performance are twin bases on which external pressures build. Internal pressures are psychological and originate in self-evaluation, the need for control, and value conflicts.

The external pressure created by interaction with other people is part of the human condition. We are social animals; we live and interact with others of our species. "No man is an island," but we don't like everyone we meet, nor are we liked by all. In private social settings we freely choose the people with whom we associate, but the work place is a different situation. Our associates are chosen for us, and the choices are not always to our liking. Will Rogers said he never met a man he didn't like; I say Will Rogers was either a unique human anomaly or a prevaricator.

In the corporate structure everyone has a boss; even the president and CEO answer to the board of directors and the stockholders. A boss is selected for employees, not elected by employees, and sometimes the boss-employee match is a mismatch. For many employees, bosses are a source of intense pressure because they have a major and continuous influence on one's career. Articles and indeed entire books address how to manage, impress, or simply tolerate one's bosses; employees often wage pragmatic campaigns to win their boss's attention and approval. Part of a superior's job is to exert subtle or not-so-subtle performance pressure on subordinates, but often bosses are so subtle as to be ambiguous. These people rarely detail assignments or even expectations; they assume employees know what they want. Trying to read the boss's mind is a terrible predicament; employees are expected to act but are unsure of the action to perform. Working for such a person is much like playing Russian roulette with your career.

Another common boss-centered pressure has roots in employee egocentricity. The match between supervisor and subordinate may be ideal, with mutual liking and respect, but ambitious people are arrogant about their abilities and are often jealous of the boss's power and position. I've never met a corporate person who didn't feel he could do his boss's job better than the boss. With this attitude employees become frustrated and irritated working under someone they consider less qualified than themselves.

Bosses also encounter people pressures. The Biblical admonition "Judge not that ye be not judged" is strong in our socialization, but corporate managers are required to hire, fire, and evaluate based on their personal judgment. Most are sensitive to the impact that has on the lives of others and agonize over these decisions. The firing process is particularly upsetting for some executives. When one has power over others' lives, the responsibility is awesome and pressure-packed; the resulting stress causes many sleepless nights. Handling pressure induced by work superiors, subordinates, and peers is a point of pride for most employees. This "people skill" is rated on performance reviews and is considered in promotion decisions. Employees may have the skill, but it doesn't alleviate the pressure and stress.

Employees' major people-oriented pressure is family pressure, and it is not as easily handled as work place pressure. The home/work balance is delicate, and when the balance is upset, the scales normally tip in favor of work. Families complain, and the pressure builds. Normally, employees react to these pressures by becoming defensive about their work; they rationalize their choice of job over family by emphasizing how important their work is for the entire family. Nonetheless, pressure from families causes powerful stress in the lives of corporate employees, and this pressure is constant.

The second building base of employees' external pressure is the need to perform well in the job and show results. In the corporation the bottom line is supreme, and the bottom line for employees is job performance, both for themselves and for their bosses. In some cases entire staffs are fired because the department isn't performing up to expectations. Performance is basic to the ideals of meritocracy and essential to career progression.

Is it any wonder that performance pressures are never-ending for ambitious employees?

Achievement based on competition is the corporate game, and for some, achievement is "whether you win or lose," not "how you play the game." The competitive corporate game pits company against company, division against division, department against department, and employee against employee. The goal is to achieve and achieve better than the rest. People who choose and remain in corporate employment thrive on competition and glory in achievement; they accept the personal cost of the performance pressure as part of the game. After all, they firmly believe in meritocracy.

Everyone who is employed must do acceptable work: specific duties and tasks are required and must be done to satisfaction in order to remain employed. As union members, blue-collar workers have clearly defined duties, and they are protected from unjust dismissal. Non-union salaried employees have neither clearly regimented work nor job protection. Superiors evaluate their performance on abstract as well as concrete results; the personalities of both superior and employee reflect in the performance review. In this white-collar world employee job security rests on the individual's talent, ability, and performance, with no protection from unjust dismissal. Of course, they experience extreme performance pressure.

In the early career stages performance pressure centers on launching the career and climbing the corporate ladder. In the executive ranks the pressure is to stay on top of the business and the ladder. Executives religiously read *The Wall Street Journal* and peruse *Business Week, Fortune,* and *Forbes* weekly and monthly. They enthusiastically attend executive training sessions and physically torture themselves at leadership work-shops such as Outward Bound. (The Japanese have an executive training camp that attendees refer to as "hell camp." Each day of the thirteen-day session begins at 5 A.M. with calisthenics, led by instructors with stop-watches who patrol the ranks for slackers. The last class ends at 9 P.M. The businessmen wear plain white uni-forms and pledge to admit their flaws and correct them. Each man must pass a series of tests in order to graduate from the program.) Corporate employees are under con-stant pressure to perform well to achieve or retain their jobs. As one expert puts it, "The higher you climb on the mountain, the harder the wind blows."

Time is another heavy performance pressure. Have you ever noticed that corporate people are rarely on time? When they make an appointment for ten o'clock, never expect them before ten fifteen or ten thirty. Many ex-ecutives set their watches ahead fifteen minutes and are still late. Most spouses have learned to accept this an-noying recurrence and give a grace period of forty-five minutes to an hour. Corporate people are busy people: they have deadlines to meet, appointments to keep, planes to catch, and family obligations to fulfill. There is too little time for too many demands. Executives often re-mind me of the White Rabbit in *Alice in Wonderland* bemoaning his lateness for a very important appoint-ment.

Female employees have additional and unique per-formance pressures arising from their relatively recent forages into the corporate world. Although the number of female corporate employees is growing, they are in truth still anomalies. And laws change faster than so-cialization and emotion; it is a matter of de jure versus de facto. Women receive more attention, of a different kind, than their male peers. I am reminded of an incident related by the wife of a company president. She attended a business banquet at which her husband presented awards to outstanding salespeople. As each person came to the podium for individual recognition, her husband shook each man's hand and kissed each woman's cheek. After returning to their room, the wife pointed out that each salesperson did the same job and received the same reward but her husband treated them differently. She ended by advising the president to "either shake everyone's hand or kiss everyone's cheek—one or the other, not both." The husband was surprised and disconcerted because, being the ultimate geltleman, he hadn't realized the disparity in his congratulations; it was simply a natural reaction.

Women achievers are highly visible in the corporate world and are often used as symbols and tokens. This visibility is certainly applicable to black women because they fit two categories of equal opportunity employment simultaneously, black and female. Women's professional and private lives, as well as their physical appearances, are carefully scrutinized and subjected to open discussion and sometimes office gossip. They must learn to deal with unearned praise and criticism plus unwanted attention and condescension. A common complaint among female employees is that they must work longer, harder, and better than males to achieve the same goals. Being a token or symbol of a minority produces extreme performance pressure and often demands an exorbitant personal price.

For spouses the external pressures directly related to corporate living are less obvious but can be quite numerous and profound. Among these pressures are repercussions discussed in earlier chapters on long hours, relocation, and business travel. In his book *Anxiety and the Executive*, Alan Schoonmaker wrote "But, the wife receives the greatest stress and they deserve most of the credit for keeping families together."[2] Family stability is a primary concern for wives, but wives (mostly unemployed wives) experience other pressures directly associated with their husbands' careers. Hanna Papanek discussed what she termed the "two-person single career," in which only the male is officially employed, but formal and informal company demands are placed on both husband and wife. She stated, "A pattern of pressures is generated for both members of the couple which is closely related to social mobility, mobility within the employing institution, loyalty, and interpersonal rivalry."[3] Both Schoonmaker and Papanek referred specifically to wives, but today career women are prominent in the corporate scene. What about their male spouses?

In my judgment there is a vast difference in pressure and stress felt by male and female spouses of corporate employees. Male spouses usually have their own careers and rarely feel any strong obligation relative to their wives' employment. If they do feel obligation, it is a matter of attending some business/social function. Companies don't exert pressure nor do male spouses feel pressured to take an active role in their wives' careers. Of course, there are exceptions to this generalization, as some male spouses now relocate when their wives receive promotions. But this is still the exception rather than the rule. On the other hand, female spouses, whether employed or unemployed, are expected to accommodate and participate in their husbands' careers. Schoonmaker's and Papanek's exclusion of male corporate spouses in their theories holds true and applies, even today, only to wives of corporate employees.

The concept of the two-person single career is seldom discussed in business circles, but the situation exists. Early in my husband's career, while at a business dinner, his boss came over and invited me to take a short walk. I soon realized the purpose: Mr. Boss suggested that I spend more money buying for myself, the children, and the house to "encourage" my husband to sell more and get more commission in order to pay the bills. I had a difficult time matching the boss's serious demeanor because my emotions were walking a tightrope between hysterical laughter and exploding anger. The dinner was, in fact, a sales contest prize won by my husband for his achievement.

Commonly mentioned external pressures for spouses are entertaining and attending business functions, but these pressures aren't felt uniformly by all: some like it, some do not. Many women truly enjoy giving parties, entertain beautifully, and take pride in their accomplishments. Other spouses resent having to entertain because they are uncomfortable with their abilities or they feel used. I admire and envy anyone who loves to entertain; it is a God-given talent in my eyes. But those who dislike entertaining have a valid point too. When entertaining businesspeople, the wives do most or all of the work, and their employee/husbands get all of the credit. The parties are normally referred to as "John's party," not Mary's, or seldom even John and Mary's party.

The attitudes of attending spouses are sometimes clouded by pressure exerted by the host and hostess, usually the boss and his wife. Overt coercion robs people of self-determination, and spouses aren't immune to corporate coercion. One Christmas we received a beautiful engraved invitation to a party at the boss's home. Handwritten in the corner was the message: "Expect to see you here." I asked my husband if this was an invitation or a royal decree. Managers' wives can be as demanding of subordinates' wives as the managers are of the employees. Some, but certainly not all, managers' wives cast themselves in the role of Mother Superior of their own private convent. One wife told the story of her collision with the domineering wife of a corporate VP. Mrs. VP was giving an afternoon tea to welcome the wives of new employees. Sue received her invitation, but the date conflicted with a previous engagement, so she called to decline. Mrs. VP asked the reason, and Sue told her of the other date. After giving a lecture on priorities this Mother Superior suggested that Sue would be wise to cancel the other appointment and attend the tea. Although she greatly resented the overt pressure, Sue did as she was told.

Rookie couples rarely entertain, but they are expected to attend business/social occasions to which they're invited. In middle management, entertaining becomes part, and an accepted part, of a corporate wife's job description. Unspoken demands to entertain or attend functions increase with job level. In addition, spouses are called into action to entertain and occupy wives of visiting businessmen; entertaining strangers can be stressful but dear friendships sometimes result. Entertaining and the previously mentioned effects of long hours, relocation, and travel are definite external corporate pressures on spouses. But ask any executive if the company expects anything from spouses and the answer will be an emphatic _no_.

Internal pressure is the second and heaviest category of pressure experienced by ambitious couples. It is psychological, coming from within and originating in socialized mores, needs, and insecurities. Value conflicts—the struggle between what one does and what one feels should be done—are a source of internal pressure. We are all socialized with a distinct set of values and behaviors, and these individual teachings often conflict with doing business corporate-style. The "deal" is all-important in many companies, and sometimes it is indeed a "shady deal." Kickbacks, gifts, stock tips, privileged information, and graft thrive in the corporate environment, and most employees confront such situations at least once in their career. One's ethics are sorely tested at times, especially when doing business in a foreign country where such practices are an accepted and expected part of business. The pressure is there and also the money.

Another example of value conflict is the carnival atmosphere in which employees sometimes find themselves when attending business functions at home or on the road. The effect of group or peer pressure is amazing. An employed friend tells the story of attending a surprise birthday party at the home of a business associate and his wife. The birthdays of the couple fell on the same day, and attendees were to bring two gag gifts. Everyone was enjoying the fun until time for the last gift. It was a surprise gift given by one couple as the finale of the evening: a dance performed by "strippers," a man and a woman. Some of the people enjoyed the presentation while others sat in stunned silence, but no one left. My friend was embarrassed, mortified, and felt her values had been compromised. In relating the tale she stated that she was "so embarrassed I wanted to crawl under the coffee table, but it was glass-topped and everyone would see me anyway." Employees occasionally find themselves in compromising situations not of their own choosing, and the pressure to be "one of the gang" is tremendous because the career is involved.

The balance of work and family also brings personal values into conflict. As stated earlier, this balance is delicate and often tips in favor of work. Families complain, and employees feel guilty, because most Americans are taught that families should have top priority in one's life. Employees worry about the effects of their actions on the family unit and about their relationships with individual family members. Female employees, especially, agonize because they were reared to feel that the emotional stability of the family, individually and collectively, is their primary responsibility. Most are constantly torn between their socialized need to be home with the children and their career and/or financial needs.

Career women, regardless of whether they are married or are living with someone, have another concern in addition to the children. A woman's place is no longer just in the home; her place is everywhere. But socialization is tenacious, and although people may intellectually disavow it, most still subconsciously feel that in the man/woman relationship the man is or should be dominant. Many women in the corporate world function under opposing pressures of striving to succeed but being afraid of success. A woman often feels that if she is more successful than her mate he may feel devalued, and the relationship might be threatened. Conversely, researchers find that men are primarily concerned about their relationships with the children and have little concern for spouses, because most male employees feel their marriages are secure regardless of neglect.

Maintaining self-control and gaining control over others are self-applied internal pressures of corporate employees. These needs for control come as much from environment as from socialization and are important to businesspeople. In the business environment people seem to be constantly "on," striving to say the right thing, do the right thing, look the right way, and make the right impression. Although a business group sometimes resembles a squad of automatons, behavior is definitely noticed, and self-control is mandatory. At a weekend function I attended a young couple evidently had had a quarrel; they were both sulky and withdrawn. That night at the banquet the young man was visibly upset to the extent that he bent a spoon in half. Nothing was said to the young man that weekend, but two weeks later he was no longer with the company. Such anger is frightening anytime, but in the business world lack of self-control can be fatal.

For managers particularly, the ability to manipulate and control the actions of others is a decided advantage. The word *manage* is synonymous with control; thus a manager is a controller and a manipulator. For promotion to executive ranks an employee must be able to persuade others to perform desired actions. This ability is an innate talent for some and a learned skill for others. Salespeople, especially, are manipulative; to make a sale, the client must be persuaded to buy. Regardless, internal pressures to gain and maintain control over themselves and others, including their families, are characteristic of most corporate employees. A former vice-president of human resources agreed that the archaic but still prevalent corporate evaluation of potential promotees is "If they can't control their own families, how can I expect them to manage people?"

Perhaps the most stressful of all the internal pressures is the incessant self-appraisal of ambitious employees. Because their careers and job security depend on their own resources and performance, self-evaluation and self-doubt are ever present. For these people, best efforts never satisfy; they always feel that a little more time, work, travel, money, and funnel-vision will surely improve results. Ambitious people continually question, compare, and evaluate themselves against others: Do I know enough? Can I keep up and keep ahead? Am I doing a good enough job? How can I improve my position?

Although most corporate salaries are quite adequate, money too is a pressing matter. Corporate couples find that as positions and salaries increase, so do material acquisitions. It's the "keep up with the Joneses" syndrome—a home and life-style equal to, perhaps better than, others of their rank and position. Although unverbalized, these matters preoccupy employees subconsciously, inducing internal pressure and stress.

As employees get older, age and health become pressure-packed concerns. All people go through a middle-age transition in which they confront the aging process, but age and health suddenly become overwhelmingly important to older employees as younger employees avariciously wait for open promotion slots. Even those who feel secure in their jobs worry about impending retirement, sickness, future security, and even death. Older men often see any health problem as a personal weakness that could negatively influence career progress and position. Therefore, such problems must be covered up, secretly overcome, and/or completely ignored. Middle-age and older corporate people are consequently most susceptible to self-appraisal and comparsion.

Corporate wives have their share of internal pressure. Although leading nontraditional lives, they tend to judge themselves by the traditional standards of their mothers, who usually were not in the corporate environment. The majority of women hide their feelings and internalize their resentment. Then they feel guilty about their unhappiness and depression and blame themselves for the negative effects of the life-style. When asked, almost all corporate wives proclaim their own happiness and satisfaction, but these same women will say that most other corporate wives are unhappy. Part of the corporate wife's duty is to "put on a happy face," at least in public. The facade goes with the role, and most women play their roles to perfection, enduring the pressure to be the ideal, traditional wife.

An ominous internal pressure for many corporate spouses is the fear that their behavior and actions will reflect negatively on their husbands and affect their careers. A corporate wife often sees herself merely as a representative or an appendage of her husband and a person without individual identity. Consequently, most wives feel inadequate and uncomfortable in business atmospheres, tolerating rather than enjoying the occasions. They are constantly on guard about the impression they make, never feeling free to be themselves. They are careful to be gracious and interested in others but will express no strong personal opinions.

Robert Seidenberg surveyed fifty top executives, asking them to define the attributes of a good company wife. Adjectives such as *selfless, cooperative, gracious,* and *accommodating* were used, but *intelligent* wasn't cited even once. These executives defined the negative traits as being a shrew, a show-off, and/or a pusher.[4] Although female spouses feel they are complete nonentities at a business/social affair, they nevertheless feel on display, scrutinized as to looks, dress, manners, and behavior. Businesspeople show little interest in them outside of mandatory courtesy. Spouses, as a group, have little in common because they see each other so seldom. The general consensus among wives is that their only importance to other employees is how well they complement their husbands, and their only importance to other spouses is for comparison. Not all spouses or even all female spouses share these feelings; some are very gregarious and enjoy these occasions, although guardedly. But all spouses know that anything they do or say might be used against their mates. The pressure is on to put a well-pedicured best foot forward.

Although there are many pleasant pressures in life, the external and internal pressures cited are decidedly unpleasant and are inherent in corporate employment. As Dr. Selye stated, unpleasant experiences cause stress, which in turn can cause physical and mental discomfort. The prevalence and persistence of stress in our society hasn't escaped the attention of researchers and physicians. Stress management is now written about in newspapers, magazines, and books; seminars and programs proliferate in the private and corporate sectors. Most company-sponsored programs are specifically for employees. Spouses are either ignored or it is assumed they have no stress. Findings show that stress can have a variety of symptoms but the following are the most common:

1. Physical illness of all types
2. Weight gain or loss
3. Inability to concentrate
4. Craving for or lack of interest in food, sleep, sex
5. Irritability
6. Increased smoking or drinking
7. Emotional extremes

Experts suggest managing corporate stress in such constructive ways as music in the work place, long lunches, afternoon vacations, leisure sports, and hobbies. If these methods don't work, employees should try to detach or remove themselves mentally from the stressful situation. If all else fails, quit. All are good suggestions, but many corporate people manage stress destructively by resorting to pills and alcohol or a combination of both to relieve the symptoms they choose to ignore. Executives make up a significant part of the more than 10 million American alcoholics, and most started on this path by having a drink or two to "unwind" at the end of the day. The major stress symptom for spouses seems to be depression, and many seek relief in hidden drinking and pills. Rarely does one read or hear of an unemployed spouse having "stress." Employed men and women may have stress, but unemployed women have "depression."

The pressures on corporate people are the stimuli that activate fear, and the result is stress. *Fear* is an unpleasant word, but no other word will suffice; *apprehension* is too mild and *terror* too strong. Most writings on corporate pressures never use the word *fear*, although there is always an underlying shade of it. In his book *The Gamesman*, Maccoby listed three sources of employee fear: lack of performance, lack of knowledge, and lack of control.[5] Fear ensues when security is threatened, and the job security of corporate employees is on the line each day. What makes Dick and Jane run the "rat race"? For most couples the answer is simple. Fear.

Spillover in the Home

When a person chooses a career over a job, that career is accompanied by fear and stress that spills over into the personal and private lives of the employee and the family. Spillover might be defined as the effect that the white-collar employment of one or both marriage partners has on their lives outside the work place. Company officials deny the existence of spillover and publicly denounce any suggestion that the company infringes in any way on home life. This company attitude is particularly evident when family-related corporate social responsibility is discussed. The pat corporate answer is "Oh, we couldn't do that because it would intrude on the private lives of our employees." Yet companies subtly place such high performance and achievement expectations on employees that it is impossible for work not to carry over to the home. The fact remains: corporations and corporate employment do affect the private lives of employees and families. It's the nature of the beast and its environment.

Spillover is intrinsic to humanness, to careers, and to corporate employment. But is spillover preventable? Most psychiatrists, psychologists, and counselors will answer emphatically *yes*. Their standard position on the subject is that when employees enter their homes, all work-related thoughts and actions should be left outside the door. At the risk of triteness, this is easier said than done. In my opinion it's impossible to prevent spillover because employees are human, and we humans don't shut off our minds and bodies by simply closing a door or turning off a switch. Trying to do so merely adds more stress to the already overstressed employee.

Researchers spend an enormous amount of time and money analyzing the corporate work/home relationship; most end up merely analyzing the roles and actions of wives in relation to their husbands' work and the corporation. Many researchers assume the marital relationship depends primarily on wives because it's their traditional role. Furthermore, they absolve the husband of any responsibility for that relationship because of his traditional role as provider and head of the household. I'm convinced that researchers, in analyzing the corporate couple to date, have used traditional work/home standards—blue-collar, agricultural, and private employment—to analyze a nontraditional work/home lifestyle—corporate employment.

For most people work provides the necessities of life, and because work makes living possible, the demands of that work dictate where and how life is lived. Traditionally, most jobs have been nontransient and stable; the jobs and the workers stayed in one location, and moving was rare. Each day the worker went to the plant, the doctor went to his office, and the farmer went to his fields; each night they returned to their homes. The family was a solid unit of father, mother, and children who ate, slept, and lived together every day. This traditional life is not the corporate life. Because the job demands it, the corporate employee and his family are transient and mobile. Traditional rules and roles should not be applied to corporate families because their way of life is no longer traditional. The transient, mobile life-style affects the roles of both husband and wife, and responsibility for their relationship should be shared by both.

Nevertheless, there is one common thread I find in all corporate homes: spillover. Various couples manage the spillover differently, but its existence is universal. Employment spillover takes three forms: physical, mental, and behavioral,[6] and each includes pleasant and unpleasant aspects. While reading _The Wall Street Journal_ recently, I glanced at a cartoon that clearly illustrated a case of physical spillover. Two bewildered women stood looking at the inert man sound asleep on the sofa as one woman said to the other: "Sometimes I wish *I* could have a hard day at the office." Physical spillover is the bring-home product of an employee's physical and mental expenditure at work. The nightly routine of vast numbers of employees is to come home, have a drink, have dinner, start reading the paper, and fall asleep on the sofa. This routine is so familiar to spouses and children that it is seldom questioned. I find that this nap after dinner has become as traditional in corporate homes as the family dinner used to be.

In *The Wall Street Journal* survey of executive wives, women referred to the effects of physical spillover on the children rather than on themselves. One said, "The good hours of his day are used up by the time he comes home. The children would like his attention, but he puts them off." Another related that her husband was rarely home, and when he was, he was too tired to make time for the children's needs.[7] Employee exhaustion isn't necessarily the result of a bad day at the office; exciting, stimulating events can also be quite tiring. Regardless of the source, the physical costs of corporate employment spill into the home and demand payment from family time and relationships.

Mental or emotional spillover is a subtle interloper in the home; its presence is difficult to identify, but it is nonetheless felt. It is the mental ghost that comes home with the employee and permeates the home atmosphere, inhibiting interest, interaction, and conversation. Mental spillover occurs when employees come home in body but not in mind. It is the mental baggage of the workday: problems, fears, worries, and defeats, solutions, hopes, joys, and victories. In my research I ran across a phrase used by a spouse that aptly describes the mental spillover situation; the employee was said to be "psychologically unavailable." What a nice description—courteous, yet intelligently accurate. I've often considered having signs printed reading, "Psychologically Unavailable," so when my husband comes home with this malady, the entire family could easily recognize the situation by the posted sign.

Mental spillover can be destructive for corporate families because when employees are preoccupied with work, they exhibit little or no interest in family members or family affairs; they hear but don't listen. Their sensitivity, intimacy, and involvement are retarded. As a result, family members often interpret employees' symptomatic silence and withdrawal as anger. And indeed anger sometimes does erupt from employees, families, or both because an ambiguous "I've got a lot on my mind" isn't a sufficient explanation for the preoccupation and lack of interest. Mental spillover is a powerful force, capable of inflicting hurt and alienation on the entire family.

Behavioral spillover, however, is manifested in obvious and often blatant employee actions. Some corporate employees, especially managers and executives, expect their business power, prestige, and importance to transfer into the home environment, and they tend to interact with wives and children in the same manner as with business peers. Manipulation and coercion may be accepted and often demanded behaviors in the office environment, but they are ill-advised in the home.

Examples of behavioral spillover can include happiness, teasing, laughter, and joking as well as bringing office work home, expecting deferential treatment, interacting impersonally with loved ones, hiding feelings, and being dictatorial and demanding in requests. Men are more susceptible to behavioral spillover than women because their socialization tends to validate "tough guy" behavior. They are reared to be unemotional and decisive, to be problem solvers rather than problem understanders. More than half of the executive wives surveyed by *The Wall Street Journal* reported that job pressures and demands had seriously affected their husbands' temperament and behavior at home, because they brought the closed way in which they related at the office into the marriage and home. As one spouse put it, "He is careful with his feelings, afraid to be vulnerable with me."[8]

The amount of spillover is said to vary with age and career stages. Researchers tell us that young people in the early or rookie career stage experience the most spillover because they are so pressured to establish careers that they treat their private lives simply as support systems for their careers. Middle-level career stars supposedly have a little less spillover because the employees are becoming more sensitive to their families and they have less pressure. Top-level career coaches are said to have the least spillover because employee pressures are less, they are more secure, and families become of major importance in their lives.

I agree that age mellows reaction and experience lessens spillover's severity. But I heartly disagree that spillover itself lessens with career advancement or age. I find that regardless of age ambitious corporate employees, particularly men, subordinate their private lives to their professional lives. In the rookie career stage employees and spouses rarely recognize spillover as part of the chosen corporate life, feeling it is a personal rather than a career-oriented issue. In midcareer, stars may recognize the effects of spillover but deny its persistence. Most stars believe that spillover is purely situational and that its effects will disappear when the situation or problem is resolved. In the later stage coaches recognize and accommodate spillover as a facet of the life-style; they simply have learned to live with it and therefore handle it better.

Second, in my opinion ambitious corporate employees do not gradually shift their priorities from work to home over time. Pressure is present in all career stages, and as a rule pressures increase, not decrease, as employees climb the corporate ladder. The vast majority of top executives and spouses admit to far greater pressure now than in earlier career stages. Executives may be mentally more sensitive to home and family, but priorities remain the same and so do actions: work first, home second.

Office spillover has a serious and heavy impact in corporate households, but the reverse is not true. Spillover from the home to the work place rarely occurs. When spillover of home to office does happen, it is usually because events at home—such as death, divorce, or illness—are personally traumatic. Such reverse spillover also can result from family reaction to proposed career decisions, such as relocation, promotion, and demotion. These incidents of home spillover into the office are situational and have no continuing disruptive effects on the office environment. In essence persistent spillover is a one-way street that dead-ends in the home.

Summary

White-collar corporate employment is a career that demands accommodation in and combination of personal and professional lives. Although this career is a life progression for both the employee and spouse and requires personal investment and commitment from both, the career becomes part of an employee's personal identity. Because the career is so personal to employees, they inadvertently bring the effects of their work into the home, thereby impacting on spouses, children, and the home environment.

Stress is a direct result of the pressures and fears inherent in corporate employment and the accompanying life-style. Both employees and spouses experience external and internal pressures. External pressures are based on performance and interaction with people, whereas internal pressures emanate from value conflicts, need for control, and self-appraisal. Because corporate employees have no protection against unjust dismissal, fear plays a major role in transforming pressure into stress. The combination of pressure and fear produces stress.

Stress is evidenced at home in the employee's physical, mental, and/or behavioral spillover; and spillover impacts on marital relationships, family relationships, and the home environment. Spillover comes from work to home but rarely does home life spill into work life. Corporations, as abstract entities, deny any intrusion into the private lives of their employees, but the working conditions produce stress and spillover that bring the corporation into the home and greatly influence the family's lives and relationships.

8

GAME PLANS AND TEAMMATES

COMPANY PRACTICES AND PEERS

The office is the world in miniature, a condensation of the good and bad with the same human strengths and frailties. It is the mini-world in which corporate employees live their professional lives and from which emanates the corporate influence on spouses and homes. A company has its own culture, society, and mores and also its own philosophies, prejudices, and power plays. Corporate work places have a commonality of traits that manifests in each office environment and is part of office culture. Astute, ambitious employees learn to identify and contend with these common office undercurrents, and spouses learn to recognize and accommodate the effects of the office in homes and relationships. The office is no better nor worse than the world at large, and corporate survival depends on the couple's ability to meld with this mini-culture, benefiting from and using the positives while tolerating and understanding the negatives.

American corporations are founded on opposing philosophies. The ideals of individualism and meritocracy are basic in hiring and promoting employees, but the ideals of collectivism and teams are fundamental in operating and transacting business. For employees the work environment produced by this dichotomy is emotionally confusing and sociologically conflicting. Success in professional life depends on one's ability to be an individual and a team player at the same time. It may sound simple, but the execution of such a feat is an exercise in discipline and manipulation. Let's examine why the ideals of individualism and collectivism conflict and how this conflict affects the employee's work life and work environment.

Each year corporations search the country and raid the campuses in their quest to hire that year's brightest and best graduates. Each applicant's scholastic records are carefully scrutinized for outstanding academic and extracurricular achievements because such successes occur through individual effort and portend the stereotypical ideal corporate employee: the individualistic, ambitious achiever with a deeply instilled belief in meritocracy. During the hiring process promises are made and accepted by both parties, and the match is made. The new corporate employee enters the business world ready once again to prove personal value and gain promotion through familiar socialized methods and the ideals of individualism that brought the successes of the past. Then the shocker comes. Corporations demand teamwork, not solo performances.

America is a sports-oriented country, but the majority of our people aren't team players. We all have engaged in team sports at one time or another, but team playing was either part of a high school physical education program or simply for fun and relaxation, not a work philosophy. When we think of teamwork in an occupation, we think of professional sportspeople, not corporate employees, because we were socialized to the belief that personal success in the business world comes from stand-alone individual efforts. Individualism is our culture and our attitude. The Japanese culture, on the other hand, is extremely collective or team-oriented. Remember how the kamikaze pilots shocked us because of their willingness to sacrifice themselves individually for their collective cause? Since the end of World War II Japan has stunned the world with its technological and industrial prowess, sending American corporations and business scholars scurrying to discover their secret. One such scholar, William Ouchi, studied Japanese management techniques, and in his book, *Theory Z*, stated that a culture of teamwork must precede teamwork in actuality.

Teamwork depends on trust: team members are accustomed to depending on others and being depended on by others. This necessary trust is built into the company culture and philosophy, and it strengthens as employees integrate their work and social lives, socializing as well as working together. Because of trust team members work well together, and the credit for results is shared by the group. Ouchi's research showed that in the few American companies that typified his "Z" culture and management, team employees have long-term commitments to their working relationships and anticipate a lifelong career with that company. The companies have a much slower promotion rate and much less job turnover.[1] Teamplayers are collectivists, not individualists.

Thomas J. Peters and Robert H. Waterman, Jr., also addressed the business team philosophy in their book *In*

Search of Excellence. They agree that attitudes, climate, and culture must be right for the team concept to work well in a company. Effective teams have four important elements: membership is limited to less than ten people, membership is voluntary, duration of the team is very limited, and the team sets its own goals. These authors describe teams as unstructured and chaotic, with shared purposes, internal tension, and competitiveness underneath.[2] In my dictionary competition means opposition and tension means strain. Is it possible for shared purposes to overshadow opposition and strain and produce harmonious corporate teamwork?

Ideally, teams should work well, accomplishing goals while spotlighting individual talent and effort. But does the ideal hold true in reality? Corporate people talk a good game, but playing by the rules of that game is something else. They espouse the virtues of teamwork because it's the company "party line" and it's politically wise to support this philosophy, at least verbally. It's a great idea for someone else, but actually working on a team project is a different matter.

The current crop of "baby boomers," people born in the 1950s and 60s, are an example of the contrast in philosophy and implementation of that philosophy. After growing up in the socially chaotic 60s, these young people enter the corporate work place with collectivist values but individualist job goals. They believe in participatory decision making and teamwork, much like Ouchi's Theory Z, yet they want flexibility, autonomy, and personal growth in their jobs. Most of today's young employees are highly competitive and impatient to get to the top. This impatience leads to reduced company loyalty and increased job-hopping. A vice-president of human resources was quoted in a *Business Week* article on these "baby boomers": "They don't see any corporation as a place they will stay for the rest of their career, and they're likely to move on if they don't achieve what they want within a certain time frame. . . . They are more committed to their profession than to the company."[3]

In the corporate work place collectivism and individualism clash when communal work begins. Employees have difficulty in controlling individual competitiveness and submerging into teamwork. Participatory decision making is ideal as long as they are the ones who okay the final decision—being a team player is great as long as they are the quarterbacks calling the plays and receiving the greatest recognition and credit. Teamwork is chancy and sometimes dangerous for the career. A person might be working with eight people on a project, but if just one of the eight is more concerned with personal goals than team goals, the cooperative effort dissolves into eight individual efforts competing for credit and prominence. In such instances the exception becomes the rule, and teamwork becomes survival of the fittest. On the other hand, it is often the case in teamwork that one person ends up doing all the work, and the team as a whole gets shared credit. Teamwork is at best a "sometime thing."

Another opposing philosophy of the corporate work place is the supposed employee egalitarianism in which all employees have equal opportunity and equal pay for equal work. In actuality the corporate work place is not egalitarian at all, not even for men. Once again, it's a matter of de jure and de facto; the law says there must be equality, but in practice employees are not treated equally. It is common knowledge that Title VII of the 1964 Civil Rights Act prohibits employment discrimination because of color, race, sex, religion, or national origin and that the Equal Employment Opportunity Commission was established to enforce Title VII. But discrimination in the work place has survived both the law and the enforcement. Emotion and socialization cannot be legislated, and men still do not consider women as peers. Korn/Ferry, an executive search firm, and the Graduate School of Management at UCLA conducted a study of three hundred senior women executives. The results showed that these successful women managers feel they are not rewarded fairly and that their sex is the greatest barrier to success. This study shows that these women do not earn equal pay for equal work, and national statistics confirm this as true for the majority of women employees.

But for corporate employees as a group, both male and female, there are other more blatant corporate practices that smack of elitism rather than egalitarianism, and these practices evolve from usually unwritten, informal, but corporate-backed policies of mentorship and sponsorship. In Ouchi's idealistic Theory Z company, mentoring relationships between young and old employees would develop naturally. But in most corporations executives are encouraged to play mentor or sponsor roles to selected corporate juniors.

There are functional differences between mentors and sponsors, although the terms are often used interchangeably, and one person can be both. A mentor is a teacher, coach, and role model who shares skills and knowledge with a younger, selected employee. Mentors make introductions, advise, and train their recruits to move and work effectively in the corporate system. A mentor relationship is sometimes more than purely professional; mentors and their protégés often form friendships and socialize outside the work place. A sponsor is more of an authority, even parental, figure who directly influences a recruit's career progression. Sponsors are public relations people for their recruits, defending and praising them, assisting in their achievement, and actively working for the protégés' advancement and promotion.

The mentor/sponsor system is very much a part of the corporate work environment. Ralph Turner, as quoted by Rosabeth Kanter, commented on these practices in terms of "contest mobility" and "sponsored mobility." The contest mobility corporate system is the egalitarian practice of equal opportunity for advancement for all employees or promotion on the basis of individual performance and talent. Everyone has a chance to grab the carrot. Sponsored mobility is the practice of "elites" or executives choosing protégés early and then guiding, teaching, and inducting them into the elite ranks.[4] Sponsored mobility is predetermination of who gets the most desirable jobs—not exactly what one would call equal opportunity.

For the corporate protégé, there are many advantages in having a mentor/sponsor, but there are "catch 22s" as well. Advantages include the power gained from the backing of an influential executive, an inside track on information and promotions, valuable exposure and training, protection from critics, and rapid career progression. The disadvantages include the dangers of being too visible, becoming too dependent, and being known as somebody's "boy" or "girl," which could cause damage later in the career. Young comers also have to be very careful not to flaunt their power, and they must live up to the expectations of others. For women the mentor/employee relationship is often construed as sexual rather than professional. But the biggest danger for all young climbers is that if one's mentor/sponsor falls from grace, a common occurrence in corporate life, the protégé usually falls also.

Mentors and sponsors are often listed by employees as requisites for corporate success, and they are definitely advantageous for young employees. Nonetheless, many people are called for corporate employment, but few are chosen by mentors and sponsors, and these few have a decided edge. Regardless of idealistic philosophy, the corporate work place is not egalitarian.

Work Peers and
Office Politics

Corporate employees, being citizens of the microcosmic office world, interact with work peers, stratify themselves into groups, and vie for power and position through office politics. Peer acceptance and relationships are important because the work is interrelated, and peer assistance is mandatory for task accomplishment. In addition, these interactions are evaluated on formal performance reviews. Executives depend on their managers to put plans and policies into action, to transform decisions into specific acts, and to carry on daily business operation and productions. Managers need their subordinates' support to execute those actions. The office is an interwoven action center dependent on peer cooperation. Some employees work well together, some don't. But an employee's peers are a power base necessary for success.

In any society people form groups based on similar interests and common traits, and the same is true in the office. Researchers find that employees form homogeneous groups based on social background, similarity of work, and company experience, but competition and vying for prominence are still prevalent. Members of such groups feel a close kinship, and the influence of the group on members can be powerful.

Christopher Hegarty and Philip Goldberg, authors of *How to Manage Your Boss*, defined three types of worker groups characterized by energy (job interest) and confluence (cooperation): (1) low energy/low confluence: employees in this group have no interest in their job or assisting their work peers; (2) high energy/low confluence: these people are interested in their jobs and career success but do not assist or cooperate with others; (3) high energy/high confluence: team players such as these do their jobs well while cooperating and assisting others.[5] I would term these groups simply workers, competitors, and team players. And with groups come politics.

Office politics can be defined as the art of manipulating situations and peers to gain assistance for personal career benefit, a scheme for advantage. Office politics is an accepted fact of office life, and most employees confirm that career progression is virtually impossible without playing politics. Besides, the political moves of peers affect employees whether they choose to play or not. Office politics is a mystery to most employees; they can neither define nor recognize the process, but they unwittingly play a role in its execution. Let's take a look at the process of playing politics.

Information is essential to playing the political game; it is the coveted asset and/or ammunition of an adept politician. The game has three important stages. First, you must acquire information and knowledge relative to the business. Be a willing listener, read newspapers and magazines, and remember what might be useful to yourself or fellow employees. Second, swap and trade useful information with others. When you give information, be sure you acquire some information in return. Remember who knows what and who can do whatever. Third, act on the personally useful information. Become a storehouse of information on where and to whom to go to get things done. Learn to circumvent the bureaucratic system and discover the hidden power. When your storehouse of information and knowledge becomes more valuable than your job skills, promotion should follow.

Ideally, office politicians can enhance their positions without damaging others, and they can assist others to do the same.[6] This type of politician certainly belongs in the team-player work group. But such political virtues are rare. The more common office politician belongs in the worker or competitor work group, dissatisfied or power-hungry. These types of employees play a rough game and consequently give office politics its unfavorable reputation.

Information is the necessary tool for office politicians, and gossip is the flood-stage channel through which both useful and malicious information flows. Secretaries usually form alliances with other secretaries, and this group is acknowledged as an informal information system. Their superiors assume secretaries are apolitical; therefore, bosses use secretaries to disperse news before formally issuing the information. Management uses this gossip channel to gain employee reaction prior to announcing a change, to soften the impact of bad news, and to gain knowledge of employee activity. Secretaries have knowledge without power, and some use their privileged knowledge to gain prestige and status among their group. Being a conduit of information for the boss may be an informal job description, but unless discreet, a secretary is quickly fired.

Malicious gossip is commonly used by members of the worker and competitor work groups to retaliate against and damage peers in order to gain personal political advantage. Women employees are familiar victims of political and/or personal gossip. Jealousy is as prevalent in the work place as in the larger world, and gossip is a common tactic in both. In situations of intense competition the "fittest" who survives often does so by using gossip to undermine competitors. In answer to a letter to "Dear Abby," Abigail VanBuren wrote that animals and birds "know intuitively who their friends are. Would that man were so blessed."

Office politics are so commonplace that different forms have acquired distinguishing names. Here are some examples:

1. "Deadwood dumping" is a game played by many executives and managers. Most executives hate to fire people, and sometimes it's against company policy to fire. But what if a subordinate is unproductive or troublesome, how does one get rid of such an employee? An executive writes a glowing report on the employee, praising virtues and omitting faults. Then the report is sent to a fellow manager who needs people. Trusting the executive's judgment, the manager takes the employee and ends up with the "deadwood." In addition to getting rid of the unwanted employee, this tactic is also used to undermine the strength of a competitor's staff.

2. "Empire building" is a maneuver used by power-hungry professionals whose basic rationale is "the more people and functions that report to me, the more powerful and important I am." This politician devises a scenario to show that the problems of another department can be solved by moving the functions and people into his/her department or "empire." This political move is

an ego trip for the executive to gain power and status while downgrading a competitor's position and influence.

3. "Cover your ass" or "CYA" is a protective measure familiar to all employees and most prevalent in team projects. While working in conjunction with others, these politicians pretend to agree with and work toward team goals while covertly throwing up roadblocks to the team's progress. As a general rule, these people secretly document their suggestions, communications, and actions. The primary motive for CYA is to off-load responsibility in case of failure, but it is also used to devalue and, with luck, eliminate competitors within the team. If this is accomplished, then the politician can move a trusted cohort into that key slot.

A middle-level executive related this incident to me concerning his education in office politics. While assigned to the corporate staff of a major company, Harry was mulling over an idea to improve product dependability. But he made a fatal mistake; he mentioned the idea to a work peer in casual conversation. The peer assured Harry that the idea was inoperable, but the next day the "friend" took the idea to his superior. The idea became a very successful policy. Harry's friend was praised for his innovativeness and received all of the credit for Harry's idea. Harry quickly learned not to discuss his ideas with peers.

Office politics and peer relations are usually cooperative "I'll scratch your back if you'll scratch mine" interactions and can be productive and gratifying for all. But in highly competitive situations the politics can and usually does get dirty, the gossip grapevine buzzes, and the infighting gets rough. For employees the office is indeed a mini-world where survival sometimes becomes more important than doing the job.

Sex in the Work Place

And now there is sex. Sex has been present in the office since the first female secretary gathered her long skirts in hand, climbed the stairs, and took her place behind the typewriter; but with the recent influx of women to all ranks of the corporate mini-world, sex has become a business issue. Suddenly, corporate sexual game playing is causing reactions in offices, homes, and media. The issue is no longer confined to the discreet office affair between the boss and his secretary; office sexual politics now includes power struggles in addition to the traditional emotional struggle. And neither struggle is discreet.

Women are going or returning in droves to paid employment. Added to the numbers of single working women, over 50 percent of the nation's married women are now in the work place. But, in spite of the increasing female employment, the corporation is still a male bastion, resenting, resisting, and often refusing to accept women as equals. (Secretaries are okay because their jobs are assistance, not competition.) As a result, sex is used by both men and women to gain personal advantage and power. Men blame the women, and women blame the men.

Both sexes encounter problems in the legislated asexual work place, and both counter by making sex a factor. Men play sexual corporate games, trying to put women in "their place," and women play games trying to establish their positions. Yes, some men do slow or block the progress of career women, but some women use their sex to unfair advantage. Let's examine some typical attitudes and behaviors of both.

Generally, corporate men cannot relinquish their stereotypes of women. Women are emotional, sexy, cute, and supportive, or harsh, ugly, domineering, and self-centered. Men describe female peers in emotional and physical terms and rarely use terms commonly applied to male peers, such as smart, professional, authoritative, sly, and "with it." Women are aggressive, but men are competitive. Most men simply don't know how to react to women outside the traditional roles. So men play games to reduce their discomfort and try to force these women back into more familiar roles.

Rosabeth Kanter, author of *Men, Women and the Corporation*, described the roles in which female employees are cast by male employees. The "Mother" is the emotional support for all problems, doling out sympathy and assistance. The "Seductress" is the sexual fantasy luring men with her attractions. The "Pet" is both mascot and cheerleader for the males, never a threat. The "Iron Maiden" is the tough female, competent but threatening, always to be shunned.[7] The guys can platonically love the Mother, desire the Seductress, and protect the Pet, but the Iron Maiden demands equality—probably "one of those Gloria Steinem women"—therefore, she is politely avoided. The first three female roles meet little resistance from the men because the male superiority complex remains intact. The threat comes from the Iron Maiden because she refuses to play the male ego game by traditional rules.

It is generally accepted that the corporate games men play are masculine dominance and identity rituals, and woe be unto the woman who rejects the rules. She is sweetly abandoned to her own resources and becomes the prey of corporate predators. It's difficult for female employees to acquiesce to these stereotypes and still gain and retain respect, because men refuse to take them seriously. A magazine article quoted one woman on this subject as saying, "How can they take my presentation seriously when their eyes never leave the buttons on my blouse?"

Most male sexual games are of this "Me Tarzan, you Jane" type, although sometimes the game goes too far and becomes sexual harassment. In this case women have legal recourses, but few are inclined to go this route because it's messy and can destroy careers. When stymied by sexual games, most women back away from the discrimination and start job shopping, hoping for and often receiving promotions by changing companies. The Korn/Ferry–UCLA survey asked women executives how they made it to the top. They replied: changed jobs often, took high-risk/high-reward assignments, moved, and "did not make waves by backing unpopular people, pressing women's issues, or jumping ship to go back to school."

On the other side of the sexual coin, women aren't above playing sexual corporate games either. Just as our culture teaches men to view women in supportive, nurturing, and sexual roles, our culture also teaches women to be supportive, nurturing, and sexual. The only type of competition little girls learn is to compete with other girls for male attention and favor. A woman's adversaries are other women—not men, who are the prizes, protectors, providers, and power. Such deeply ingrained attitudes and mores are mental prisons in which existence is difficult, but escape is even more difficult, fraught with unfamiliar, disorienting danger.

In truth, some corporate women exploit their sexual attractiveness and characteristics to attain personal and career goals, and some do try and often succeed in "sleeping their way to the top." Consciously or subconsciously, they accept their socialized, stereotypical roles in the business world as well as the social world; they are the nurturing Mother, the supporting and protected Pet, and the flirtatious, sexually alluring Seductress. They too look with disdain, disgust, and perhaps a little fear on the Iron Maiden.

Regardless of the degree of participation, all male and female employees are affected by the sexual games played in the office. Basically, these games are sexual power struggles: women use sex to gain power and men use it to retain power. For both, flirtations, flattery, and sexual innuendos can be turned into techniques of control that in reality have nothing to do with sex as an expression of emotion. Men learn business power techniques from other men, but women have no such power role models and revert to the instilled technique of using sexual ploys to gain the desired results. In essence, both have difficulty relinquishing social roles for business roles.

Whatever the psychological or sociological basis for these sexual games, such interaction between the sexes is the stuff relationships are made of, and these relationships sometimes develop into office affairs. Although it is true that sexuality depends on the person, and sexual liaisons can develop in any environment, the office affair has its own mystique and is so commonplace that it belongs in the Hall of Office Folklore Fame. Let's dissect the typical boss/secretary relationship to find the seeds that might grow into a full-blown affair.

The boss/secretary relationship is perhaps the most personal office interaction of all. A secretary's job is specifically to aid and assist, to do the nitty-gritty, mundane detail work in order to free the boss for creative mental and physical activity. Secretaries are helpmates, and female secretaries are often referred to as "office

wives." This metaphor is quite appropriate. Most secretaries not only perform business duties, but many also
perform such personal services as paying bills, buying gifts
for spouses or children, running personal errands, planning parties, and house-, baby-, or dog-sitting while boss
and spouse are away.

When these very personal services are added to the
close, confidential work situation, the relationship between boss and secretary invariably lifts out of the purely
business realm. The familiarity becomes a personal bond
that over time can develop into a serious emotional tie.
Going through pleasant and unpleasant work and personal times with their bosses, loyal secretaries begin to
empathize or feel with their bosses: defending, protect-
ing, supporting, nurturing, and eventually loving. Male
bosses assume an innate loyalty from secretaries and often
feel a personal responsibility and caring for them. In essence, the relationship elevates from business assistant
to surrogate wife. Most boss/secretary relationships remain at this platonic level; others accelerate into affairs.

But the boss/secretary affair is passé; it has been part
of the business scene for many years and thus has become a discreet but familiar happening. Today liaisons
between work peers and the effects of such liaisons on
the work place are sending shock waves throughout the
corporate world. Love affairs among corporate workers
are nearing epidemic proportions, as shown by a *Redbook
Magazine* survey in which more than 50 percent of the
working women in their late thirties admitted to having
affairs with work peers. Evidently, Robert Seidenberg's
often-quoted statement is correct: "Work is very sexy."

For years the common corporate colloquialism regarding sexual relationships was "Don't fish off the
company pier." But with today's prevailing sexual attitudes, this directive is often ignored. Since more and

better-educated women have entered the work place, the office atmosphere has become charged with sexual energy and power game playing. Working together and sharing the excitement and pain of business ventures are indeed a type of bonding, heightening sexual attraction. This bonding, combined with revised sexual attitudes, increases the potential for and number of executive love affairs.

The December 1982 issue of *Working Woman* magazine contained an article entitled "A Matter of Convenience" concerning the sexual attitudes of some career women who, intent on career success, have little time or energy for marriage and deep commitment. The answer to this dilemma: have a part-time liaison with a married man. Most of the women interviewed for the article said their affairs happened for several reasons: the men were "safe" (married) and attractive, the men had power, they shared common interests, and the liaison might further the woman's career. The author closed her article with: "Indeed, for some ambitious women bent on spending most of their energy on work, married may be just the way they like their men. As long, that is, as they're married to someone else."[8]

My intention in reviewing this article is to point out attitudes, not to condemn career women for immorality (although I must admit to disgust at the complete disregard of the married man's wife and to the callousness of the author's proposal). Whether the instigators of such affairs are male or female, such liaisons do not occur single-handedly. There must be agreement of both parties, and the culpability must be shared by both the man and woman. Even "the world's oldest profession" wouldn't have become nor would it continue to be a profession without willing clients.

Work peer pairings are so pervasive that they have

evolved into an important management issue because of the effects these liaisons have on other work peers and the company. As one author said, "Love may be blind, but others are not." Research shows that feelings of jealousy, anger, abandonment, and distrust surround the lovers, and anxiety abounds in the work place. Eliza G. C. Collins, senior editor of the *Harvard Business Review*, states that "love between managers is dangerous because it challenges—and can break down—the organizational structure." But most companies don't interfere in such relationships unless sexual harassment, job performance, or conflict of interest are involved. The recommended solution in this event is that the lower-level employee must go, which normally means the woman.

No, sex in the office is not new, but opportunities are greater. Researchers prognosticate that the number of affairs will increase. There are no clandestine relationships; high emotions are not easily hidden, and others sense the situation even though evidence is absent. As with other office politics, employees are affected by the action whether they play the game or not. Each office is a world in miniature, and although I've concentrated on the negative aspects of the environment, many of the same positives are found here that exist elsewhere. Regardless of the prevailing atmosphere, the work place is where corporate employees spend the majority of their time and energy; the positives, like all positives, are taken for granted, but the negatives irritate.

Work Peers/Corporate Spouse Relationships

Office events and peers directly affect employees, and most of these effects enter the home as internal and external spillover, as discussed in the preceding chapter.

But aside from the spillover, spouses too are often directly affected by their mates' work peers and events. Although spouses aren't officially employed by companies, they necessarily have some contact with their mates' peers, and these contacts have personal impacts for wives. Once again I must qualify by stating that male spouses have fewer impacts because they have less interaction with their wives' professional lives.

Most wives are reluctant to discuss their attitudes about their husbands' work peers because they're afraid of sounding suspicious and jealous. Wives are not in the corporate environment, but they nevertheless are affected by their husbands' activities and relationships with others. Commonly, these women deal directly with results and backlashes: results of their husbands' interactions with work peers and backlashes of those interactions from the peers themselves. For example, peer acceptance is important to careers and being "one of the guys" often entails participation in such activities as stopping for a drink at the local bar after work. The results can be chaos: dinner is prepared, children are fed and bedded, husband arrives slightly inebriated, dinner is prepared once again, wife is angry, and husband goes to sleep. If this scenario isn't bad enough, when Mrs. Corporate Wife sees one of the "fellows," she must smilingly endure snide remarks and double-entendre comments about the night on the town or the latest communal trip out of town. Male work peers are sometimes irritating and hurting thorns in a corporate wife's side. Spouses, male or female, have little choice other than to deal with the results and backlashes. Aside from drastic action, they have relatively no power to change a mate's behavior and are often accused of being untrusting and not realizing the importance such camaraderie has for the career.

But a female spouse is more comfortable with her husband's male work peers than with his female peers. As stated earlier in this chapter, women are socialized to compete against other women, and reciprocal uneasiness dominates the meetings of career women and career wives. Most wives are both idealistic and realistic about their husbands' female co-workers. Idealistically, wives accept and applaud women's right to equality in the work place, but realistically, they acknowledge the personal threat of close working relationships between their husbands and other women. Most wives use business/social occasions to meet the women of the office, but often their attempts fail because there is so much uneasiness and so little understanding.

In my long experience as a corporate wife I've had contact with numerous career women. Most are quite relaxed and comfortable talking with their peers but are rather guarded with spouses. Such reactions are understandable because unemployed spouses and working women usually have few common interests, or so it is assumed. The most difficult of all female peers to talk with and get to know are the Iron Maidens. Although these career-dedicated women are to be admired for their achievement and courage, most ignore other women, especially wives, to the point of rudeness. It's as though they're afraid to be seen talking with another woman or afraid they might find something in common with her. On one occasion my husband called to ask me to join him, an associate, and a business visitor for a drink after work. The visitor was a woman whom I had been most anxious to meet. She had begun her career as an engineer when female engineers were very rare, and she progressed to the presidency of her own company. Eagerly, I rushed to the meeting only to be greeted by a very cold stone wall. After the introductions the woman, for all her intelligence and success, completely ignored my existence, talking only of business issues and directing all comments to the men. I have known her for many years now and even spent a weekend with her and her husband, but each time we meet it's an instant replay of that first meeting. I'm always pointedly excluded from the conversation—unless I ask questions about how she got where she is today.

Conversely, secretaries are eager to be pleasant and accommodating to spouses, but wives are often purposefully distant. A natural jealousy exists between a businessman's wife and his "office wife." The wife is often critical and suspicious of the secretary's motives, and the secretary is just as often snide and condescending about the wife. The close relationships between the boss/wife and the boss/secretary are much like an emotional triangle of two women and one man. Secretaries often berate wives to others for not understanding how busy their bosses are and for calling the office too often. They honestly feel they know and understand their bosses better than their wives do. Almost all wives are leery of secretaries, feeling they intentionally pry into their private lives and sometimes cause friction between husbands and wives. And this can easily happen.

Most corporate wives with whom I'm acquainted rarely call their husbands' offices, but one woman related this story, which she believed to be a deliberate subversive secretarial action. Jan had an understanding with the secretary that the secretary was never to put her calls through to her husband if he was busy or in a meeting unless Jan stated that the call was important. One day Jan called while her husband was touring the manufacturing plant with some important visitors, so Jan told the secretary that it wasn't important and she would call later. The secretary replied that she would have the boss return her call when he came in. Five minutes later the husband frantically returned her call. The secretary had raced out to the plant, found her boss, and informed him in front of his visitors that his wife said to call her immediately. When he realized the call was not an emergency, the man was irate with his wife for the interruption of the tour and his embarrassment in front of the visitors. That night Jan explained the sequence of events, but her husband was reluctant to believe that she had told the secretary the call was unimportant. Such things do happen.

As related earlier, office or business sex affairs have become so commonplace as to become a management issue, and much material has been published lately on this subject. What is most distressing to me is that in all of the articles and books very little reference is made to the spouses of the married businesspeople involved in such affairs; it's as though they are simply nonexistent. But spouses do exist and are more sorely affected by these liaisons than the companies are. Unemployed wives, especially, are very vulnerable; they can end up alone, their lifework destroyed, and with little or no means of financial support.

As far as divorce is concerned, corporate marriages are said to have a good track record, but the impact of office affairs echoes in many corporate homes. Wives are concerned and rightly so. Some wives state they have no trepidation on this issue. In my opinion these women are either superb diplomats or superb fools. The business world abounds with marriage-destroying temptations, and employees usually spend more of their lives at the office than at home. When one compares the wife at home with the career woman at work, the contrast is glaring. Necessarily, wives are frequently associated with problems: children, bills, emergencies, responsibilities, do-it-yourself repairs, and all of the other pressing matters that arise in the course of maintaining a home and family. Career women have a certain aura of joie de vivre, quite the opposite of problems: excitement, achievement, ambition, sophistication, and fun. Sharing accomplishments with a carefree career woman is certainly more interesting and pleasant than pulling crabgrass from the lawn with an overloaded wife. Although such comparisions smack of paranoia and insecurity, the contrasts are obvious, and the employee must choose between the two.

A corporate wife friend, Kate, has a dear sister who was for many years a single career woman. As an inexperienced young corporate wife, Kate would tell her sister how threatened she felt by the women with whom her husband worked, pouring out all her insecurities and fears. Kate's sister would soundly upbraid her, saying she had nothing to worry about and shouldn't feel threatened. Years later, after having married a corporate employee, the sister came to Kate and apologized, saying, "I never really understood what you were going through. Now I do because I see things from the other side of the fence."

Although spouses aren't physically part of their mates' professional life, office policies, activities, and work peers affect both employees and spouses. The most persistent and easily accommodated effect is the spillover that invariably comes home with employees. But the interaction spouses have with work peers and the influence these peers can have on spouses' lives and marriages can be upsetting and sometimes destructive.

Summary

Corporate employment can be sociologically confusing for employees because corporations operate with opposing philosophies and policies. Companies hire people based on individual talent and achievement and then expect them to become team players; they espouse equality in the work place, but instigate and support mentor/sponsor systems based on elitism. Because we Americans are taught individualism and egalitarianism, these collectivist and elitist corporate practices are confusing and often conflicting for many employees.

Offices are microcosms of the larger world. Each office is distinct, but all have common traits, one of which is office politics. The essence of office politics is information, and to "play politics" one has to acquire and use pertinent information to gain advantage. The political arena is the interaction between work peers and groups. Gossip, as prevalent in the office as elsewhere, provides a constant flow of information for both good and bad political games. Sexual politics is also a factor in the work place, but most sexual games are played for power rather than sexual favors. Still, the office affair cannot be overlooked, because the number of affairs is increasing and causing so much concern that the sexual interaction of corporate employees is now a managerial issue.

Most office events and relationships impact on employees through stress and spillover, but spouses too are affected by corporate policies, politics, and peers. Although not officially employed by the corporations, spouses, especially unemployed spouses, are bystanders who can become victims of office politics and corporate sexual games.

9

THE FINAL SCORE

REWARDS AND RISKS

The preceding five chapters presented the principal problems and hardships of working within the corporation and living the corporate life. In an effort to depict corporate living honestly, the negatives were emphasized to point out that this life-style, like all others, has pros and cons, negatives and positives. But where does this dark-skies, uncorporate-like attitude bring us? What good does it do to dwell on the down side?

No job is perfect, but the demands of the corporate environment can have a prodound impact on employees, one that frequently echoes through them for a sometimes severe secondary impact on spouses and children. Yes, there are corporate casualties, but there are also corporate champions. Opting for employment with a large corporation is a life decision; one must be willing to take the risks to gain the rewards. But the abstract employment contract, that unwritten understanding between company and recruit of what is required and received, contains obscure fine print that few recruits fully comprehend. In the recruit's excitement at being selected by the corporation and his or her eagerness to accept the offer and launch the career, the dangers are often unknown or unacknowledged. This chapter is addressed to the lament, "If I had only known."

Psychology and psychiatry are valuable yet imprecise sciences; one human being cannot actually go into another human mind and determine that a certain factor or event directly caused a certain psychological reaction. However, the corporate environment is an intense incubator that can forcibly nourish a personal tendency, either positive or negative, into full-grown victory or disaster, a catalyst spurring a reaction that might never surface in a different set of circumstances. This possibility of negative reaction is the gamble, the risk that all corporate people take whether they are cognizant of the facts or not.

Let's take a look at this gamble and evaluate some of the risks and rewards of corporate employment. Those of us already in the corporation might find a new insight and those considering corporate jobs might discover points to mull over before, rather than after, their decision.

The Up Side

Opportunity: the rewards of corporate employment might be broadly defined in that one word. Corporations offer no guarantees, but they do offer opportunities for individual fulfillment of potential, bringing psychological and material rewards. Corporate demands are high and employment risks are many, but no other business institution offers such opportunities without a personal monetary investment. The major rewards to be gained through corporate employment are training and experience, financial security, and personal growth.

A corporate career begins with training. During that period the employee isn't working or producing for the company, but he or she receives a salary in addition to the training. The trainee's formal education gives general knowledge; companies train in specific techniques, and more important, they train the employee in the proper application of those techniques. Knowledge without application is like a lamp—it does nothing until turned on. Corporate training turns on an employee's knowledge and talent. A company invests a great deal of money in an employee's training, and the return on that investment is the eventual productivity of that person. Later, as the employee works and produces, experience enhances his or her trained knowledge. The combination of knowledge, training, and experience becomes an irrevocable personal asset that can never be repossessed by the company. Companies may get the results, but employees own the skills. Those skills are marketable to other companies, usually at a higher salary because the new company doesn't have the original training investment. In fact, most employment contracts now require recruits to remain with the hiring company a stated number of years to ensure return on the training investment. One company with which I'm familiar requires three years' employment from new recruits.

Over time astute, ambitious employees manipulate their career paths to obtain training and experience in many phases of the business. This is the path that leads to the top, and as these employees progress, their value to the company, their skills, and their marketability to outside companies increase. Many of today's entrepreneurs are yesterday's corporate trainees. They worked in a corporation for a time, honed their skills, and then resigned from the corporation to invest their experience and assets elsewhere. The training of corporate employees equates with the apprenticeship of some blue-collar workers: it teaches a lifetime trade or skill. The trainee is the fertile ground, the training is the seed, and the resulting career is the plant that produces life-sustaining fruits: skills, money, and future opportunities.

Financial security is another plus obtained from corporate employment. Corporations ask much from their employees, but the monetary compensation ranges from quite adequate to very good. Depending on individual performance and company profits, periodic raises and/or bonuses over the years can substantially increase the starting salary. In addition, many companies offer company stock options and educational programs in which employees may participate. Stock option programs allow workers to purchase a stated amount of company stock at a guaranteed price, usually well below market prices. For employees wishing to further their schooling, a corporate educational program normally pays tuition fees, with the stipulation that employment is continued. A similar program offered by some companies allows employees' children to compete for company scholarships. All of these financial rewards are reflected in the affluent life-styles and educational levels of both parents and children. Entrance into and benefits from such financial programs usually depend on employee vestment, the specified period of employment required before becoming eligible for participation. These and other special programs are often known as perks or "golden handcuffs."

Health, dental, and life insurance and retirement

plans are another type of financial security and are often referred to as the corporate "protective umbrella." The value, both mental and financial, of insurance and retirement are inestimable, depending primarily on the individual's need for assistance and his psychological need for security. Employees have the security of good insurance coverage, and it's worry-free. Most retirement plans are based on matching contributions, both employee and employer paying into the fund. On retirement the employee has a guaranteed income, the amount dependent on employment time, level, and contributions. If a person chooses to leave the company after a certain period of time, the contributions made to this fund can be withdrawn in lump sum, much like closing a bank account, or the money may be left in the fund and received later as regular retirement pay. For many contemplating an employment change, leaving the "protective umbrella" and the security of corporation benefits is psychologically upsetting. Some never leave and others go only to companies offering the same or a better umbrella of security.

Corporate employment provides people with opportunities for personal growth and social mobility. The financial compensation enables them to broaden their cultural experience, which stimulates them intellectually and socially. Corporations provide worldwide travel/work experiences for employees; the corporate couple sometimes receives personally unaffordable tastes of luxury through company-sponsored award programs. And all the while the frequent-flyer bonus points are adding up for additional free transportation. Even relocation offers growth opportunities: new people to meet, new territory to explore, new cultures to learn, new experiences to enjoy, new facilities to use. It is a sophisticated way of life that offers exposure to and options for personal growth. The secret is to make the most of the best and the least of the worst.

Corporate employment is a conduit through which upwardly mobile high achievers can obtain these rewards with no financial investment. It offers outstanding opportunities rarely found in other employment, but one must be willing to meet the demands, take the risks, and pay the personal price to gain the rewards.

The Down Side

The major risks lurking in the corporate environs might be lumped under one general heading: psychological. Psychological risks are by no means the only perils, but they are the ones I consider most prevalent and most destructive for corporate employees, spouses, and children. Of course, this is not to say that all who suffer emotional upset do so as a direct result of corporate employment. But the magnitude of psychological upset among corporate people is surprising and therefore deserves attention. Although accommodation of and reaction to the life-style varies individually, I maintain that the corporate environment nurtures negative tendencies and enhances the risks of negative psychological repercussions.

Risk: Career/Ego Damage

As stated earlier, corporate employment is not simply a job; it is a career, part of an employee's identity; and career damage causes ego damage. A stymied career is the most common cause of ego damage because it is seen by others as well as felt by the employee. Any employment involves the risk of disappointment: the job didn't fulfill expectations, one's skills were inadequate, or the pay was too low. But career disappointment is damaging when the employee feels penalized unjustly, feels no control over the situation, and has no recourse within the organization. Stymied careers abound in the corporate world and take three basic forms: dead-end jobs, demotion, and termination.

A dead-end job is blocked job mobility. Promotion stops, and the probability of future promotion is greatly decreased or completely negated. In this situation ambition urges the employee to keep climbing, but he looks up and there is no next rung on the corporate ladder, no new challenge, no place to go. Opportunity is passing or has passed him by. Others come and go but he remains stable, growing old in the position, gaining seniority in that work level. Then the questions start: "What happened to my dream? Where did my career train run off the fast track? Why me?"

People end up in dead-end jobs for several reasons, all of which seem unjust to the employee involved. A common reason is the individual's choice of employment. One's chosen career may offer little opportunity for advancement at the outset. For example, clerical jobs have notoriously short career ladders, and the same is true of many highly specialized job positions. When the dead-end situation is a matter of choice, little or no damage occurs. Damage does occur when employees receive unsatisfactory performance reviews and/or make unfortunate political alliances. These people find themselves stagnating, they lose out in the competitive race, and are demoted or relegated to unchallenging but necessary duties.

A third circumstance involves employees, typically

salespeople, who perform well, rise quickly, and arrive at the top of their field but can go no higher on the company pyramid because they lack well-rounded experience in all phases of the business. Such employees are great sales executives but know little about manufacturing, engineering, finance, or human resources. At this high departmental level employment crossover into another area is rare, so the executive remains stable in his position with no place to go. Later the executive is "promoted" into a manufactured position with a title but little responsibility or is quietly demoted. The ultimate dead-end is a vice-presidential position; there can be only one president at the tip of the corporate pyramid. The choices here are stablizing in the VP slot, going to another company, or retiring. Company morale and the VP's ego rarely allow demotion or termination, but sometimes a title-retaining, nonproductive position is made available.

Although dead-ends are general knowledge among fellow workers, the person in the dead-end retains public posture or "face." This is not the case with demotion; demotion is open humiliation. The demotee loses face and is often the object of peer pity. It's an embarrassing situation. Even if the employee is relocated to a different place, news of the action travels by company grapevine and arrives at the new location before the employee. To avoid the embarrassment and to mend their egos many employees take the only escape route open, resignation. Resignation is a drastic and sometimes ill-advised step because in some cases the stigma of demotion can be overcome and the career might be rebuilt. But the odds of this gamble are not encouraging.

Termination—being fired—is the greatest ego-damaging corporate risk. Corporations jealously guard their "employment at will" privilege: the corporate right to fire whomever and whenever they please. At present there is no job protection for corporate employees outside Title VII of the 1964 Civil Rights Act. The fear of termination is always present, but actually being fired is a devastating blow. Fellow workers and friends tend to assume incompetence as the reason for dismissal even though the termination may be the result of an acknowledged reduction in work force, a company merger or buyout, a facility relocation, or a political power play. Suddenly, co-worker friends disappear; all association with the disengaged employee stops. Our society treats termination in the same manner as a social disease; the victim is literally shunned. In my opinion such work-peer reactions involve more than heartlessness. When a friend is fired, the remaining employee faces the truth that he or she could be next, and this uncomfortable personal truth motivates the dissociation.

Dead ends, demotions, and terminations force employees to confront themselves through intense self-evaluation, and no matter what the final truth, the end result is ego damaging. Employees are embarrassed, scared, and depressed; they experience a strong sense of failure and powerlessness; they lose self-confidence and feel a complete loss of control over their lives. Aside from the ego damage, a stymied career mars the résumé, and both ego and résumé are important factors in any future job hunt.

Demotion or termination affects spouses in subtle ways. Usually, a spouse's main concern is for the mate and the ego damage that might ensue. This concern normally surfaces as anger at the company and bitterness about the injustice rather than sympathy. But beneath this outward show of anger lie fear, insecurity, and perhaps a bit of unadmitted resentment of the mate. A lengthy suspension of salary is undeniably a threat to the present standard of living and future security. Spouses are ashamed of and only grudgingly own such thoughts, but the fear is nonetheless in their minds. The equation of job termination with social disease is as common to the corporate couple as to their friends; the couple feel somehow degraded and worry about what their friends will think. Some wives react to demotion or termination with open hostility and angry outbursts; others experience anxiety attacks and depression. But as a general rule corporate spouses are very supportive of their unemployed mates, encouraging them to put away the past and go forward to better circumstances.

These three types of stymied careers are common occurrences in today's corporate life. Reciprocal loyalty of company and employee was common in the preceding generation, but it's now a thing of the past. Voluntary and/or mandatory career changes are so familiar that periodic shake-ups are becoming just another part of the corporate game. Most employees are sensitive to the omens of an impending demotion or termination and make a change voluntarily instead of waiting to be fired. It's the mandatory change that stymies the career, mars the résumé, and damages the ego. My axiom about these career events is that if you choose to play in the corporate sandbox, expect to get sand in your eyes occasionally.

In accommodating the corporate life-style wives too risk severe ego damage, but their psychological damage doesn't occur in relation to specific events such as demotion. For a spouse ego destruction is often a slow process, much like the constant drip of water that eventually wears away a stone. The constant drip is the continual displacement of her personal wants, needs, and goals; the eroded stone is her sense of personal identity and/or self. Recognition of ego erosion seldom comes until one asks the questions "Who am I, what am I, and where do I belong?" If the answers are "I'm Mrs. Executive, I'm my husband's wife and my children's mother, and I belong with my husband and children," ego erosion or complete loss of self are likely. All of these answers may be true, but this concept of one's identity is not true personal identity—it is identity by proxy, coming through someone else rather than through the person.

Loss of self occurs when one repeatedly submerges or abandons one's own needs and feelings in order to help someone else fulfill his or her needs and goals. This description is typical of the traditional unemployed wife and particularly typical of the unemployed corporate wife. Employed spouses display fewer symptoms of this malady for one obvious reason: they maintain a personal identity through their individual jobs. But even the employed corporate spouse is susceptible to both ego and career damage when relocating for the mate's career benefit; then it's back to zero just like the unemployed spouse. The needs and goals of family members take priority in the life of the supportive spouse; her goal is their success. Over time she gradually and unknowingly relinquishes personhood and becomes an extension of the employee/mate's personality and identity, basking in reflected glory but usually harboring bitter resentment.

For spouses ego damage can result from the overload and neglect incurred by long hours, frequent travel, repeated relocations, negative spillover, and office affairs. Once again I stress that not all spouses incur ego damage and loss of self, but the corporate environment elevates the danger. In this setting submerging oneself in the mate's career, supporting and assisting his goals, and becoming an extension of his personhood is often the easiest route for corporate wives. But this route is also the road to self-destruction.

Risk: Depression and Crisis

Depression is epidemic in all segments of the American population. Although it can be a singular problem, unrelated to the work environment, the incubating corporate climate provides perfect conditions for the development and spread of this illness, and the incidences of depression within this community are astonishing. According to the National Institute of Mental Health one out of every five people in our country has depression. Such figures normally are based on "reported" cases, people who actively seek help. I conjecture that corporate people make up a significant portion of these cases and that more cases of depression are unreported than reported. Most mental health experts state that depression is two to six times more prevalent in women than in men, but I disagree. A truer statement is that women seek help for their depression and other illnesses more frequently than men do. Men tend to shun help unless a crisis makes it mandatory. I believe that men have as much depression as women, but it is often unreported and/or misdiagnosed as some other malady. And the majority of corporate employees are men.

Most employees ignore their conditions because their symptoms are often masked in behaviors approved by both the corporation and society. One psychiatrist stated, "The workaholic is often running to hide depression." Studies show that high achievers are more prone to high depression than are others, but whereas doctors routinely look beyond women's visible symptoms to discover depression, they are much less likely to do so in men. The workaholic may suffer from stress or burnout, certainly not depression.

Another contributing factor in the relatively low reported incidences of male depression is the "tough guy," macho attitude that prevails in society and in the corporation. Male executives, managers, and employees are expected to be tough, and female workers are striving successfully to meet the same standard. This attitude considers illness a character weakness, especially if the problem is mental or emotional. A *Fortune* article candidly addressed the subject of executive depression and crisis by describing the corporate tough-guy ethics as "self-punishing." John DeLuca, director of the medical department of Equitable Life, was quoted: "It's not appropriate in a corporation to admit your concerns or problems. I think that's *the* major executive crisis—their inability to have one."[1] Counselors retained by corporations report that depression and anxiety are quite common in corporate ranks, but reliable statistics are difficult to compile because when an employee seeks help, it is usually at an outside, private source. Corporate people are so sensitive about employers and work peers knowing of their problem that untold numbers pay for such services out of their own pockets rather than file for company insurance payment.

The same is true with alcohol and drug abuse problems. Accurate statistics are lacking, and it's difficult to judge the extent of substance use and abuse relative to the corporate environment. The National Council on Alcoholism estimates between 6 percent and 10 percent of America's work force are alcoholics whose drinking seriously interferes with their work. But a 1979 Opinion Research Corporation survey showed that 18 percent of top- and middle-management executives admitted having some concern about their own drinking. One thing is sure: the life-style is conducive to drinking. Meetings held outside the office, whether business or social, are planned around the cocktail, and the after-work drink "to relax before dinner" is part of the coming-home ritual in most corporate homes. Alcohol is considered a necessary tension reliever by employees and spouses. It is, in fact, a depressant, and overuse can be dangerous, especially if the user is already depressed or combines alcohol with other drugs.

Alcoholism is by no means confined to employees; many corporate spouses are quiet and unnoticed drinkers. Maryanne Vandervelde, an author, psychotherapist, and corporate wife, stated that most corporate wives seen in outpatient therapy present symptoms in one of two categories: depression and alcohol or drug abuse. [2] Alcoholism among spouses is seldom recognized because the heavy drinking is done at home, alone. I have a dear friend who I never realized was an alcoholic until she paid us a weekend visit and asked for a beer before breakfast. Alcohol is always available and indeed takes its toll.

Employees can carry heavy emotional baggage: guilt induced by neglect of family, job pressure and stress, and adverse career events. Depression might be disguised in such applaudable symptoms as working long and hard, but one insignificant event can trigger an emotional crisis or breakdown, for which the prognosis is not good. Experts estimate that only one of three executives hospitalized with severe emotional problems returns to the same position. Employee depression can occur at any age and career level, but it appears more often in mid-life when self-evaluation is more intense. Midlife normally brings a feeling of time running out to accomplish desired goals. This feeling is abetted by the prevalence of dead ends, demotions, and terminations among this age group. In Japan terminations are rare in the corporate culture. Even so, a recent newspaper article related that in 1983 the suicide rate of Japanese men in their fifties was 34 percent higher than in 1982, and men in their forties and fifties made up 40 percent of the entire country's suicides. These are the men who rebuilt Japan after the war, bringing their country from destruction to front-rank status in world economics, the men who awed the world with their single-minded dedication to job and employer. Although suicides are culturally more accepted in Japan than in the United States, these statistics are nonetheless disheartening. A Japanese social psychologist stated in the article that "a burn-out phenomenon is common among them. They are driven to devote themselves to their work until they burn out. Naturally, they become worn out, and a simple matter may cause them to commit suicide." Is this the work ethic Americans strive to emulate?

As for spouses, their individual roads to depression are built aimlessly and unknowingly while aiding, assisting, and accompanying their mates on the corporate climb. These roads are paved with the stones of anger, bitterness, resentment, loneliness, and loss of self. The "good" spouse never complains; she quietly accepts the circumstance, internalizes her feelings, and adds another stone to her road to depression. As the years progress, the road gets longer and the destination nearer. Bouts of mild depression, commonly described as moving blues, travel widow loneliness, and empty nest syndrome, serve as signposts along the way. Astute wives observe these warning signs and alter their course, but numbers of corporate wives simply forge ahead to the ultimate breakdown.

The previous chapters enumerated five of the problem areas that negatively impact on corporate wives. Of these five, relocation is the most severe and psychologically dangerous. Spouses are terribly vulnerable after a move. They continue their roles as support systems for family members but have little or no support for themselves. The loneliness of a new home can be overwhelming. All of the bitter feelings accumulated and internalized in the past surface, and severe depression and total breakdown become very real possibilities for these trailing spouses. If a woman chooses to be a martyr, the corporate life-style will certainly provide the stake and build the fire.

Risk: the Child Wager

The influence of the rootless corporate life on children is at best unpredictable and at worst catastrophic; one simply cannot be sure of the outcome. There is practically no reliable information on the subject because to date psychological and sociological researchers have devoted too little time and thought to the problems of the corporate family, particularly corporate children. Problems that appear with these children are too quickly and easily filed under traditional adolescent problems with no investigation for causation beyond the obvious symptoms. Corporate children are not traditional; they live life on the fast track just as their parents do. They have no home in the traditional sense, just a progression of houses and locations. As adults, they will never introduce anyone as a friend "I grew up with." Yet to my knowledge, adequate research about these children is lacking.

Children of the corporation are privileged. Their social stratum ranges from middle to upper middle and even to upper class. They grow up in affluent economic circumstances and are accustomed to the more expensive, if not the finer, things of life. Their neighborhoods are the corporate ghettos that proliferate across the country. The houses are pleasing and expensive, built to sell quickly because the resident turnover is enormous, but the neighborhood is a ghetto nonetheless. The people are homogeneous, all corporate families, all transient, all of about the same job and salary level. Only the name of the employer differs. Parents indulge their offspring with things to compensate for little time spent with them and for their transient lives.

Local schools show the influence of the life-style. At one time our family lived surrounded by automobile executive families in a subdivision eighteen miles outside Detroit. It was customary that on the sixteenth birthday, each automobile executive's child received a company car and a new replacement every six to twelve months thereafter. The local high school parking lot was a quiet sea of TransAms; inside was an angry ocean of problems. Partying was the main teenage entertainment in the area. Each week party locations, generally at the home of out-of-town parents, were posted on the bulletin board, and literally hundreds of kids attended a single party. At one party, so the rumor went, the "fun" got out of hand and a dining table was thrown through glass doors. Drinking, drugs, and skipping school were common activities. One would like to think of this as an extreme example, but the affluent corporate teenage world is a rarefied atmosphere.

Such children grow up quickly, and compared to traditional children, they are quite sophisticated. Thanks to affluence and relocations, they are usually well traveled and have broader exposure to the world. Flying across the country to visit friends in a former location is the thing to do in the summer; meanwhile, they keep in touch by telephone, not by letter. Generally, corporate children seem unafraid, at least on the outside. But adolescent problems are rampant in corporate families, and in my opinion many of these problems have at least some roots in the transient way of life. Robert Seidenberg dubbed children as the "passive passengers" on the corporate fast track. During a move almost all children experience moving blues and minor depression. The younger ones tend to be confused, frightened, and insecure, often exhibiting evidence of internal troubles. With teenagers the problems associated with relocation center around social upheaval and frustration, and the symptoms of depression are more visible, often causing terrible strife within the family unit.

Studies have shown that peer acceptance and confirmation is extremely important to adolescents and are necessary for proper emotional and intellectual growth. Teens often react with anger and resentment when required to move and give up their peers. Most teens' anger eventually subsides, but some become openly rebellious either before or after the move. Many refuse to move, requesting to stay with a friend and finish out the school year. This is a tough decision for parents and child, but if arrangements can be made, it's sometimes the best solution. Other angry teenagers threaten to run away from home, and some actually carry out the threat. If this happens, it results in enormous hurt and damaged relationships among family members. Normally, adolescents react to a move with resentful acquiescence, withdrawing from the world into their rooms and themselves. But this reaction also can be very dangerous if the withdrawal is prolonged, turning into loneliness, despair, and severe depression.

Moving into a new community is difficult for teenagers. Just at the age when their need for peer acceptance is greatest, transient teens must relinquish friends and start anew as outsiders. Generally, the adjustment to the new place is more difficult for girls than for boys. Girls are more inclined to form cliques or exclusionary groups. Admittance to such a clique takes months, and many times acceptance is denied completely. Even at this age young girls vie with others for male attention— any new girl, especially if she's pretty, is seen as a threat rather than a possible friend. Boys are less prone to form cliques, and this makes acceptance easier. Proficiency in some sport is an excellent passport into a new location; jocks are welcomed.

Regardless of the reception, children of high achievers feel extreme pressure from parents and themselves to assimilate and become outstanding in the new location. But feelings of loss and isolation are inevitable for both girls and boys. The self-imposed and parental pressures to gain acceptance, combined with feelings of loss and isolation, sometimes result in severe teenage depression. Since 1955, the approximate time massive corporate migration began, adolescent suicides have increased an astonishing 300 percent. In the age group of 15 to 19, suicide is the second leading cause of death after traffic accidents, many of which are suspected suicides. The highest rates of teen suicides are found in Phoenix and Dallas, both Sun Belt areas experiencing exploding populations due to corporate relocations. One corporate bedroom town outside Dallas has been shaken by eight teen suicides in one year. Twenty years ago this town was an agricultural community with a population of three thousand. Today it is a typical corporate ghetto with more than one hundred thousand residents, well over half of whom have lived there four years or less. The heartbroken parents of one suicide chose to have their son cremated. Having moved five times, the mother was quoted as saying, "Where would we bury him? Where is home?"[3]

All this negative rhetoric is perhaps an overstatement of the situation. The percentages of such dire incidents related to relocation may be very low, but no one knows for sure. The purpose is to present the possibilities candidly, not predict probability. These dreadful problems surface in noncorporate and corporate families alike, and we all rationalize that it could never happen to us. In my opinion the stresses of corporate life raise the odds that it might happen to us. Rearing children in this environment remains a game of chance with few guidelines but very high stakes.

Summary

Corporations offer opportunities for psychological and material rewards that few other employment choices can match. Training and experience increase employee productivity for the company, but the employee gains skills that can be marketed to other companies or used to start a private business. This training is expensive for the company but very valuable for the employee. Another corporate reward is financial security. Salaries are quite adequate and provide an affluent life-style for families. Other financial benefits include the "golden handcuffs" of stock options and educational programs and the "protective umbrella" of insurance and retirement plans. Finally, corporations facilitate personal growth through intellectual, social, and cultural exposure. Most corporate people become quite sophisticated through travel opportunities and relocation, and this sophistication is reflected in other areas of their lives.

But there are also dangerous psychological risks involved that apply to spouses and children as well as to employees. The three major risks are ego/career damage, depression, and the detrimental effects on children. Since one's career is part of the ego, psychological damage can result when careers are stymied, often unjustly, through dead-end positions, demotions, and terminations. Termination is especially painful because it not only damages the ego, it mars the résumé and inhibits obtaining new employment. Dead ends, demotions, and terminations are common occurrences in the corporate environment.

Spouses too run the risk of ego damage through the loss of self or identity, with the unemployed spouse running the greatest risk. Loss of self is likely if a spouse habitually submerges or abandons her personal feelings and needs to assist someone else in fulfilling his needs and goals. The spouse whose life goal is someone else's success is in danger of losing personhood, becoming a mere extension of that other person, and allowing herself to be a victim.

Depression can affect any member of the corporate family. Employee depression often goes unrecognized and unreported because the symptoms are disguised in socially accepted and company-encouraged behaviors such as working long hours. The corporate environment is conducive to the use of alcohol by both employees and spouses. It is the focal point of off-site business meetings and social occasions. Spouses are most vulnerable to depression during a relocation; internalized bitter feelings from the past often surface at this time and combine with loss and loneliness. Depression becomes a real possibility.

Rearing children in the corporate community is a gamble; one never knows what the outcome might be. Too little research has been done on this subject, and therefore, reliable information is scarce. Nonetheless, children are often the true victims of life-style; they have little or no control over the course of their lives because of their age and dependency. Negative reactions of children can cause dire consequences for the entire family.

Corporate employment is an individual choice, but unless both the pros and cons are considered, it is a biased decision that later might be lamented. No one can say for sure that the life-style is *the* cause of personal problems, but if tendencies exist, it can have an incubating effect on them. It is vitally important that prospective employees and their spouses be educated, either by our schools or by the corporation, to the risks as well as the rewards of corporate employment. If the pitfalls are posted before employment, corporate families would be aware of the dangers and might possibly circumvent the hazards, thereby avoiding some of the personal hardships associated with living the corporate life.

PART THREE

NEW

GAME PLANS

Human beings are unique, many-faceted creatures with both objective and subjective natures. Each of us has the practical, objective ability to think and act and the emotional, subjective ability to sense and feel. Being social creatures, we pass to following generations the accepted mores of subjective attitudes and objective behaviors. But there is a glaring anomaly in this socialization process: we socialize our children unequally, along sexual lines. Female socialization emphasizes the subjective nature of humanness, sensing and feeling; male socialization stresses the objective nature, thinking and acting. Because of biological differences we assume psychological differences and socialize sexual mores rather than human mores. In our society it is generally accepted that women are more subjective than men, and men are more objective than women. This sexually selective socialization often impedes complete and balanced development of both aspects of human potential. Both women and men are oversocialized as sexes and undersocialized as human beings.

Human history is a sequence of evolutionary mental and physical changes. Time and environment alter attitudes, attitudes alter behaviors, and behaviors alter lives. Sociological theory tells us that in order to survive, social structures and institutions must change and adapt with changing environments and attitudes. The same is true for socialization, but socialization changes much more slowly than time, environment, and attitudes; it always lags behind, holding onto the comfortably familiar past.

As commercial institutions, corporations are altering their practices to accommodate the shifting business times and environment. As social institutions relating to their people, corporations change more slowly, although gradual change is occurring. But the slowest change of all is in corporate people themselves, most of whom are still living their lives according to their sexually selective socialization. This is outdated and inappropriate preparation for the modern, nontraditional life that millions of corporate people live. It dictates sexual roles and rules that are ill-fitted to their environment and circumstances, and it inhibits the mutual communication, understanding, and supportiveness between employees and spouses that are so important to personally rewarding marital relationships. As a result, this traditional socialization magnifies and intensifies the problems and hardships innate in modern corporate life.

A new game plan is needed. William James, the distinguished American psychologist and philosopher of the late 1800s, once wrote, "The greatest discovery of my generation is that human beings can alter their lives by altering their attitudes of mind." James wrote of his generation, but this truth knows no generation gap; his words are as valid today as in his time. For employees, spouses, and the corporation itself, altering lives by "altering their attitudes of mind" is long overdue.

10

THE CORPORATE EMPLOYEE

A WHOLE PERSON

As a corporate employee, you are among the chosen. You are all the adjectives previously used to describe corporate employees in this book: intelligent, high-achieving, sophisticated, enthusiastic, and above all, ambitious. You are also pressured, stressed, and overworked, and you often experience feelings of guilt. You lead two lives: one professional, the other private. Each day you juggle these two lives in the hope of emerging a well-balanced, whole person. But the proper balance of success in both lives is elusive. Many times you're a success at work and a failure at home, or you're a success at home and a failure at work. However the scales tip, guilt results.

Being a corporate employee entails obligations, just as being a husband and father carries responsibilities. The requirements of both the professional and the private roles are prescribed, and little alters these respectives duties. But something can be done to bring the two into a better balance and alleviate some of the guilt feelings. After years of striving most employees eventually decide that a perfect balance of work and family is unattainable; many give up trying. And they are right; constant and perfect balance between the two is impossible. But an averaging out, a mean, *is* possible, and attaining that mean is the secret of successfully living the corporate game.

Although this sounds simple enough, it is not—especially for the male employee. This mean is attained more through subjective awareness and understanding than through an objective division of time and energy. A mean balance between work and family demands subjective changes in attitudes followed by objective changes in behavior. For men the difficulty lies in their sexually selective socialization to objective rather than subjective thought. Attaining an average balance is quite possible; it simply requires men to take full advantage of their human potential by learning to use their subjective natures more effectively.

As executives, you are trained in problem solving and decision making. Why not use the same techniques to strive for a solution to the work/home balance? Because this problem is more subjective than objective, there is one difference in the sequence of problem-solving steps. Basically, there are four steps to follow: (1) defining the problem, (2) defining the options and choosing the desired outcome, (3) gathering accurate relevant information, and (4) instituting a plan of action based on that data. In business problem solving, listing the outcome options normally follows gathering the relevant facts, but personal problems usually necessitate definition of the options and choosing the desired outcome before data gathering. The desired outcome dictates whether or not action should be taken. But be forewarned: an open mind and complete self-honesty are prerequisite to seeking a solution to the work/home balance, tapping into the dormant subjective assets of your humanness, and reducing the chronic guilt feelings.

The first two steps of this exercise—defining the problem and choosing the desired solution—are relatively easy. Most employees realize a work/home problem exists; they are bothered by their spouses' anger and their own guilt feelings. Research finds that feelings of guilt about families are common among executives, but most tend to define this problem in terms of someone and something else rather than in personal terms. They say their wives are unhappy because of the job or they nag because of the long hours. Such problem definition is an evasion of personal responsibility by off-loading onto another. Define the problem in specific, personal terms and admit ownership of it. A better statement of the situation might be: "My marital and family relationships are unhappy because of the work/home balance, and as a result I also am unhappy and experience guilt feelings." State the situation without assigning individual blame and focus on what is personally upsetting.

Then move on to step two by listing foreseeable outcomes of the situation. For example, without taking any action the circumstances might remain the same or become worse with continued or increased uneasy relationships and personal guilt; the situation rarely improves without action. At the extreme, divorce and dissolution of the home are possibilities. Status quo, escalation, and/or divorce are all negative, inactive options. If one of these is the desired outcome, the problem-solving process stops and no action is taken. But if the choice is to try to resolve or at least to ease the unhappiness and guilt, then action is required; and the problem-solving process moves to step three, gathering accurate, relevant information about the causes of the problem.

Here again, when searching for causes, keep it personal. Ask "How have my attitudes and actions contributed to the problems?" rather than "What does my spouse think and do to cause the problem?" A primary tenet in subjective problem solving is to realize that one individual cannot change another's attitudes and actions; each person can change only his or her own. With this in mind start by honestly exploring your personal motivations and behaviors in relation to the work/home balance.

Gathering Revelant Data

How do you evaluate yourself at balancing your personal and professional lives? Self-evaluation is difficult even for women, socialized to subjectivity. Most people evade such soul-searching unless or until some crisis occurs that makes it unavoidable. We all tend to picture ourselves as we would like to be, not as we really are. Facing up to the fact that we're not perfect can be rather disconcerting, throwing us into a tailspin. But unless we honestly recognize our motivations, priorities, goals, and behavior, our personal decisions are handicapped and unrealistic. A person with an inaccurate self-evaluation cannot make good personal choices, just as a businessperson with incorrect information cannot make good business decisions.

The contemporary public image of executives confuses many corporate employees; they have difficulty separating themselves from that public image. They become so engrossed in adapting to the image depicted by society, the corporation, and the media that they neglect the soul-searching required to determine who they really are, what is really important to them, and how to go about achieving personal satisfaction. Assuming the employee is male, society imposes objective, macho socialization; the corporation enhances these decisive, emotion-denying traits and initiates him into the career success syndrome; and advertising reaffirms behavior by emphasizing his importance and glorifying executive status. (Television advertises overnight mail to become a successful executive and stomach remedies once success is attained. Executive cologne, at forty-five dollars for four ounces, is available "for the chief executive or those merely aspiring to corporate distinction.") Adopting these publicly accepted attitudes and behaviors of the executive image may gratify one's ego, but it avoids self-examination, evades personal responsibility, and usually intensifies personal work/family problems.

Dr. Roy Menninger, president of the Menninger Foundation, wrote an article, "Responsibility to Self,"[1] about the need for executives to honestly examine and compare personal attitudes and values to personal behavior. In the article Dr. Menninger posed several questions as guides to gaining self-knowledge. Using his guidelines, I offer the following questions that relate directly to employees' work/home balance. All are subjective and require honest appraisal.

1. What are your life goals? Corporate employees are trained to define objective, long-range business and career goals; they strategize and outline the necessary actions and steps to succeed. Defining such business goals as making x amount of corporate profit in ten years is followed by action plans to increase sales and decrease expenses. A career goal of being CEO in twenty years is based on outlined accomplishments and promotions. But most corporate employees are unfamiliar with defining subjective, emotionally satisfying personal goals. The

meaning of life goals becomes clearer as one questions what he really wants to accomplish in life. Personal value systems are tested by asking such thought-provoking questions as which are more important, material things or emotional relationships, and what are one's personal priorities.

2. Do your priorities reflect in your actions? As stated earlier, every corporate employee I know swears first place to his family, but his actions often do not bear out this testimony. Dr. Menninger also commented on these public protestations to the importance of family and went on to say, "Indeed, it could be fairly said of many of you that you are married to your job, not your husbands or wives, that you are invested in your colleagues, not your children, that you are committed to your business, not your society. The point is not that these imbalances are wrong, but that it is quite probable that they are decidedly inconsistent with your own statements about what is important and what constitute your personal priorities."[2] B. C. Forbes, founder of *Forbes Magazine*, once compared ambition to a horse. If the rider keeps a proper rein and guides the horse, the horse can carry him far. But giving the horse too much rein can land the rider in a ditch. Do you give your ambition too much rein? Most dedicated executives put their own mental and physical needs last on the list of priorities. Ask yourself, "How do my actions compare to my stated priorities?"

3. From whom do you receive emotional support and to whom do you give such support? The word *emotional* is scary to most employees because many equate emotionalism with weakness. Early psychosexual socialization teaches that girls, the "weaker" sex, are emotional; they cry. Boys must never cry or exhibit emotion for fear of being a weak "sissy." In the corporate world "emotional" is a derogatory descriptive word that can se-

verely retard career advancement. Yet all human beings are emotionally sensitive; even men need emotional nurturing and occasional strokes to ensure psychological stability. Giving and receiving emotional support are not signs of weakness or inadequacy; emotional support is the essence of productive human existence. Who knows you best, shares your victories and defeats, feels your joys and sorrows? Who's always in your corner in your fight against the world? These are the ones who give the vital but usually unrecognized emotional support. But do you reciprocate or do you emotionally isolate yourself out of fear of appearing weak?

4. What is the quality and consistency of your marital and family relationships? Evaluate these personal relationships. Are you satisfied, or is something lacking? Can you depend on them for emotional support and, just as important, can they depend on you?

5. Is your sense of responsibility out of balance? Of necessity, most employees spend more time and energy working, but nights and weekends are presumed as family time. Do you allow your work habitually to infringe on home and family time? Do you accept the responsibility for these choices or do you off-load the responsibility by making alibis? Evaluate your decisions on long hours, travel, relocation, and other work-related issues. How often do work needs displace family needs and vice versa? Remember, honesty is mandatory to self-knowledge.

After plowing through these subjective questions, do your actions really reflect what is most important in your life? Regardless of your answer, you deserve congratulations for enduring the exercise, delving into the subjective nature of your being, and experiencing honest, emotional thought. In the scheme of applying objective, business problem-solving techniques to the personal problem of the work/home balance, confronting one's "self" is the "gathering accurate, relevant information" step. Now is the time to move into the final step of exploring and instituting action plans for improvement.

Maintaining Bridges

Communication is a bridge between two people. Like all bridges, communication requires attention and frequent maintenance to keep the connecting span in good working order. Communication is the basis of all interpersonal relationships, but it is vital for a rewarding marital relationship. In the business world communication is a skill, but in the home the skill must evolve into an art form that utilizes both the objective and subjective elements of human nature.

Babies are born with the ability to communicate based on their wants and needs. Mother and father instantly recognize hungry, happy, or hurting because baby lets them know by crying or smiling. Emotional sharing is inborn. Yet somewhere along the road to maturity this innate part of our nature becomes devalued, hidden deep inside in the effort to become strong, tough, commanding, and objectively decisive. Denying emotion is a decided asset in the business environment, but it can be a destructive liability in the home. The emotional bond between two people normally is the essence of the marriage. If emotional sharing through communication is allowed to lapse and fall into disuse, then the relationship itself is endangered. A gap occurs, leaving the spouse and possibly the children on one side and the employee on the other. The family becomes separate people who share the same living space but not their lives.

For job security corporate employees learn to communicate effectively with their peers and clients on an objective level. For psychological and familial well-being corporate employees must relearn the art of subjective, emotional sharing through communication. This is no easy task. One does not simply decide to start sharing feelings, emotions, and thoughts; it is not a machine that starts by flipping the "on" button. This type of communication doesn't just happen, it must be learned, worked at, and constantly maintained. Psychological counselors define maturity with two major components: the achievement of self-sufficiency and the acceptance of dependency. The word *dependency* relates to the human need to share an emotional bond with another. But our culture teaches men that emotions and dependency are negative traits; they must be unemotional, action-oriented, and completely independent. For most men it is indeed a difficult task to reactivate the long-dormant human trait of emotional sharing.

The sharing process begins with recognizing and accepting feelings and emotions as intrinsic to both men and women. Become aware of and comfortable with feeling and thinking. Ask "how do I feel?" as well as "what do I think?" about a specific issue. Feeling may seem the direct opposite of logic, but combining feeling with logical thinking often results in realistic appraisals and decisions at the office as well as at home. Having learned to accept feeling without embarrassment, the next level is learning to verbalize those feelings.

Verbalizing feelings is perhaps the most difficult part of the entire process for corporate employees. How does one express emotional feeling without appearing weak or sentimental? Keep in mind that we are talking about communicating with a spouse at home, not a working peer in the office. Most wives welcome knowing how you feel and what you think. Women normally view subjective talk as personally complimentary, as a way of saying "I trust you with my inner thoughts and feelings." Second, emotional sharing allows a wife to fulfill her socialized and perhaps biological need to nurture, to understand, and to encourage. Last and most important, communicating your feelings to your wife strengthens emotional bonds. As a general rule, the male fear of revealing feelings and being considered weak is totally unnecessary in the home; sensitive, intelligent women consider subjectivity an asset rather than a deficit, even in men. A man who is secure enough in his maleness to share his feelings is a treasure, not a handicap. Feelings are not a weakness; they are a strength.

Interpersonal communication usually encompasses words and actions, but expressing one's feelings doesn't have to be an overly emotional outburst or a weepy display of sentimentality. There are other methods that some find more comfortable, but just as effective. It is quite possible to communicate feelings while controlling emotions. A friend of mine who is a counselor related a personal incident with her adult son that showed this communication technique. The son had done something that made the mother extremely angry, and a confrontation followed. But instead of initiating an emotional tirade she stated clearly and simply that she was very angry with him and matter-of-factly told him what he had done and why she was angry. By this method my friend expressed her feelings, eased her anger, and felt much better; but she controlled her emotions and avoided a residue of bitterness between herself and her son. Businesspeople are adept at communicating plainly and unemotionally with clients; it's a matter of semantics. Why not use the same technique to express feelings in unemotional terms? "I am very angry with you" is much better than calling hateful names, and verbalizing the fact that you've had a rotten day at work is better than kicking the cat. It's a matter of what words are chosen and how they are used.

But remember that the communication bridge between two people is a two-way street; listening skills are as important as speaking skills. Once again, let's compare business listening skills to home listening skills. With the exception of casual conversation, most co-worker communication is problem-centered, usually business but sometimes personal. If it's business, you objectively hear all the facets of the problem and immediately go into the solving mode. The same is true if a co-worker comes to you with a personal problem. You hear him out, perhaps sympathize, perhaps make suggestions, but you're rarely upset about someone else's problem because it doesn't affect you on a personal level. Employees are usually comfortable with this objective style of communication—action-oriented problem solving. The situation is personally nonthreatening, you know what reaction is expected of you, and you are well trained to handle it.

However, many men become frustrated by purely subjective conversation with wives or children. For example, a tired man comes home from work to find a tense wife. After the children are in bed, she complains that the kids have been demons all day, leaving her nervous and exhausted; it's been a hard day. Husbands usually react in one of four ways in such a situation. The man who is in touch with his subjective nature can listen instead of just hearing. He realizes that when his wife tells him of her day it releases and eases her tension. He can't change his wife's bad day, but he can understand her feelings and empathize. The other reactions would ordinarily come from a man who is uncomfortable on a feeling level: (1) he hears her out and then either drops or changes the conversation, ignoring or being unaware of her need for consolation; (2) he reacts with anger— "Well, what do you want me to do about it?"; or (3) he falls back on familiar problem-solving techniques—"You have got to be more strict with them." These last reactions are normally rooted in the frustration of not being able to control the situation with positive actions as one does at the office. Lack of interest, anger, or patent solutions are defenses against the showing of feelings through concern, understanding, and love. Rather than recognizing that their wives are simply sharing emotions and asking for understanding and empathy, many objective men interpret the communication as a demand for physical actions or practical solutions. Anger especially is often a defensive reaction that masks feelings of helplessness.

Here are some basic guidelines regarding communication between husbands and wives:

1. Express your feelings; don't be afraid of revealing your inner thoughts and emotions. To feel is to be alive, and your spouse already knows you are human. It is quite possible to express feelings without being excessively emotional.

2. Listen for the other's feelings; don't just hear the words. Sometimes mere words do not convey the depth of emotional importance; listen for voice tone and watch for body language.

3. Practice understanding; don't always problem-solve. It's impossible to "solve" someone else's feelings; it's up to them to work through their own. Learn to empathize more and criticize less. If in doubt whether to under-

stand or problem-solve, trying understanding first. Your spouse will usually ask for your help if a solution is needed.

4. Have an open mind; don't be defensive. When talking over a sensitive issue, having an open mind can lead to mutual understanding and supportiveness, but defensiveness leads only to argument. If a person becomes defensive of his or her position, constructive communication ceases. The best solution is to point out the defensiveness and postpone discussion until another time when emotions have cooled. After both parties have had time to consider the issue and their reaction, the subject usually can be approached with more open-mindedness.

5. Accept your spouse as an individual with personal feelings, needs, and goals. She may be "your" wife, but she is her "own" person first. Don't tell her how she should feel, what she should want, or what she should do. This robs her of personhood.

6. Play fair. Leave your competitiveness for the office and the tennis court. Communication is not a game of one on one, with each trying to outscore the other. In true communication there is no winner or loser, so don't play King of the Hill.

Relearning emotional sharing and building or repairing gaps in the communication bridge takes time, dedication to the cause, and cooperation from one's spouse. If the communication gap began long ago and has widened over the years of corporate life, joint counseling should be considered. Resentment builds up over the years and needs release, but turning communication into a bitter sniping battle is very destructive to the relationship. Counselors are trained in communication techniques; they are moderators and facilitators who can lay out the ground rules of fair play and guide communication into constructive channels. A few sessions with a qualified counselor can teach a couple valuable communication techniques that outlast the basic issue, carry over into everyday application, and enrich personal and marital relationships. Many corporations now have employee assistance programs (EAP's) through which counseling might be obtained. These programs will be discussed in the final chapter of this book. But whether through company-sponsored programs or private sources, counseling can provide constructive guidance for the corporate couple wishing to restructure and revitalize their relationship.

Responding to a spouse's subjective feelings with objective communication techniques is at the root of corporate spouse resentment; she is left feeling cut off, shut out, and uncared for. It can severely damage the marital relationship and sometimes leads to divorce. Male corporate employees expect and indeed require understanding and support from their wives, but many men do not give or are unable to give understanding and support because it calls for verbal emotional sharing. But if a bridge of communication and emotional sharing is established and maintained throughout the corporate career, problems can be eased and midlife transitions can be less traumatic. However, this bridge requires considerable use to remain strong and stable. It is like good silver: the more you use it, the brighter it gleams; if stored away for future use, silver develops tarnish, and the communication bridge develops gaps. Dr. Menninger defined love as "a capicity to care. . . . it implies a willingness to invest ourselves in others, to be involved with them, to listen to them—in short, to care about them."[3]

The Positive Use of Spillover

When speaking of the positive use of spillover, I always recall songwriter Roger Miller's statement: "Some people feel the rain, others just get wet." In chapter 7 the types of spillover and its negative effects on the family were discussed. Most families "just get wet" from spillover. Spouses resent the corporation, its intrusion into the home, and their mate's devotion to career. Employees feel guilty about family neglect and become defensive of work activities by relying on alibis. Everyone loses: employees, spouses, and children. In chapter 7 the question of whether or not spillover is preventable was asked, and in my opinion the answer is that spillover is intrinsic to corporate life and cannot be prevented. But I believe that although spillover often has negative effects, it can be used more positively to "feel the rain" rather than "just get wet." Positive spillover can be an emotional link between an employee and his family that leads to sharing common life goals, establishing mutual understanding and supportiveness, and strengthening marital relationships.

Communication is the key. Many authors have used the door as a symbol of the barrier that they believe should exist between employees' private and professional lives. They state that when an employee enters the door of private life, the door should be closed on his professional life. I disagree with such a separation of the two lives because it divides an employee down the middle, fragmenting his or her wholeness and personality. The communication key unlocks the dividing door, acknowledges the importance of the work life, and accepts both the private and professional sectors as aspects of the employee's entirety rather than distinct divisions. The success of positive spillover depends on the employee's willingness to share his professional life with his spouse and the spouse's willingness to participate in that life. Mutual trust, respect, and confidentiality are essential to this sharing; business discussed at home must remain at home. But with these prerequisites, using spillover positively through communication can benefit both employee and spouse.

A good starting point to using spillover positively is to talk with your spouse about your ambitions, career goals, and feelings about your work. Give her the opportunity to realize how important your job is to you, not just how important you are to the job. Enlist and show appreciation for her support based on understanding and caring rather than duty and obligation. In short, invite her partnership, participation, and assistance in mutually defined life and career goals and let her know that you value her opinions and contributions.

Next share information about the job, the environment, and work peers. Taking fifteen minutes at day's end to share work events, problems, and interactions can act as an outlet for an employee's built-up stress and provide a cooling down process to facilitate the transition to home life in mind as well as body. But one must remember that the object is to share, not to use the spouse as a dumping ground for all of the day's anger and frustrations. Second, although the spouse isn't directly involved in the work situation, her somewhat disinterested opinions can provide a different view of the situation that often stimulates new thoughts. Regardless of the spouse's response, merely verbalizing the issue helps the employee clarify and focus his thoughts. Finally, spouses need to know and understand more about their mates' professional lives to avoid social blunders at business/social affairs. Merely being familiar with names and positions of work peers can mitigate discomfort, and even a surface knowledge of business projects enables a spouse to follow the conversation.

There are three major advantages of positive spillover for both employee and spouse. First, positive spillover enables spouses to become more familiar with the company and its policies and problems. A corporation profoundly influences the lives of spouses and children through its policies and job requirements, and many of these influences are negative. For this reason many spouses tend to blame the company for all of the negatives of their life-style without stopping to consider the benefits and opportunities the company provides. Through positive spillover families gain more knowledge about the company's functions and its reasoning. With this knowledge families become more understanding of the "whys" and less antagonistic toward the company.

The second important advantage is that through communication a spouse becomes more involved in and develops a better understanding of the employee's professional life. She begins to realize that the work is not just a job; it is her mate's career and therefore vitally important to his personal sense of well-being as well as to the family's security. This realization often alters a spouse's attitude toward the employee and the work. Understanding the demands and importance of work life doesn't necessarily bring acquiescence to or agreement with those demands, but it can temper reactions. Most spouses welcome knowing more about their husband's "other" life and value the trust he shows through the sharing.

The final advantage of using spillover in a more positive manner is that it encourages an employee to diligence in balancing work and family as spouses and children become more appreciative of his efforts and more understanding of the problem. It's not easy to be the employee in the middle, with work pulling one arm and the family pulling the other; maintaining difficult equilibrium requires strength. But a family's appreciation and understanding rewards the effort. Using spillover in an honest, positive manner can set up a chain reaction: communication → understanding → appreciation → diligent effort → improved work/home balance.

Spillover is a given in the lives of corporate couples, but the effects of spillover depend on the individuals involved. Positive spillover must be based on personal integrity; the motivation should be an honest effort for improvement, not a self-serving sales pitch. It demands willing, reciprocal communication between employee and spouse, both sharing and receiving. Positive spillover will not solve all problems, but it will help corporate families to "feel the rain" rather than "just get wet."

Be Practical

Corporate employees are normally good "people" persons; that is, they enjoy others, they are considerate of others, and they know how to interact with others for mutual benefit. These qualifications are necessary for successful corporate careers, and the same qualifications are necessary for success in marital and family relationships. So let's look at the problem of the work/home equation with a little more objectivity. Let's be practical and apply some business acumen to relationships with spouses and children.

1. Common courtesy. Business relations are based on courtesy, and it pays big dividends. But employees often forget that showing respect and courtesy to family members is even more important because it involves long-term relationships. Business deals are here today, gone tomorrow, but family is forever. The much used quote from *Love Story*, "Love is never having to say you're sorry," has misled an entire generation of young Americans. Love is frequently saying you're sorry, meaning it, and striving never to do the same misdeed again. To assume the understanding of another is avoidance of personal responsibility. Remember to show spouse and children at least the same concern and courtesy you would show a business client.

2. Use the telephone. Telephones are communication tools and are invaulable in business dealing, and the same is true in family dealing. Simply picking up the phone and taking two minutes to communicate can calm fears, cool angers, cancel hurts, and cement relationships. Your plane arrives late—call home; you're detained at the office—call home. If the party runs longer than planned, excuse yourself, find a telephone, and quickly call your spouse; no one will ever know. Frequent calls home while on business trips can lessen the distance, and a no-reason call in the middle of the workday translates into caring. A call requires thoughtfulness but takes little time and effort. The telephone is one of the world's great inventions; take advantage of it.

3. Time management. Schedule time for spouse and family, and don't let work infringe unless it's a dire emergency. Businesspeople would never think of arriv-

ing two hours late for an appointment or canceling an important meeting with a lame excuse about family obligations. But employees often arrive home late or cancel family outings and celebrations with a perfunctory "I have to work." Time management is a hallmark of successful corporate people—why not apply the same importance in managing time with the family? Let them know you do have time for them. Our daughters used to have a standing date with their dad. Each Saturday morning Dad and one daughter went out to breakfast together. The girls are grown now, but they still fondly recall their Saturday morning dates with Dad. Mortimer R. Feinberg, psychologist and author, and Aaron Levenstein, professor of management at Baruch College, wrote: "If an executive decides that family responsibilities are tasks that only he can handle, then the home can take as firm a place in his schedule of activities as any other of his non-delegable activities. And the same principle applies as with all other non-delegable tasks: If a conflict of demands requires that one must be neglected at a given moment, there is a clear understanding that the executive must compensate for the omission at the earliest possible moment."[4]

4. Sales pitches and orders. Nothing infuriates and hurts spouses more than being manipulated like business clients or managed like secretaries. It puts the marital relationship on a professional level and is devoid of personal feelings and involvement. The spouse normally feels degraded, as if she is no more important to you than anyone else. Sales pitches are common when relocation is proposed. Talk with her about the issue; don't try to sell her on it.

5. Honest dealing. Share your professional life with your family. You care about your spouse and children and want to know what goes on in their lives. The same

is true of them; they care about you and want to know about your life too. When work/home conflicts arise, discuss them honestly and openly. Hiding behind alibis is rewarded by distrust. Family members instinctively recognize alibis for what they are—lame excuses—and most spouses and children feel patronized and betrayed by alibis. Don't take advantage of your family's trust in you by using excuses just because you don't want to be the "bad guy." Being an honest "bad guy" is better than being an untrustworthy husband or parent.

6. Closing the deal. When negotiating a contract, that contract must be beneficial to both parties. If you want love, understanding, and support from your spouse, you must be willing to give love, understanding, and support to her. Modern corporate marriages survive better as partnerships than as autonomies. The secret to all good contracts is mutual understanding, mutual support, and mutual benefit. The same is true of good corporate marriages.

An executive can transfer many, but not all, business skills to the home. Communication and people-handling skills, especially, must be subjective and more personal, but these skills can be usefully transferred to work. The combination of emotional sharing, positive spillover, and practicality can produce improved marital and family relationships. And as these relationships improve, the home/work balance normally improves too. Even though the scales sometimes tilt, honesty in these relationships promotes understanding, which in turn moderates an employee's feelings of guilt. As a corporate man would say, "It's a win-win situation."

11

THE CORPORATE SPOUSE

ACTOR OR
REACTOR?

For many years writers and researchers described wives as the long-suffering victims in the corporate game. In most cases this depiction was appropriate. This was the role to which the wife was reared, and she executed her duties to perfection. It was easy to describe her, to feel sorry for her, and to be angry about her plight, because most wives quietly fulfilled their prescribed destinies without complaint. Those who refused to play victims were few, and those few were openly criticized by both society and other corporate wives. But women are finding that this traditional role is neither gratifying nor rewarding; in fact, living the corporate game by traditional rules is often psychologically destructive. Although many women tenaciously hold to tradition, others are creating new roles for themselves. These spouses still encounter the same problems and demands, but they do not quietly accept the circumstances and react in the prescribed manner. They are demanding recognition as individuals and equal partners in their marriages. Which are you? Do you play a meaningful role in the corporate game or are you simply part of the game equipment? Are you an actor or a reactor?

Reactor Spouses

The first two sections of this book outlined the general career levels of corporate employment and the problems common to the life-style. Each chapter discussed both the positive and negative repercussions that might occur for employees, spouses, and families. Often these effects seem overwhelmingly negative, especially for spouses. Loneliness, anger, bitterness, hostility, responsibility overload, depression, loss of identity—the list of negative effects seems dreadfully endless. One wonders how spouses arrive at such circumstances and why they endure it. Were they reared to masochism?

No, women haven't been socialized specifically to masochism, but I believe instilled psychosexual mores have inadvertently led to this aberration. Women sometimes become victims of their own choices because those choices are founded on socially accepted female rules and roles that in earlier times and social environments might have contributed to a women's personal happiness and fulfillment. But these traditional rules and roles are inappropriate and indeed are often detrimental to modern women in the corporate environment.

Traditional socialization of male dominance and female dependence leads to subconscious acceptance by women of such folklore as the husband is the breadwinner and the wife is the homekeeper; a wife goes where the husband's job takes him; the marriage relationship is the wife's responsibility; a woman is nothing without

her man; and a man's home is his castle. How often have
women heard the Bible story of Ruth and her mother-
in-law misapplied to the situation of wives saying to
husbands, "I'll go where you go. Your people will be
my people." Female dependence is often based on socialized insecurity: women subconsciously doubt their
ability to survive without a man's beneficence. In the
corporate marriage a spouse who chooses to comply with
the traditional, who chooses to accept her husband's
dominance, and who chooses to be dependent also may
be choosing to be a victim.

No sane person consciously chooses victimism; it isn't
a life goal or a considered decision. A woman begins her
life as a corporate wife with all good intentions and much
love; she does what she was told would bring happiness.
She wants to be a good wife and mother, a helpmate to
her husband and a role model for the children. She sees
herself as a glowing example of womanhood, certainly
not an unsuspecting victim. But her path to victimism
is much like her husband's staircase to success: one step
leads to another, and each is taken because of someone
else's need. She was taught to nurture others, to sub-
merge her needs and fulfill the needs of others, to be
the good wife and mother. She was taught to be a reactor, and victimism is the destination of most reactor
corporate wives. Let's consider the personal traits of a
corporate wife at each progressive step toward victimism.

Step One: No personal goals—"Your success is my
success." Many spouses enter corporate marriage unprepared for the life, their heads and hearts filled with romantic dreams of devoted husband, bright children, and
a lovely suburban cottage with swing set and sandbox in
the backyard. Their only personal goal is "happiness" that

can be obtained only through the happiness of others: happy husband, happy marriage, happy children, and happy home. Therefore, Mrs. Reactor devotes herself to supporting the goals of her husband and children; their life is her life, and their happiness is her happiness. This is the traditionally supportive wife referred to in part I. She is not a career woman. Although she may work, usually part-time, the happiness and success of her husband and children are the purpose and focus in her life.

Step Two: No personal time—"You come first." Mrs. Reactor is so busy facilitating success and happiness for others that she has little time left for personal interests and growth. Usually, she is a very busy lady, but her activities center on doing for others: shirts to the laundry, planning company parties, driving to the airport, chauffeuring the kids, working for the PTA benefit. Since she has no specific personal goals, any leftover time is spent with friends or on hobbies, but husband and family duties always come first. She immediately cancels her plans to accommodate others; she is always available for duty. If employed, she is supermom and superwife, working all day but maintaining the home as if she had no other job. This reaction encourages and abets corporate employees' long work hours and travel and results in responsibility overload and loneliness.

Step Three: Displacement of personal wants and needs—"You're more important." As Mrs. Reactor progresses down her path to victimism, she invariably allows her needs and desires to be displaced by those of husband and children. Mrs. Reactor was taught that "good" wives must be supportive, understanding, and caring, so she supports, understands, and cares to the point of self-sacrifice. *Their* needs always take priority.

She rationalizes this reaction by telling herself that their needs are important, hers are unimportant, and that "it really doesn't matter." But subconsciously, it really does matter. This displacement of personal wants and needs often results in anger, bitterness, and hostility toward the company, her mate, and herself. Of course, all of these emotions are internalized, unexpressed for fear of being selfish and causing unhappiness for others. This spouse reaction commonly applies to long hours, travel, relocation. His career and success is more important than her own well-being. Career women who give up their jobs and relocate for a mate's career are especially vulnerable to anger and bitterness while trying to secure a position in the new location. Displacement of personal wants and needs is the first major sign in becoming a victim.

Step Four: Abdication of self-responsibility—"You know best." Since her husband is the breadwinner and dominant member of the family, Mrs. Reactor puts her life in his hands, hoping that whatever he decides will be best for her and the children. Even when she feels the decision is wrong, she is afraid to challenge it because such a challenge might damage his career and cause problems in her marriage. Therefore, she accepts whatever he decides, giving him complete responsibility for the lives of the entire family, including her own. As cited earlier, this spouse reaction is almost traditional in corporate marriages when relocation is comtemplated. Even though she may oppose the move, may know it will be harmful, and may never really agree to the move, she rarely says no. What she does say is "You know best." In her efforts to please others and ensure their success, Mrs. Reactor relinquishes self-responsibility and self-determination. She allows her husband or others to make decisions that vitally effect her life. She goes along, and in doing so she loses her sense of self.

Final Step: No power or control of personal life—"You hurt me." With this final step Mrs. Reactor arrives at her destination: victimism. She feels locked into her situation, buffeted by circumstances, and powerless to act. All of the anger, bitterness, and hostility internalized along the path surfaces, and depression usually results. She feels victimized by the corporation, the corporate life-style, and her husband, and indeed she is a victim. But most corporate victims never realize they allowed themselves to become victims by slowly giving up their personhood and putting responsibility for their lives into their husbands' hands.

As stated in chapter 9, I consider loss of self to be the most personally harmful of all possible risks, and loss of self is a hallmark of most reactor spouses. Mrs. Reactor *continually* displaces her personal needs and submerges her feelings in order to help her husband attain his needs and goals. In doing so she loses touch with her inner self. Such people eventually become unable to define personal goals, needs, desires, opinions, and even their identity except through someone else. I somewhere read this description that is typical of a person out of touch with her inner self: "She never knew what she wanted, only what she didn't want. But, in life, unlike math, two negatives do not produce a positive."

In defining loss of self the key word is *continually.* The danger lies in always, every time, giving up one's own needs to meet the needs of others. There are many times in life when others' needs must take precedence over our own, and sometimes we put others first simply because it makes us feel good about ourselves. The situation that causes concern is when a woman never acts for herself but only reacts to someone else. In the corporate marriage and life-style it's difficult for a spouse to hold onto a strong sense of self. The much easier path is to let husband and corporation take responsibility for her. All she has to do is react to their expectations and fit into their mold; life isn't so bumpy that way. Yes, the path to victimism is the easiest, but most corporate spouses pay an extremely costly personal toll at the destination.

In Search of Self

Losing touch with one's inner self is at the base of most of the ill effects spouses encounter in a corporate marriage. In my opinion loss of self is the principal factor in the depression that is so prevalent among corporate wives. But the loss isn't irreversible; a sense of self can be regained. Sometimes crisis, such as depression, intervenes and makes the retrieval of self mandatory for psychological survival. In such cases professional counseling is needed; other people freely choose and greatly benefit from counseling assistance. Many corporations now offer EAPs, through which counseling might be obtained. But for the majority of women, getting in touch with one's inner self comes through personal determination and effort. Regardless of the method, it is not a simple task. Women are taught dependency, and dependent relationships retard personal growth and self-knowledge, as well as undermining the sense of self.

As a preamble, it must be understood that having a sense of self, or authenticity, is not the same as being self-centered or selfish. Authenticity might be defined as coming from the center of one's being, the knowing of who and what you are. It is the capacity of being individual while maintaining the ability to have close, caring, interdependent relationships. Self-centeredness results when concentration on self becomes so engrossing as to deny, block, or damage loving relationships with others. Self-centeredness is Superman and Superwoman, so involved with doing their own "thing" that they become incapable of relating to another on an emotional level.

There are three equally important aspects to having a sense of self: self-knowledge, self-management, and self-responsibility. All three sound awesome. Thoughts of Shakespeare's "to thine own self be true" come to mind and raise the specter of profound philosophy. This alone is enough to frighten the faint-hearted, but finding out about oneself need not be so difficult. Self-knowledge is honestly analyzing thoughts, actions, and personality in order to define strengths, weaknesses, goals, needs, and feelings. It is simply being honest with yourself about yourself.

Among corporate spouses loneliness is a major and valid complaint. Loneliness is especially troublesome for those who have lost touch with their inner selves. Such people experience loneliness more deeply because they are cut off from themselves as well as from others. But solitude is essential to self-exploration and self-knowledge, and these lonely times are a good place to begin the search for self. Learn to be alone instead of lonely. Reactor spouses often rely so much on others for meaning in life, for fulfillment of needs, and for pleasure that when alone they feel abandoned, empty, and unloved. They

feel anonymous, without identity or purpose. Feelings
of loneliness can be quite frightening. Aloneness, on the
other hand, can be energizing and revitalizing when one
uses the time to get acquainted with the inner self. Analyze and evaluate yourself, your situation, and how you
came to be where you are; assess what is happening in
your life, both inwardly and outwardly. Are you satisfied with the course of your life or are you unhappy and
depressed? Do you control your life or do you simply
react when someone else pulls your string? Define what
you want to do with your life and what you want from
life.

The most important aspect of self-knowledge is this
definition of purpose, of what is important to you as a
person. But merely knowing yourself changes nothing;
acting on that knowledge is the substance of a sense of
self. Learn to set personal goals. Those goals may be going
back to school or starting a business. Or they may be
the same goals you have always subconsciously worked
toward, for example, being supportive for the accomplishments of husband and children. That's okay; just
make sure you consciously set this goal for yourself and
realize that this goal is your personal choice, rather than
your sacrifice.

Self-management, the second part of the sense of self,
is just as necessary as self-knowledge. Nena and George
O'Neill wrote, "If you don't manage yourself, then by
default either circumstances or other people will manage you."[1] Corporate spouses are good managers; they
have to be. Of necessity they manage the home, family,
and usually the finances, and many work full-time outside the home. They are always scurrying, but usually
they scurry to someone else's demands. Such reactors

allow husbands and children to dictate the course and circumstances of their lives; then they complain of lack of control. By letting others make decisions for her, a reactor gives away control over her life; then if the decisions prove adverse, she blames those "others" for her misery. Self-management is taking control of your own life, determining your own course, and making your own decisions. This doesn't mean selfishly demanding your own way; sometimes self-management is compromise or even compliance with the wishes of someone else. The important point is to know you made the decision to act independently—to compromise or to comply. John D. Rockefeller once said, "There is no feeling in this world to be compared with self-reliance. Do not sacrifice that to anything else." A woman manages her own life when she makes her own choice, whatever that choice might be.

The final necessary ingredient for a sense of self is self-responsibility. There is an old saying, "You made your own bed, now lie in it," which essentially means to take responsibility for your own actions and life. Once you know what you want and decide your course, you must take responsibility for the outcome, good or bad. There can be no off-loading the blame onto others. Self-responsibility is based on courage and maturity. It means you are accountable to yourself for yourself; you are able to explain your actions and accommodate the results of those actions without excuses. Self-responsibility gives one security; you know you can and will, if necessary, take care of yourself.

It is difficult, but not impossible, to maintain a strong sense of self within a corporate marriage. The essence of self lies in knowing you have a choice, making a choice, and owning responsibility for that choice. It is not the decision that counts; it's realizing you made it.

Supportiveness and
The Modern Spouse

Supportive is not an obscenity. Previously in this book, the word has been used in reference to the traditionally supportive wife whose whole life revolves around husband and children. Some are happy and satisfied with their lives; others, such as the reactor wives, are unhappy. It is my belief that all wives in marriages based on mutual love and caring are supportive, regardless of how they are categorized: unemployed or employed, traditional or modern, reactor or actor. Sacrifice is not a synonym for support; there are other ways of being supportive without being sacrificial.

In *The Gamesman* Michael Maccoby quoted one gamesman as saying, "It is very unusual for someone to get ahead in the corporate world if his wife does not support him."[2] The executives surveyed for *The Cox Report on the American Corporation* cited that "being supportive and encouraging" was the most effective way that their spouses aid their careers.[3] Whether admitted or not, most wives are just as intelligent and success-oriented as their executive husbands, and regardless of her personal employment status every corporate wife I've met thinks her husband's career success is important and supports him in his efforts. But this support can take many different forms. In addition, whether admitted or not, corporate men depend, but are never completely dependent, on their wives for career support, and most of these men are supportive in return. The form and degree of individual or mutual supportiveness within a corporate marriage is relative to the relationship itself.

The type of support given by today's corporate spouses is as individual as the spouses themselves. In the past most wives supported their husbands in more physical and objective ways, such as moving, entertaining, and relieving them of home and parental obligations. They understood little about their husbands' jobs or careers, and many didn't particularly want to know or understand. But circumstances in the corporate marriage are changing. Although corporate spouses of all ages still support their husbands in many or all of the traditional physical forms, they are becoming more aware that psychological support for a husband's career is just as important and sometimes more important than moving across country, attending a company party, or staying at home while he travels. Women with a strong sense of self and a marriage based on mutual love are forging innovative ways to be supportive without sacrificing themselves on the altar of career. And the marital relationship usually benefits.

Mutual psychological support springs from communication, mutual sharing of personal feelings, goals, and dreams. It is working together as a team rather than living separate lives. Find out what makes him tick, how he feels about his work, and what he wants from his career. Understand and accept his need for achievement. It's important to his ego, it's part of his personality, and it's probably what attracted you to him in the first place. Encourage him to talk with you; learn to listen willingly and intelligently. Every corporate spouse knows that work spills over into the home, so why not make positive use of it? Sincerely ask about his work and what is going on to cause his moods. Find out about this man to whom you're married.

Just as important, give him a chance to learn more about you: how and what you think about yourself and the marriage, what you really want to accomplish with your life, and what is necessary for your fulfillment and personal identity. Tell him that you expect him to be as supportive of your needs and goals as you are of his. Be specific and don't talk in euphemisms. Instead of relating that you want to be "happy," tell him in exact terms what you believe will make you happy: a better home/work balance, remodeling the kitchen, going to work or back to school. Many spouses have trouble being open with their husbands; such reactor wives tell only what they think their husbands want to hear. Is it any wonder that numbers of husbands don't really know their wives, only their own image of them? Tell him how you feel and what you want. Don't expect him to read your mind; tell him. And don't try to read his mind; ask him.

Supportiveness often takes different forms for unemployed and employed spouses, but this doesn't necessarily mean that one is better than the other. Unemployed wives have more time and energy to assist their husbands' careers. But the difference between the modern unemployed spouse and the traditional unemployed spouse is attitude. I found in interviews that most modern wives exhibit a stronger sense of self than in the past. Even though they don't work outside the home and they give both physical support and psychological support to their mates, most wives realize the importance of being independent within an interdependent relationship. One unemployed wife in her early thirties stated, "When he takes a bow, I take a bow too." She was saying that she and her husband are in this together, and they both realize and acknowledge her contributions to his career. They work as a team, and both are finding fulfillment. And why not? It is her choice not to work at a paying job, she shares the rewards of his accomplishments, and she does whatever she can to assist his career. But she is not dependent on him to make her life worthwhile, and there are limits beyond which she refuses to go. There are sometimes conflicts, but the relationship remains strong and steady, interdependent rather than spouse dependent, mutually supportive rather than spouse supportive.

Working or career spouses normally offer more psychological than physical support simply as a matter of logistics. After a full day at work they have less time and energy for physical support. It takes time, effort, and hard work to plan, give, and clean up after a company party. Working wives can offer little of this kind of support. Moving, in particular, causes problems. What the working spouse can and does give is psychological support, empathy, and comradeship. Being in the business world herself, her understanding of his need for achievement and his career demands is sharper; she can relate better to his professional life than the unemployed wife can. The reverse is also true; husbands can relate more easily to the lives of working wives than unemployed wives. Dual-career couples have a shared link between their lives that single-career couples rarely have. The success of the dual-career marriage often depends as much on mutual support as on mutual love, but even then most dual-career corporate marriages encounter severe problems.

Mutual supportiveness is based on mutual caring, respect, honesty, and understanding. The concept of being mutually supportive is general, not necessarily constant. There are times when one gives or receives more support than the other, times when one must give in for the sake of the marriage, times when a stalemate prevails and hurt feelings result. This is reality. But it is the norm that affects the relationship, not the singular events.

Talking It Over

Communication is a major source of conflict in most marriages, according to a study conducted in the middle 70s by the Family Service Association of America. Of the couples interviewed, 87 percent pinpointed communication as a primary problem; sex (44 percent) and money (37 percent) rated much lower. Many people think that to communicate is to give information, and this is often the basis of problems between wife and husband. The English word *communicate* derives from the Latin word *cummunicare,* which means "share," and sharing entails giving and receiving. When both married partners communicate, they share information with each other; each must be as willing to listen as to talk. Marital communication should be talking with, not talking to. It is much harder to accomplish than communication between people of the same sex because of the previously mentioned difference in socialization—subjective versus objective. In addition to talking and listening, successful communication involves accepting without argument or criticism the validity of the other's feelings and opinions. Here are some commonsense guidelines that women might use to facilitate the bridging of sexual communication gaps.

    1. Learn to express yourself more objectively. Cor-

porate wives often state that they can't "get through" to their husbands and often come away feeling stupid and inane. Practice using as few "feeling" words as possible. For example, when discussing impersonal, unemotional issues and events, say "in my opinion" or "I think" instead of "I feel" or "I sense"; most men relate better to opinions and thoughts than to feelings. Remember that men learn to surpress feelings, and in the business environment feelings are taboo. Some men automatically close down the minute "feel" comes into the conversation.

2. When verbalizing feelings, be specific. Men are used to dealing in specifics, not abstracts. If there's a problem, he needs to know exactly what caused it and how it developed. When relating feelings, women often get so wrapped up in the emotions that the reasons become obscure. Take time to think the feeling through by, first, identifying exactly what you feel—angry, sad, hurt, happy, whatever—and, second, what brought on the feeling. When verbalizing, state both how and why you feel. Example: "I feel hurt and angry when you stop for a drink with the guys and forget to call. I feel unimportant to you."

3. Verbalize without accusations and listen without defensiveness. Now is the time to use "I feel." Feelings come from within yourself; those feelings may result from someone else's actions, but other people don't dictate your feelings. Take responsibility for your own feelings, "I am angry" or "I am hurt," rather than accusing, "You make me angry" or "You hurt me." Accusations immediately put people, male or female, on the defensive. When he talks, listen with an open mind, not with a chip on your shoulder. The purpose of communication is better understanding, and understanding requires open-

mindedness. If he says you nag too much, accept his feeling as valid whether you nag too much or not. Defensiveness leads to argument.

4. Verbalize rather than act out emotions. Above all, control your emotions. Don't cry or become angry. Emotional acting-out cancels the issue under discussion as both parties focus on the action rather than the issue involved. Overreacting emotionally stops communication, and the basic problem remains unresolved. If emotions erupt, try to agree to postpone the issue until another time when emotions are calmer.

5. Don't beat a dead horse. This is perhaps the most common error wives make in communicating with husbands. Feeling they are not "getting through," they go on and on and on trying to make themselves understood. Be sensitive to your husband's body language, and the minute his eyes, posture, or movements show you he has clicked out or shut down, stop. Better yet, stop before you see these signs. Remember that communication is not just one person bombarding the other with words. Businesspeople are very conscious of time, and their conversations are concise and to the point. Your husband will listen better if you state what you have to say without overkill and then shut up and let him think about it. He'll tell you if he doesn't understand.

6. Choose an appropriate time for communication. The time can make or break communication efforts. Unless the matter is urgent, don't call him during work hours or force conversation immediately on his arrival at home. Most businesspeople resent unnecessary interruptions from home during the workday, and once at home most need time to unwind and relax. Many corporate wives find that after dinner, early morning, or weekends are the best times. Never start an important or

sensitive conversation knowing you will be interrupted in a short time; urgency often short-circuits good communication skills.

7. Play fair. Communication isn't competition, trying to score points and defeat the opponent. It is sharing of information for better mutual understanding, problem solving, and general conversation. Snide, sarcastic, and intentionally hurtful remarks lead only to resentment, ego damage, and impasse. Don't play Queen of the Hill.

Establishing communication or reestablishing lapsed communication takes time and patience. Professional counseling is helpful and often needed. If the problems are severe but the relationship is good, professional counseling can facilitate communication efforts. Talking it over is not a cure-all for the problems that arise in the corporate marriage. It increases understanding, but it cannot alter anything. Improving communication and understanding is a good starting point, but only change changes.

Choices and Changes

In reviewing the written material for and about corporate wives during the 1960s and most of the 70s, I'm always amused and more than a little angered by the advice given to wives by some of the well-respected writers who just happen to be male. Their sage opinions included being patient until your husband retires, getting involved in community volunteer work, and accepting your husband's gifts and favors. One insightful writer was much more practical: if you're lonely or afraid when your husband is out of town, buy a dog and install a burglar alarm. In other words, quit griping and make the best of your situation; it's not so bad. Blanket advice can be dangerous. Individual personalities and situations differ; what works for one person might destroy another's life. My only advice to corporate wives is to realize that each woman has choices in her life.

When speaking of living the corporate game, women so often state, "I had no choice," and each woman honestly believes this. There are times when this statement is true; no one chooses birth, accidents, death, or other people's actions that may affect our lives. But adults can and do choose the course of their own lives; everyone has options about the way life is lived. When a person feels there is no choice, it's usually because that person is unwilling to take the risk and pay the personal price that another option might demand. In saying "I have no choice," you are in reality making a choice. You are choosing to let circumstances or someone else make your choice for you and control your life; you choose dependence over independence and reaction over action.

The choices of life are not always to our liking; sometimes we face situations in which all options seem negative. In such situations we still choose whether to (1) do nothing, let circumstances control, and endure the consequences, or (2) choose a course of action, take the risk, and work to improve the situation. In the corporate marriage, relocation usually presents such a situation. Both the company and the employee want the spouse to move, but the spouse doesn't want to go. The spouse faces three difficult options: (1) acquiesce, let the mate and company make the decision, and hope for the best; (2) refuse to move, take control of her own life but risk damaging the marriage and career; or (3) search for viable compromises, which in this case are usually few or nonexistent. I would speculate that in 90 percent of such situations spouses choose to go along with the move. The important point of this scenario is not the choice that is made; the importance lies in knowing that she made the choice and owning the responsibility for that choice. Even if she moves when she really doesn't want to, she retains control over her own life by realizing that in this instance she chose to let others determine her life's course.

Spouses are usually ambiguous about their corporate life-styles; they like some facets of it and dislike others. They enjoy the good and cope with the bad, thinking there is nothing they can do to change the circumstances. There are times in everyone's life when coping is necessary; we cope until we can do something to improve the situation. But coping as a way of life is reactive living; it is the middle ground between moving forward or backward. Coping accomplishes nothing but maintenance; it neither solves problems nor changes situations. But changes involve risks, even if those changes are personal.

If a person is unhappy with the course of her present life and if some crisis forces her or she independently decides to make changes in the way she lives her life, those personal changes will echo through her marriage, her husband's career, and her relationships with others. These are the risks a corporate wife must consider when deciding to assert her sense of self and take control of and responsibility for her own life. In close, ongoing relationships such as marriage a change in the behavior of one person of necessity causes a change in the behavior of the other. Personal change upsets the existing balance in a relationship, and a new balance must be found for the relationship to continue. The mate's reaction to a spouse's change may be very positive; he may recognize the personal growth, welcome it, and be willing to seek a new balance. Or his reaction may be very negative; he may feel frightened, threatened, and insecure with her new assertiveness.

According to Nena and George O'Neill, if the change of one affects the other negatively, then the changer has three options: (1) give up the change and go back to the former relationship balance, (2) divorce, which brings both emotional and economic impact, or (3) gamble on the change, encourage the partner to change, and try for a new, more equitable relationship.[4] This third option, the reformed relationship, is the renegotiated marriage pattern mentioned in chapter 2.

Choosing change is risky, and a spouse should evaluate the risks, be willing to face and accommodate the outcome, and decide if the gamble is worthwhile. Dependent, reactor spouses may long for change, but they often retain their familiar marriage patterns out of fear of unguaranteed outcomes. The O'Neills believe that if the relationship is based on caring and sharing, couples can adapt to almost any change with positive results. Psychotherapist and author Maryanne Vandervelde says there is much evidence to support this belief and optimistically states, "A wife who tries to combine some measure of freedom with her corporate role tends to bring life and excitement and stimulation into her marriage. This almost always results in better communication, and if the marriage has any solidity at all, the relationship will be enhanced."[5]

Changing the course of one's life doesn't just happen; it occurs only over time and through personal determination and systematic effort. Each individual must choose for herself if, why, and how she changes, but there are some general and rather abstract suggestions one might consider in making these choices. First, let the past go. The present is life; the past is gone and the future is maybe. For all of us the past consists of joys and regrets; retain the joys as pleasant memories, but release the regrets because they can negate the present and future. Preoccupation with "if only I had or had not" accomplishes nothing. As for the future, today's plans and dreams for tomorrow are wise and constructive, giving purpose and direction to life. But dreams alone accomplish nothing; it is the active living of today that attains the goals for tomorrow. The O'Neills said it best: "Time spent in regretting missed opportunities makes us triple losers: we can't change the past, we lose present living time and we affect the future."[6]

Next search for, develop, and retain your sense of self. Self is your most precious possession; be proud and vigilant of it. Find out about yourself, set priorities for yourself, and be protective of that self. Whether you choose to change your life's direction or not, reclaim intimacy with and responsiblity for yourself. Loss of one's sense of self is a silent but malignant disease that preys on unsuspecting victims. Supportiveness does not have to be sacrificial.

If or as you change and take more control of your life, beware of overacting to the point of selfishness. Carefully consider the issues on which you make a stand; compromise and compliance are choices too. Totally abdicating your role as corporate spouse can be extremely hurtful and embarrassing for your husband. If the relationship is important to you, temper your change with consideration. Distinguish between the personally damaging and personally rewarding parts of your role; make the most of the best and work on the rest.

Finally, refine your sense of humor. Corporate life situations are sometimes seriously silly. I recall one such incident in my own marriage. A niece was coming for a visit, and my husband and I were to meet her at a certain location. When we arrived, the teenager was nowhere to be found. Visibly upset and thinking I had misunderstood the instructions, my husband exploded: "Incompetence. I'm used to incompetence at work, but this level of incompetence . . ." My first reaction was anger, but as I looked at him, so pompously serious and businesslike, I broke out in laughter and threatened to pour a soda on him. It relieved the tension, and he too laughed as he realized how silly his reaction was. Then we took constructive action on the situation. The niece had forgotten where she was to meet us. My husband and I often recall this incident with shared laughter. A sense of humor is an asset in all marriages, but in the corporate marriage it's almost a necessity. Humor can often neutralize an explosive situation. Most important, learn to laugh at yourself.

In the corporate marriage based on mutual respect and caring, the spouse's purpose for change will be resolution, not revolution. The goal is mutual supportiveness, mutual communication, and mutual change. It is seeking to be an individual within an interdependent relationship rather than a dependent individual.

12

THE CORPORATION

FAMILY FRIENDLY

Corporations have people problems, but most corporations don't even recognize the existence of these problems. Employee functions, rewards, and penalities are major concerns for every employer, but the emphasis is on employees, not people. The people to whom I refer include spouses and children as well as employees; they are part of the corporate culture because they too have a relation to the corporation, albeit secondhand. And here's where the unrecognized people problems lie. There's a corporate colloquialism that goes, "If it ain't broke, don't fix it." This is the attitude most companies take toward their relationship problems with the corporate family, but that attitude goes one unspoken step beyond the adage to "and if it is broke, ignore it; maybe it will fix itself or go away." Companies are quick to mend the breaks in employee relations but are reluctant to acknowledge any link or obligation to the corporate family.

The preceding portions of this book outlined the major problems that employees and spouses encounter in the corporate environment. Purposefully, the company point of view and the benefits for company, employee, and spouses were stressed. Suggestions were offered individually to the employee and spouse as to how they might personally ease some of the impacts of the problems associated with the corporate life-style. Now let's concentrate on the corporation—what it does and what it might do to improve the circumstances of that life-style.

Motivation and Productivity

A motivation might be defined as that inner urge that spurs a person to act and obtain personal wants and needs. Motivation stimulates action. A corporation produces goods and services to obtain the desired profit; profit is their motive, their reason for existence, and their need for survival. But corporations are institutions, and as such they are inanimate. They exist but they cannot act for themselves. Therefore, a corporation depends on its employees to act for it. Employees, in turn, produce or act for companies to satisfy their own wants and needs.

Psychologist Abraham Maslow proposed a hierarchy of human needs or motives for acting. In diagram form his hierarchy of needs resembles a pyramid consisting of five levels, each building on the last. The base of the pyramid is the human physiological needs such as food, water, and air that are necessary for survival; the second level is security and safety needs such as clothes, shelter, law, order, and stability. The third level is love and belonging needs: family, friendship, caring. The fourth level is esteem and self-esteem: recognition and self-respect. And the top level is self-actualization, the full and whole development of personal potential. The importance of these needs in a person's life is in ascending order: the lowest or physiological needs are the most important, and self-actualization is least important. The first two levels of needs—physiological and safety—are termed basic needs, and the last three levels—love, esteem, and self-actualization—are growth needs. Maslow believed that the higher or growth needs are sought only after the basic needs are satisfied. [1]

Maslow's hierarchy of human needs greatly influences the research and understanding of motivation. In relating this hierarchy of needs to ambitious, high-achieving corporate employees, Maslow's priority ordering of needs must be modified. Most research pertaining to ambitious employees agrees that needs for esteem and self-esteem come before needs for love and belonging. Ambitious high achievers, especially men, place personal success, esteem, and self-esteem needs before personal relationships, love, and belonging needs. Therefore, the pyramid structure for these employees would be (1) physiological needs, (2) security and safety, (3) esteem and self-esteem, (4) love and belonging, and (5) self-actualization. Let's apply this modified needs model to the corporation's efforts to motivate its employees to increased productivity.

Corporations do a superb job of fulfilling employees' basic needs. They pay good salaries that enable their people to obtain the necessities of life. For the security and safety of their employees, companies offer retirement plans and health, dental, and life insurance; they even provide security guards at the office. Indeed, corporations excel in providing the basic human needs in return for employee production. But as Maslow says, after these basic needs are met, people turn their attention to personal growth needs. Realizing this, corporations attempt to motivate increased employee productivity by meeting the esteem needs of level three. They offer recognition through promotions and titles and self-esteem through achievement opportunities, usually with good results. Once these esteem needs are met, the corporate employee then looks to level four for motivation to produce or act. But this is where most corporations stop short in their attempt to motivate increased employee productivity. With the exception of a few innovative companies American corporations refuse to provide incentives that assist their employees in attaining their needs for love and belonging, for family, friends, and relationships. In fact, corporations generally work in direct opposition to those needs, and this opposition to or ignoring of employees' needs for love and belonging inhibits employees' personal growth, closing the door to increased productivity for the company.

Although the United States leads industrial nations in absolute productivity, our growth of productivity per man-hour lags behind that of West Germany, France, Japan, Canada, and Britain. Our rate of productivity per man-hour began slowing in the 1960s and between 1978 and 1980 that growth was negative. According to a survey of executives conducted by the U.S. Chamber of Commerce in 1980, workers' attitudes ranked third, after Federal government regulations and inadequate investment, as a reason for slow productivity growth.[2] Pick up any business paper or magazine and there will be some mention, if not an article, about productivity and worker incentives. These are major concerns in today's business world. Corporations depend on employee productivity, and they are forever searching for new gimmicks to motivate employees to better productivity.

There are three methods of motivating others to action, and corporate managers use all three.

1. Motivation by fear. Physical threats do not work in the corporate environment, but psychological threats work very well. These threats are rarely spoken; they are a subliminal part of the company initiation, culture, and philosophy, all of which are abstract. Fear of career reprisals is pervasive and generally acknowledged among employees. Remember the example of company training in chapter 1 where a slide depicted a late worker with the caption "Sales is not a nine-to-five job." The slide didn't say that you must work ten or twelve hours a day or that you would be fired if you didn't work long hours, but it did instill the message. Other examples include fear of turning down an offered promotion or move, being the first to leave the office, missing a meeting even in an emergency. Employees do have choices, but they are sometimes penalized if their managers feel they made the wrong choice. In using fear to increase employee productivity corporations threaten that employee's basic need for security.

2. Motivation through manipulation. This is the "carrot on the stick" type of motivation, and its place is undeniable in the corporation. Manipulative motivation appeals to both the esteem needs and material greeds of employees; it offers recognition and/or rewards. Who doesn't want to win a trip to Hawaii, gain a promotion and raise in salary, or move into a higher commission bracket? All kinds of gimmicks fall within this type: incentive pay, profit sharing, bonuses, stock options, and so on. Our materialist society encourages this type of motivation, and corporations make good use of it.

3. Motivation through persuasion. Persuasion is changing another's perspective and behavior by sharing thoughts, opinions, and knowledge. When persuasion is used negatively, it becomes motivation by fear and is typified by the earlier examples. But motivation through positive persuasion encourages people to meet their emotional needs by striving to fulfill their personal potential. It's a complimentary "atta boy" instead of veiled threats; it's helping to do things right instead of punishing for mistakes; it's "you can do it" instead of "why didn't you do it?" Positive persuasion is the most effective way to motivate others because it promotes that person's strength and dignity, moving beyond basic needs into personal growth needs. Positive persuasion aims at the third level and sometimes the fifth level of employees' motivational needs—esteem, self-esteem, and self-actualization.

In motivating their employees, corporations rely heavily on the fear and manipulation methods with a dash of occasional positive persuasion. Bob Conklin, motivational lecturer and author on the subject, said, "Intellect and logic do not motivate. Emotion does." Since corporations do such a good job of fulfilling employees' basic needs, employees are increasingly looking to corporations to offer opportunities to facilitate personal growth needs, and these personal needs are emotional. Today people search for jobs that offer more than money, security, and titles (levels one, two, and three of the needs pyramid). They look for jobs that recognize and assist family relationships (level four) and offer opportunities for fulfilling personal potential (level five). But the majority of American corporations refuse to ascend past level three in trying to motivate employees. They cling tenaciously to lower-level motivation, trying to increase productivity through fear (threats to security) and manipulation (rewards and titles).

Few companies attempt to provide an environment that encourages employees in their quest for rewarding relationships with families and friends. Although research affirms that an employee who is happy and satisfied in private life is more productive at work, corporations refuse to acknowledge a relationship with, interest in, or benefit from recognizing the importance of employees' private lives. Joyce Lebovitz, president of Community Introductions, a relocation and counseling firm, states, "Balance is the key to a productive employee." Corporations must move to level four of the motive pyramid if they wish to have balanced employees and open the door to increased employee productivity.

Pioneer Corporate Programs

Addressing employees' needs to attain and maintain love and belonging through family, friends, and relationships is the new frontier in employee relations for the American corporation. For many years major corporations have provided relocation assistance for their transferring employees, and they proudly point to their benevolence. Relocations upset relationships and disrupt one's sense of community, but these benevolent corporate relocation packages address only the financial aspects of the move.

Although many companies refer their employees to and pay for relocation service firms, few such firms really get involved with the individual client or seek to assist in peripheral relocation issues such as schools, day care, psychological counseling, specialized medical facilities, or spouse job placement. Once the old house is sold and the new home is bought, families are usually left on their own to sink or swim in the new location. They are literally abandoned to find needed services and face personal psychological effects of the relocation alone. This much-touted relocation "assistance" program is the extent to which the majority of corporations aid their employees in family matters.

But some companies realize or are being forced to realize that the corporate life-style impacts on the lives of an employee and his family in personal ways that go beyond mere finances and eventually affect the employee's job performance and productivity. As a result, these companies search for and find innovative ways to help employees resolve personal needs, and in doing so they move into level four of employee motivational needs—love and belonging through family, friends, and relationships. By becoming more sensitive to employees' personal lives, these few humanistic companies are the level-four pioneers with programs that include spouse job assistance, child-care centers, and employee counseling.

In the past few years the issue of spouse job assistance has commanded wide attention. As stated in chapter 5, about one-third of all corporate moves involves an employed spouse, and 80 to 90 percent of these spouses are women. These employed spouses no longer meekly relinquish their jobs and careers to trail after their mobile corporate mates; they are demanding consideration in the relocation decision and assistance from the mate's employer in finding a new position if they do move. Corporations began offering spouse job assistance for three primary reasons: to keep dual-career couples from turning down promotions and transfers, to attract new employees, and to avoid losing training and relocation investments due to resignations. It is to the corporation's benefit to offer job assistance programs.

But old attitudes still prevail. In May 1984 the syndicated newspaper column "Dear Abby" contained a letter from a trailing spouse asking, "Abby, shouldn't a company take into consideration that a wife has to give up a job when it transfers her husband? And shouldn't the company also provide a job for the wife?" Abby replied, "While relocating is no piece of cake for the family, it usually means a promotion for the breadwinner, so roll with the punches. It comes with the territory. Should the company provide a job for the spouse? That would be ideal, but it's too much to expect."[3]

It's estimated that less than 10 percent of the corporations offer this service. I interviewed an official of a major oil company who is in charge of relocations within his division. That division transfers between 400 and 500 employees a year, but the company has no spouse job assistance program. Although the need is great, the programs are few, and many of the existing programs are inadequate, offering little more than referrals and rumors of jobs. There are never job guarantees nor reimbursements for the loss of salary due to relocation.

Child-care assistance is gaining popularity among both companies and employees, but actions are slow. As with job assistance, the huge majority of corporations recognize the need and support the theory of child care but resist instituting any type of program to meet the need. There seem to be no valid statistics on the number of companies offering child-care assistance. A 1984 *Wall Street Journal* article estimated that about two hundred companies offer "full-fledged" day care at reduced rates, whereas a 1984 *Time* article estimated that one thousand companies provide child-care assistance. This assistance varies in form. Some companies simply refer employees to selected outside facilities; others reimburse them for part of the cost of child care, but with reimbursement plans income tax problems can arise. A small number of companies build and equip in-house child-care facilities. Depending on the company, employees are charged either for the full cost of running the center or a reduced rate, as low as twenty-five dollars a week.

Companies that do offer child-care assistance find many benefits: female employees return to work sooner after delivery, employee recruitment is easier, employee morale improves, and the rate of job turnover declines. One magazine article stated: "Problems among workers involving child-care arrangements can affect their productivity—and the company's profit margin." The article gave an example: a company that in the first two years of day-care operation reported a 60 percent decrease in turnover and an increase of hundreds of hours of employee productivity previously lost to absenteeism.[4]

The employee assistance program (EAP) is the third corporate pioneer effort. The first EAPs were started in the 1940s as alcoholism treatment programs and were conducted in-house by recovering alcoholics. Although the main focus is still alcoholism, the programs have now expanded to cover drug abuse and emotional, marital, family, and financial problems as well. The good news is that in 1982, there were five thousand EAPs, including one-half of the *Fortune* 500 corporations. The bad news is that most employees don't know of or don't recognize the benefits of such programs, very few spouses even realize such programs exist, and some of the programs do not include families.

The need for EAPs becomes apparent when national statistics are considered. The National Council on Alcoholism estimates that 10 percent of the nation's employees come to work with psychological or substance abuse problems that might affect their productivity. Each of these employees costs his or her company from three thousand to five thousand dollars a year in lowered job performance, absenteeism, and health care coverage.[5] The National Academy of Science estimates that $20 billion is the yearly cost of lost productivity due to alcoholism. The President's Council on Mental Health reported in the late 1970s that 25 percent of our population show symptoms of depression and anxiety, and 15 percent are in need of mental health care.[6]

There are basically three types of EAP. The in-house EAP is run by the company, usually on company premises. Some offer only referrals to private counseling, but many are run by company-hired psychologists or counselors who do short-term counseling on-site. In-house counseling is usually free unless extended treatment is needed. In that case the employee is referred to a private outside agency or professional, and the employee's insurance is used. Although some of these programs work well, there are disadvantages. Many workers are reluctant to seek help from fear of job reprisals should superiors find out, and with in-house programs such discovery is quite likely. Also, in my opinion in-house programs virtually eliminate spouse and family participation because of location.

The second type of program contracts with an outside provider of services, either profit or nonprofit, which establishes and runs the EAP for the company. The first two to four visit are free; if further treatment is required, most company health insurance plans pay the larger percentage of the fee, the employee paying the remainder. Outside providers normally give the company no information about the employee except in anonymous, general, and statistical form; the company rarely knows who participates in the program unless an employee is referred to the program by a superior. There is always the chance of an information leak, perhaps through the insurance department, but confidentiality is normally carefully guarded.

The final type of EAP is the union-run program, which focuses mainly on alcoholism and drug abuse. Superiors often refer employees to the program because of inadequate job performance, and in such cases the employee's participation is mandatory and closely linked to job retention.[7]

Although white-collar participation in an EAP is normally voluntary, superiors occasionally refer employees whose problems affect their work. Substance abuse and depression are the major problems. Some EAPs include elementary health screening, such as blood pressure and breast exams, and smoking cessation clinics. Confidentiality is crucial. Managers often try to glean information from a counselor about an employee; therefore, employee protection is vital.

Companies can help their EAPs by removing the stigma from counseling, by issuing written EAP policies, by impressing employees with their commitment to make the program both acceptable and accessible, and by training managers to recognize and assist employees in seeking help for problems. But the sad fact remains that often information about EAPs doesn't effectively trickle down to the employee and his family. My husband was employed by two large corporations during twenty-two years, but I knew nothing about EAPs until two and a half years after my husband left an EAP company.

These are the three best-known corporate efforts to motivate people through family assistance. Other programs, such as flexible working hours and outplacement, relocation and retirement counseling might be mentioned, but their application within the corporate community is relatively insignificant.

Moving Up to Level Four

Women are changing, men are changing, and although socialization lags reluctantly, our culture is changing too. Corporations know the old corporate motivational system is "broke," but most ignore the signs in hopes the break will mend itself or go away. Companies long for the more comfortable and less complicated past when "big brother's" dicta were accepted passively and obediently. But change rarely reverses itself; the new, more egalitarian culture is here to stay, and as sociologists tell us, if institutions refuse to change with the times, they die away. It is time for corporations to respond to their employees' need for psychological wholeness, but response demands acknowledgment of and respect for both employees and their families. As William Ouchi says, his hypothetical Theory Z corporation "assumes that any worker's life is a whole, not a Jekyl-Hyde personality, half machine from nine to five and half human in the hours preceding and following."[8] For survival, corporations must move into level-four motivation by altering their philosophy, culture, and environment along more humanistic lines.

A good place to start this corporate renovation is inside the office with the employees. Authors of the much proclaimed book *In Search of Excellence* emphatically state, "Treat people as adults. Treat them as partners; treat them with dignity; treat them with respect. Treat *them*—not capital spending and automation—as the primary source of productivity gains. These are fundamental lessons from the excellent companies research. In other words if you want productivity and the financial reward that goes with it, you must treat your workers as your most important asset."[9] This is the stated philosophy of most corporations, and many have written policies to reinforce the philosophy. One such policy, the open door, bestows on the employee the right to take a grievance to any official in the company, no matter how high. Although such action rarely changes the issue, the aggrieved employee has an opportunity to be heard. The open-door policy salves an employee's ego and preserves his or her dignity.

There is also a relatively new trend within some companies to emphasize personal dignity through designations as participating partners rather than company employees. A friend of mine who returned to work recently was especially impressed by the training sessions because not once was she called an employee or worker; the trainees were always referred to as "associates." She loves her job and is enthusiastic about the company because she feels a part of it. People respond to titles of respect; it enhances their status and personal dignity.

Another sign of corporate respect for employees is periodic employee communication meetings. Held on company time, these meetings give employees the opportunity to question, compliment, and/or suggest corporate actions and decisions, in open dialogue with company officials. Officials use these meetings to present new projects, programs, and policies, to review company progress, and to meet employees person to person. Normally, spouses are not invited to these meetings, which I consider a mistake. By not inviting spouses companies miss a valuable opportunity to recognize spouses as an integral part of the company, to familiarize them with the purposes and policies of the company, and to improve company/spouse relationships. Merely sending personalized announcements of the meetings to spouses lets them know they are welcome, whether they come or not.

As far as corporate families are concerned, relocations, long hours, and travel are the most worrisome and aggravating problems associated with the corporate lifestyle. These problems deserve attention. Employees and spouses do their best to cope with the repercussions, but their coping doesn't change corporate demands for performance without compensation or for moving without consideration. Following are several layman suggestions, some of which are admittedly inoperable in the form given. But the purpose is to spur innovative thinking rather than dictate policy change.

Corporations have great influence in our country; they should use this influence to initiate research into the causes of and cures for corporate life-style problems. To my knowledge there has been no corporation-sponsored research and therefore no attempt to alleviate the hardships. To start, concentrated, professional studies should be conducted on the psychological impact of corporate mobility and travel. These studies should delve into the prevalence of depression, children's problems, and the breakdown of family relationships. Based on research results, current corporate policies on work hours, travel, and relocation should be reconsidered and altered along more humanistic lines; programs should be set up to educate and assist corporate families who experience difficulties. Most of the present programs, such as spouse job assistance, resulted from employee resistance, not a sincere effort by the corporation to improve the situation. Corporate-sponsored research would establish the sincerity and creditability of their interest in humanism. Follow-up actions might include education to the life-style in the college classroom and preemployment orientation sessions for both husbands and spouses. There has been much discussion in recent years about corporate social responsibility; this responsibility should start with the corporation monitoring and improving itself.

The relocation issue is a Pandora's box of ills; the entire procedure needs reworking. I believe the base of the problem lies in the promotion selection process by which superiors designate the employee they want for a certain position. The current process puts the complete burden of the decision, pro or con, and the consequences for that decision on the shoulders of the employee. He is in the spotlight and on the spot. If he or his family doesn't want the move, the family is unhappy if he takes it; but if he rejects the move, his career is placed in jeopardy by the company. An alternative might be for the corporation to advertise rather than designate open positions and have those interested in pursuing the opening to sign up for evaluation. Employees and spouses could discuss the issue before applying, not after designation, thus mitigating the risks at home and on the job. Such a procedure would give the couple control of their own destiny, eliminate the stigma of not moving, reduce mentorism and favoritism, and provide a more humanistic and equalitarian system of promotion.

If corporations continue to move their employees indiscriminately around the country, they must prepare to offer needed social services for their people. Repeated relocations undermine and sometimes destroy social structures and connections that are necessary to psychological stability: extended families, friends, community, churches, services. But the company offers nothing as temporary replacement. After a move the corporation is often the transient family's only community connection, but as a rule it denies any responsibility to the family and offers very little assistance in settlement. With each relocation corporations might provide an orientation for families, either through a company-employed social services director or a qualified outside provider. The purpose of such sessions is to provide the transient with information about the area and where to go for assistance

I know of one company, Community Introductions, Inc., that provides a comprehensive service to corporations. The transferee and spouse fill out a needs-indicator questionnaire specifying exactly what they want and need in their new location: living areas, special schools, nursing homes, day-care facilities, churches, and other interests. An employee of the firm is assigned to the couple, researches their needs, finds appropriate contacts, and personally introduces the couple to the available services. The firm provides relocation counseling, ongoing referrals, an EAP for the entire family, and a personalized spouse-employment program that sets up appointments for job interviews. This personalized service is so successful that the firm is now expanding into other large cities.

As mentioned earlier, settlement can take as long as two years; this period is very stressful and is normally accompanied by psychological distress of one or more family members. Every corporation should have some form of EAP that includes family members. These programs should be publicized in such a manner that both employee and spouse know of the program's existence and benefits. Most EAP companies post such information on company bulletin boards and/or enclose it in pay envelopes.I would suggest mailing EAP information in letter form and addressing it to the spouse personally; brochures are just another piece of junk mail. These letters should be mailed periodically to all employees' homes, whether newly relocated or not. In addition, companies should emphasize the availability of family psychological counseling and advise the spouse of the procedure to follow.

Spouse job assistance should be more than cursory. It is predicted that by 1995 81 percent of married women between thirty-five and forty-four will be employed or seeking employment. Already spouse job assistance is becoming mandatory for most younger couples, and the need for such assistance is likely to increase. Corporations could move into this service by forming local consortiums or formalized networks of human resources department heads who meet on a monthly basis to exchange information and assistance. Each company representative would contribute a list of available job openings, and from the collected lists a master list of openings would be compiled and distributed monthly to participating companies. This formalized system would be better than word-of-mouth rumors of openings. In addition, companies should compensate the trailing employed spouse with a specified percentage of her former salary if she is still unemployed after a specified time.

The second major problem area for corporate families is long work hours and unrestricted travel. Corporations benefit from an employee's unpaid work and sacrifice of family time; companies owe corporate families recognition and appreciation for these contributions. Minimum and maximum work hours should be a matter of written policy, and all hours over a reasonable maximum should be compensated in some manner. Although it involves accounting and timekeeping snags, one suggestion might be to keep a record of over-maximum hours and add these to each year's paid vacation. Another might be to reward the couple with a free night on the town for a specified number of hours overtime. And the overtime should include family hours usurped by travel. For each two or three weekends spent on trips the family might be awarded a weekend vacation at company expense.

But there are other, more practical alternatives. Corporations could concentrate on developing or securing technology for their own use; put the "big brains" to work on finding effective methods of long-distance communication to relieve the excessive travel burden. What has happened to two-way television and teleconferencing? Why haven't these technologies been refined and put into widespread use? Corporate spouses and children are eagerly awaiting tomorrow. But immediate action can be taken to establish work-hour policies and to monitor travel more closely.

These pleas for humanistic corporate consideration are not new. In 1976 E. Jerry Walker wrote, "The corporation can no longer treat his [an employee's] wife and family as just an adjunct to his life. If corporations want to get the best out of one partner in a marriage, they would do well to ensure that the other partner is getting something out of that relationship as well." [10] Both employees and their spouses want more from the corporation than money, security, and promotions; they want an environment that nurtures caring and family values. It is time for corporations to move into level four of the human needs pyramid, acknowledge responsibility to employees and families, and sincerely strive to ease the hardships of living the corporate game.

REFERENCES

Chapter 1

1. John A. Byrne, "Careers," *Forbes*, 10 September 1984, 177–183.
2. Gail Sheehy, *Passages* (New York: E. P. Dutton, 1974), 100.
3. Paul Evans and Fernando Bartolomé, *Must Success Cost So Much?* (New York: Basic Books, 1981), 43.
4. Ibid, 46.
5. Ibid, 101–106.

Chapter 2

1. Paul Evans and Fernando Bartolomé, *Must Success Cost So Much?* (New York: Basic Books, 1981), 110–124.
2. Robert Seidenberg, *Corporate Wives: Corporate Casualties?* (New York: AMACOM, 1973), 93.

Chapter 3

1. Robert N. McMurry, "Man-Hunt for Top Executives," *Harvard Business Review*, January–February 1954, 49.
2. Ibid, 50.
3. Paul Evans and Fernando Bartolomé, *Must Success Cost So Much?* (New York: Basic Books, 1981), 77.
4. Allan Cox, *The Cox Report on the American Corporation* (New York: Delacorte Press, 1982), 268.

Chapter 4

1. Michael Maccoby, *The Gamesman* (New York: Simon & Schuster, 1976).
2. Alan A. McLean and Charles R. DeCarlo, "The Changing Concept of Work," *Innovation* 30, April, 1972.
3. Diane Rothbard Margolis, *The Managers* (New York: William Morrow and Co., 1979), 58–59.
4. E. Jerry Walker, "'Til Business Us Do Part?" *Harvard Business Review*, January–February 1976.
5. "Can Apple's Corporate Counterculture Survive?" *Business Week*, January 16, 1984, 82.
6. Frank Allen, "Wives of Executives Offer Advice to Women Marrying Rising Stars," *The Wall Street Journal*, December 18, 1981.

Chapter 5

1. John Naisbitt, *Megatrends* (New York: Warner Books, 1982), 208–210.
2. William G. Flanagan and Janet Bamford, "More Than a Moving Experience," *Forbes*, November 21, 1983.
3. Maryanne Vandervelde, *The Changing Life of the Corporate Wife* (New York: Warner Books, 1979), 67.

Chapter 6

1. John Naisbitt, *Megatrends* (New York: Warner Books, 1982), 41.
2. Barrie S. Greiff and Preston K. Munter, *Tradeoffs: Executives, Family and Organizational Life* (New York: New American Library, 1981), 81–88.
3. Ibid, 91–108.
4. Gail Sheehy, *Passages* (New York: E. P. Dutton, 1974), 176.
5. Walter Kiechel III, "The Guilt-Edged Executive," *Fortune*, 28 May 1984, 219–220.

Chapter 7

1. Paul Evans and Fernando Bartolomé, *Must Success Cost So Much?* (New York: Basic Books, 1981), 22–23.
2. Alan N. Schoonmaker, *Anxiety and the Executive* (New York: American Management Assoc., Inc., 1969), 66.
3. Hanna Papanek, "Men, Women, and Work: Reflections on the Two-Person Career," *American Journal of Sociology*, January 1973, 90, 96.
4. Robert Seidenberg, *Corporate Wives: Corporate Casualties?* (New York: AMACOM, 1973), 72–75.

5. Michael Maccoby, *The Gamesman* (New York: Simon & Schuster, 1976), 191.
6. Paul Evans and Fernando Bartolomé, *Must Success Cost So Much?* (New York: Basic Books, 1981), 16–26. Evans and Bartolomé cite four types of spillover: emotional, physical, behaviorial, and existential. From my experience I detect three major types.
7. Frank Allen, "Executive Wives Describe Sources of Their Contentment, Frustration," *The Wall Street Journal,* December 15, 1981.
8. Ibid.

Chapter 8

1. William Ouchi, *Theory Z* (Reading, Mass.: Addison-Wesley, 1981), 204–208.
2. Thomas J. Peters and Robert H. Waterman, Jr., *In Search of Excellence* (New York: Harper & Row, 1982), 126–128.
3. "Baby Boomers Push for Power," *Business Week,* July 2, 1984, 53.
4. Rosabeth Kanter, *Men and Women of the Corporation* (New York: Basic Books, 1977), 181.
5. Christopher Hegarty and Philip Goldberg, *How to Manage Your Boss* (New York: Rawson, Wade, 1980), 249–251.
6. Caroline Bird, *Everything a Woman Needs to Know to Get Paid What She's Worth . . . in the 1980s* (New York: Bantam Books, 1981), 102–104.
7. Kanter, *Men and Women of the Corporation,* 232–236.
8. Nancy Baker, "A Matter of Convenience," *Working Woman,* December 1982, 101–103.

Chapter 9

1. Walter Kiechel III, "When Executives Crack," *Fortune,* July 23, 1984, 133–134.
2. Maryanne Vandervelde, *The Changing Life of the Corporate Wife* (New York: Warner Books, 1979), 67.
3. David Gelman, "Teen-Age Suicide in the Sun Belt," *Newsweek,* August 15, 1983, 70, 72, 74.

Chapter 10

1. Roy Menninger, M. D., "Responsibility to Self," *News Front,* Winter 1975.
2. Ibid.

3. Ibid.
4. Mortimer R. Feinberg and Aaron Levenstein, *The Wall Street Journal,* June 15, 1981.

Chapter 11

1. Nena and George O'Neill, *Shifting Gears* (New York: M. Evans, 1974), 218.
2. Michael Maccoby, *The Gamesman* (New York: Simon & Schuster, 1976), 117–118.
3. Allan Cox, *The Cox Report on the American Corporation* (New York: Delacorte Press, 1982), 274.
4. Nena and George O'Neill, *Shifting Gears,* 204–206.
5. Maryanne Vandervelde, *The Changing Life of the Corporate Wife* (New York: Warner Books, 1979), 45.
6. Nena and George O'Neill, *Shifting Gears,* 109.

Chapter 12

1. Dennis Coon, *Introduction to Psychology* (St. Paul, Minn: West Publishing Co., 1980), 268–269.
2. "Unlocking The Productivity Door," *Nation's Business,* December 1981, 55.
3. Abigail Van Buren, "Dear Abby," *Dallas Times-Herald,* May 3, 1984.
4. Katherine Dinsdale, "Bringing in Baby," *D Magazine,* June 1984, 46–54.
5. Ellen Wojahn, "How to Cut $5,000 Off the Cost of Each Employee," *Inc.,* July 1984, 106–110.
6. Myron Brenton, *Help for the Troubled Employee* (New York: Public Affairs Pamphlets, 1982), 2–3.
7. Ibid. 6, 7, 16, 17.
8. William Ouchi, *Theory Z* (Reading, Mass.: Addison-Wesley, 1981), 195.
9. Thomas J. Peters and Robert H. Waterman, Jr., *In Search of Excellence* (New York: Harper & Row, 1982), 238.
10. E. Jerry Walker, "'Til Business Us Do Part?" *Harvard Business Review,* January–February 1976, 101.